Restoring the Ties That Bind

THE GRASSROOTS TRANSFORMATION OF THE EPISCOPAL CHURCH

Based on research by the Episcopal Church Foundation

Restoring the Ties That Bind

THE GRASSROOTS TRANSFORMATION OF THE EPISCOPAL CHURCH

WILLIAM SACHS AND THOMAS HOLLAND

Based on research by the Episcopal Church Foundation

 CHURCH

Church Publishing Incorporated, New York

Library of Congress Cataloging-in-Publication Data

Sachs, William L., 1947-
    Restoring the ties that bind : the grassroots transformation of the Episcopal Church /
William Sachs and Thomas Holland
        p. cm.
    "Based on research by the Episcopal Church Foundation".
    Includes bibliographical references.
    ISBN: 0-89869-379-9 (pbk.)
        1. Episcopal Church. 2. Episcopalians. I. Holland, Thomas P II. Episcopal
Church Foundation. III. Title

BX5930.3.S23 2003
283'.73'090511--dc21   2003055301

Church Publishing Incorporated
445 Fifth Avenue
New York NY 10016
www.churchpublishing.org

5 4 3 2 1

CONTENTS

FOREWORD

by Donald E. Miller,
University of Southern California

Drawing on more than 2,500 discussions with Episcopalians in focus groups and personal interviews, William Sachs and Thomas Holland conclude that there is a paradox in the Episcopal Church. At the local congregational level there is considerable vitality; this vitality, however, is in marked contrast to the sense of crisis that exists within the hierarchy of the church.

Based on media reports, one might conclude that the Episcopal Church is being ripped apart by debates over clergy blessings of same-sex unions and progressive political pronouncements by the hierarchy. A quite different picture emerged when Sachs, Holland, and their fellow researchers visited over 200 local parishes. In these conversations, they discovered that church members were animated by discoveries being made in their personal journeys of faith; they were concerned about ways in which they could more effectively pursue ministry within their church and in their local community; and they were worried about nurturing their children—the future leaders of the church.

Many of the active members of these churches were first-generation Episcopalians. They were nearly indifferent to what was happening in diocesan and national conventions. Issues that had divided the church in the past, such as Prayer Book revisions and the ordination of women priests, were ancient history. Their main concern about the church's organizational superstructure was whether they were getting their money's worth. They wanted resource materials to enhance their ministry, not authoritarian leadership.

For people who pursue their spiritual journey within the Episcopal fold, the attraction is the style of worship and the fact that they do not need to check their intellect when they enter the door of the church. They are also attracted to the centrality of the Eucharist within the Anglican tradition, and the fact that the Christian life is one lived in community; it is not a purely personal quest. In this regard, they are embracing the historic commitment by Anglicans to reason, Scripture, and tradition. But they also want something more. They desire to experience the sacred in highly personal ways. Indeed, it is this encounter with the Holy Spirit that is personally transformative and cements their relationship to the church.

Restoring the Ties That Bind: The Grassroots Transformation of the Episcopal Church is an important book for clergy and lay members who are concerned with mapping the future of the Episcopal Church. At the local level, the church is a vital worshiping community of people who are committed to experiencing God in direct and personal ways. The challenge for the church's hierarchy is to support the spiritual pursuit of its people, providing resources and exemplary models of what it means to be a faithful Christian in the twenty-first century.

ACKNOWLEDGMENTS

There is good news about the spreading of the Good News— in America in general and the Episcopal Church in particular. But we might not have known this good news without the research funded by the Episcopal Church Foundation in the form of the Zacchaeus Project. Nor would we be bearers of this good news now—in a narrative form based on the Zacchaeus Project data—but for the encouragement of a variety of friends and colleagues. A number of people have offered direction for the book, and for the research program it represents: Diana Bass, Sarah Buxton-Smith, Ian Douglas, Peter Gorday, James Kowalski, James Lemler, Martin Marty, Clayton Matthews, Titus Presler, Matthew Price, Katherine Tyler Scott, Frank Turner, and Robert Wuthnow. James Wind, of the Alban Institute, and Janet Waggoner, a former Episcopal Church Foundation colleague who serves as a parish priest in Connecticut, served as readers for parts of the book as it took form and offered helpful critiques. Donald Miller, of the University of Southern California, who graciously wrote the book's foreword, is an active colleague in several aspects of the Episcopal Church Foundation's work. He is also a valued friend. We greatly appreciate the breadth of his wisdom and the good-humored edge to his insights.

Our colleague at the Foundation's Cornerstone office in Berkeley, Ann Hallisey, gave exceptional amounts of time to reviewing this book as it took shape. Her detailed, thoughtful, and skilled critiques of our prose and our logic had a major beneficial effect. We are deeply grateful for her friendship and her expertise.

Donn Mitchell of the Church Foundation played a major role in shaping this book by his skilled efforts to edit the manuscript. Once the manuscript reached Church Publishing, Johnny Ross continued the editing process. Johnny offered thorough, talented, and good-natured advice for pulling the book into final form. We are deeply indebted to him. We express our gratitude to Frank Tedeschi of Church Publishing who understood the powerful story that this book tells and who encouraged and expedited its publication.

From its inception as a research project in 1998, this work could not have been possible without the guidance and encouragement of William G. Andersen. As Executive Director of the Episcopal Church Foundation, Bill has been unflagging in his dedication, astute guidance, and thoroughness. He serves as a model of faithful and visionary leadership for many in the church. We also thank the Foundation's board, which works closely and well with Bill and the staff. In particular, we thank Bernard Milano, board president, and George Ching and Ward Richards who guide the research and development committee.

Myra Blackmon (wife of Thomas Holland) and Austin Tucker (wife of William Sachs) have lived with this book, and with our varied professional obsessions, for a number of years. Without their honesty, compassion, and sensitivity, no amount of research would find useful expression. We thank them for their clarity, faithfulness, and unflagging support.

We also thank the churches where we and our spouses seek and find God: Emmanuel Church, Athens, Georgia, and St. Luke's Church, Darien, Connecticut. In these parishes, we find numerous friends and continuing instances of the possibilities and challenges that Episcopalians and all of religious America now face. We dedicate this book to the people with whom we worship and minister, and to all the people whom we have met in our explorations of the lives of Episcopal congregations. May they continue steadfast in the love and dedication and hope which we have discovered in such abundance among them.

1

INTRODUCTION
From Zacchaeus' Perspective

SARAH'S STORY

As a few members of an urban Episcopal church gathered to describe their congregation's life, one woman named Sarah was eager to speak. Proud of the place she now calls her spiritual home and of the people who have become her spiritual family, Sarah was bursting to tell the story of how her new life in faith had taken shape. As she did, she revealed more than she realized. More than the story of one person's growth in faith, Sarah's story also is the story of a widespread spiritual search that is reshaping American life in general and the life of the Episcopal Church in particular.

She began by describing a long walk she took one day, during which she discovered a beautiful old church. It was lunchtime, and she had been especially anxious to get out of the office that day and just go walking around. Something was going on with her. For months she had been using her lunch hour to walk and think and review the details of her life. It was a good life, she constantly reminded herself. She had much to be proud of: education, job advancements, a comfortable condominium, a circle of friends. There had been difficult moments, of course: the death of a parent had come on the heels of a job change several years ago, and recently there had been the pain of a broken relationship. But even these losses had become sources of reassurance. She had learned from these experiences and—largely by her own perseverance, she acknowledged proudly to the small group—she had eventually healed.

Increasingly, though, something had been gnawing at her that she could not understand or even identify. She sensed that her life was incomplete, that something was missing. Although she had accomplished much and survived more than she could have imagined, something still was missing. Her life seemed somehow to lack meaning, to be without roots, to be as aimless and wandering as her midday walks. She was searching without knowing how, roaming with no clear image of a goal. Something deep within her was calling her to step beyond where she normally walked. There had to be more to life. But what was it? And how could she get it? The only thing she had realized from her many walks was that this challenge was not like her others. This time she needed a sense of direction that she could not find for herself. This time she could not do it alone.

Off she went, determined that somehow she would bring back something...anything...from the day's walk. It was a beautiful spring day. Surely there would be something that might make life more than it had been.

Only a few blocks from her office in the city's small downtown district, she was surprised to come upon an impressive, Gothic church she had never noticed before. Christ Episcopal Church stood along the route she regularly drove to work. She had raced past it scores of times without ever seeing it!

Until that day Sarah would not have described herself as a spiritual seeker. She had little religious background; she felt uninformed about religion but was not embarrassed by this. She would not have seen signs or portents in suddenly discovering the church. Rather, she simply saw an open door and an opportunity to slip into a quiet, meditative space, a place to pause and reflect during her walk, a place where she could be alone. "But I didn't know what I was getting into," she laughed, then continued her story:

> The church was more than quiet space. There was the strength of its stone walls, the beauty of the stained glass, and the simple power of the altar. Organ music was playing softly, and it appeared a service was about to begin. People were gathering, and I thought about leaving but couldn't. I just had to stay in the back and watch. I was deeply moved, in a way that I never had been. Even now I can't explain it, but I felt this sense of being invited and affirmed. One thing really hit me: the faces of the people who had just received Communion. There was warmth and assurance. They were reverent and joyful. I didn't understand all that was happening. But I sensed people were being fed spiritually, and I decided to explore this church.

She decided to visit again and, expecting to be left alone to her thoughts, again entered quietly. But on her second visit, a worshiper invited her to join the others in a light lunch in the parish hall. After several visits, she knew most of the regulars at the service as well as the church's clergy. The sense of invitation deepened. In both the people and the worship, she saw something that awakened possibilities for filling the void in her life. By stages, she was drawn into this congregation, discovering the power of joining her story with the stories of others. As her journey progressed, she eventually was drawn into the parish's leadership. What had begun as Sarah's private exploration had become a shared one.

During the group session, Sarah spoke knowledgeably of Christ Church's programs and proudly of its people. "I wish I had time to tell you about our outreach and education programs. They are wonderful!" As she described life in this parish, an impressive sense of spiritual community came alive. And the source of her new commitment became clear. Recalling the path of her involvement in this congregation, she immediately returned to her discovery of worship and its centrality for her spiritual journey. "That's what drew me. I had no church home, no religious background. I still don't know much about the Episcopal Church beyond here. I just know what this church has meant to me, and that is wonderful!"

Sarah was not the only person in the group who described a personal spiritual journey that led to Christ Church. Just as she unexpectedly discovered the possibilities that participation in a congregation can bring, so have other new members of the congregation. But when they gathered to recount their spiritual journeys, more than a series of individual accounts became apparent. It became clear that these spiritual seekers have formed a powerful bond of faith community among themselves and with the older members of the congregation. It also became clear that there is a new quality to the shared faith they have together. Unlike what might be described as a status quo understanding of community that prevailed a generation earlier, this community takes steps to attract and hold people on personal spiritual quests; it is a community of change—of seekers, rather than settlers. Steadily this congregation has developed innovative forms of worship, outreach, and education; perhaps more importantly, the process whereby these areas of congregational life were changed involved more than the clergy and the handful of long-established lay leaders who would have made them previously. Decision-making involves a much broader base of the membership. Major decisions are debated openly, and there are regular opportunities for church members to comment on the direction of congregational life. More women and young adults have assumed leadership roles, with new members prominent among them. The story of Christ Church has become the story of a new group of spiritual seekers who have brought new life to the congregation.

A COMMUNITY OF PILGRIMS

While Sarah's experience of Christ Church was similar to that of other recent arrivals, older members had a very different story to tell. Unlike the newer members, many of the older were "cradle" Episcopalians—raised in the church, fully dedicated to it, and steeped in its teachings, traditions, and worldview. They could recall a time when the Episcopal Church in general and Christ Church in particular had played very different roles in the world, a time when Christ Church had been a mainstay of its community. Its members had been among the area's leading citizens. They had been strong supporters not only of Christ Church but of the diocesan and denominational structures to which it belonged. Their sense of community, though strong, was taken almost for granted, as part of the natural order of things.

Then the world in which the church and its members were rooted began to change. There were wars and social upheavals; the Episcopal Church revised its Book of Common Prayer; women were ordained; and there was growing acceptance of homosexuality. Christ Church's members feared the loss of their treasured heritage. Membership declined as disaffected members left, at times in large numbers. Several clergy also left amid conflict. The church's budget plummeted and "deferred maintenance" seemed the building's fate. Conflict and dissolution defined a once-proud congregation.

But then something remarkable began to happen at Christ Church to reverse the decline. People like Sarah began to join. Most were relative newcomers to this city; education, work, and marriage had transplanted them. Although both old and new members had experienced divorces, deaths of loved ones, and job losses, these painful changes figured more prominently in the stories told by the newcomers and served as further indications of their overall feelings of disjointedness. For most of them, the Christian faith had not always been at life's center. Few were raised as Episcopalians. Some had little religious background. Several had cynically shunned religious faith. None had expected to discover religious commitment and be drawn into such a dynamic experience of congregational life. But their outlooks had changed. Like Sarah, they had felt the lure of worship and of the ideal of working together for common purposes. Joined together in a bond that had become the center of their lives, they viewed their collective task as building a spiritual community on the foundation afforded them by this religious institution.

The older members at Christ Church clearly welcome the influx of new members, which represents a reversal in the old trend of decline. But the recent arrivals mean distinctly more than that to the older members. They fully realize that the newer members are different from themselves (i.e., not the kind of cradle Episcopalians who can help them return to the past of their glory days), and they value them on their own distinctive merits. As one older man noted, the new arrivals brought fresh spiritual energies with them, and their intense longing for community—in marked contrast to the older members for whom community always was a given—added emotional vibrancy and bright new potential to the congregation. Similarly, the newer members prize the older members for their wisdom and their historic perspective. They are grateful when those who have been around for many years, and therefore have seen several cycles in the fortunes of Christ Church and of the Episcopal Church in general, are able to reassure them when they read contentious and fractious rhetoric in national church publications, or when attendance takes a temporary dip, or when there is a slump in the local economy, which also usually means a slump in the offering plate revenues. They also are grateful to the old guard for bringing Christ Church through troubled times and preserving its precious legacy intact for the future.

The generational divide at Christ Church can be quite a source of cohesion, bringing solace and renewed energy to either side, but the differences between the groups can bring tensions, too. During the focus group, when the older members talked of the old days, they exhibited great pride in their church's long heritage and in their stalwart devotion to it through the difficult times. Rightly they could claim to have ensured Christ Church's future. Consequently, they also exhibited somewhat proprietary attitudes about Christ Church's present. But the newer members expressed a very different understanding of how the past informed the present. Though grateful to the older members for their protective stewardship (without which no Christ Church legacy would have been possible), they nonetheless consider themselves the unquestioned inheritors of that legacy. They assume that they represent the future and are intent on imprinting their own new style upon their community.

Appreciative but not always comprehending of each other, they have found common cause but not always common strategies. When the small group began to focus on current dilemmas in their community, agreement on their church's priorities and strategies for addressing them was not always apparent. Sometimes the friction among them was thinly veiled. The ties of community remained intact, but their occasionally cautious treatment of one another expressed more uncertainty than perhaps they intended to convey. The group members were uncertain about exactly how they were going to integrate a new generation's altered priorities and style with older, established priorities and styles, but they were certain that—somehow—they would.

Without knowing it, this group and the congregation of which they are members are participants in a major change in American life. Until recently, religious life has been equated with the activities of large denominations and their centralized institutional structures. Episcopalians have been among the "mainstream" Protestant denominations that have exercised considerable public influence as religious institutions. Organized like major corporate or philanthropic entities, Methodists, Lutherans, Presbyterians, Congregationalists, Episcopalians, and others have built elaborate institutional histories and complex institutional structures. For the sake of sustaining a variety of denominational programs and services, these churches maintain large staffs and office complexes. For decades, local church members loyally and unhesitatingly drew on their denomination's programs and contributed generously to the budgets that made them possible. But, as will be demonstrated frequently during this narrative, a new vision of religious life is emerging. A new kind of loyalty is taking hold.

A NEW REALITY

A major shift is occurring in the Episcopal Church. Increasingly people who define themselves as being on spiritual journeys are exploring Episcopal life and finding it inviting. The pews of many Episcopal congregations are filling with adults who are at varied stages of life but are united in their focus on life as a shared, spiritual journey. The impact of their entry into the church is becoming clear. Absorbing the foundations of Christian belief and practice, they have forged new assumptions about the church's intention. Embracing the historic Episcopal balance of traditional worship and theological breadth, they are challenging its organizational assumptions. Increasing numbers of people in its pews are better equipped to navigate local conflicts and controversial issues than many mainstream religious pundits and experts who seem immobilized. At its grassroots level, Episcopal life has moved from preoccupation with the intricacies of denominational life toward a practical focus on local community and mission. As a result, the meaning of being an Episcopalian now focuses less on being a member of a religious institution than on becoming a participant in a spiritual community.

This transition is still in process. The institutional structures and processes that have characterized the Episcopal Church for a century and more remain in place. The energies of considerable numbers of talented people are being devoted to reviving and refining those structures. This book is not a challenge to those structures or to those who work to improve them. By drawing the data from those whom these structures intend to serve, rather than from the structures themselves, this study has been able to locate a new underlying reality for the church.

The purpose of this book is to describe nothing less than a new reality that, gradually but steadily, is remaking the church from the grassroots level up—a revolutionary initiative that is local rather than institutional and spiritual more than religious. In describing this rebuilding, as indicated by our research data, we also will examine what this rebuilding might mean for

Episcopalians and Americans. The fulcrum of this narrative derives from data indicating that the church's basis is shifting from an inherited emphasis upon the forms of religious institution to the challenge of building local, spiritual community. This book does not applaud or decry this major transition. The authors have no axe to grind with religious institutions in general or with the Episcopal Church in particular. The intent is simple: to report the results of face-to-face interviews with thousands of Episcopalians who have disclosed their perceptions of church life today and to interpret those disclosures.

Until relatively recently, this transition in American life—though a significant one—has not been easy to perceive; that is because the forces propelling it have arisen gradually and, more importantly, occur only at the grassroots level. But by looking closely at life in local churches, our researchers have begun to discern an emerging new shape of the Episcopal Church. As people awaken to faith and become incorporated into Episcopal congregations, there are expressions of fresh resolve for mission and outreach. There are also signs of a new wave of religiously inspired public purpose. At its root this new linkage of personal faith, community, and ministry represents efforts to achieve practical forms of religious, psychological, and social wholeness. The themes of journey, formation, and incorporation are prominent and find novel forms of expression. In short, the ties that bind the church together are being restored. As this happens, the former ideal of belonging to a religious institution is being recast as participation in a local spiritual community.

THE ZACCHAEUS PERSPECTIVE

This major shift toward a new form and purpose of religious life cannot readily be perceived through old lenses. It can only be seen when one adopts a fresh perspective. Several years ago, innovative research by the Episcopal Church Foundation began to create that new perspective. This research was called the Zacchaeus Project because it sought to emulate the experience of Zacchaeus recorded in the New Testament in Luke 19:1–10.

Zacchaeus is described as a superintendent of taxes who was very wealthy. He was eager to catch a glimpse of Jesus, but he was short and could not see over the crowd Jesus had drawn. Luke records that Zacchaeus ran ahead of the crowd and climbed a sycamore tree. From that perspective he would have a clear view as Jesus passed by. In fact the clear sightline also gave Jesus a clear look at Zacchaeus. When Jesus came upon the sycamore tree, he called Zacchaeus down. The man who sought a better view changed from observer to participant. He welcomed Jesus into his home and became a follower. By taking a different perspective, one that drew him away from the crowd, he saw and was seen by Jesus.

The story of Zacchaeus models the new experience of faith and new perspective on religious life of many people now in Episcopal churches. Like Zacchaeus, many people today break away from the crowd to see Jesus anew. Having found Jesus from a new point of view, they hear and accept his invitation to follow. A noticeably altered life then arises. Faith is no longer a private refuge; it forms new ties to others and new responsibilities to them. Likewise, the church is no longer just an institution. Though there must be committees and boards, they are not ends in themselves. Though there are professional religious leaders, all people in the church share in guiding it. On the surface, the shape of religious life retains much of its formal appearance. But for increasing numbers of people in Episcopal pews, the institutional forms point beyond themselves. The goal of those of us who served as Zacchaeus Project interviewers—a team consisting of the authors of this book and five others—was to discover a direct line of sight to the people who gather in Episcopal pews. Although some clergy and some who represent the church's official structures and affiliated institutions also were interviewed, the constant focus of the project was upon local congregations and the people they attract. We went to over two hundred locations and spoke with more than 2,500 people, sometimes in focus groups, sometimes in individual conversations. The majority of these interviews were conducted in the congregations of nine

Episcopal dioceses chosen by a diverse national advisory panel to ensure a representative cross section of the church. Our sites varied considerably according to theological and social views, worship, and style of leadership. As the number of interview transcripts multiplied, the researchers, advisory panel members, and the project's management team began to meet regularly to review the data being amassed, examine all possible interpretations of that data, and develop appropriate conclusions. As findings emerged, they suggested issues which required added attention. As a result, we expanded our list of sites to determine whether the larger sampling would confirm the initial trends our data revealed.

The findings of this work are easily summarized. Happily, there turned out to be pervasive vitality among Episcopalians at the local level. In the hundreds of congregations we visited, consistently strong patterns of worship, education, and ministry were in evidence. Of particular note was the clarity with which Episcopalians emphasize the centrality of the Eucharist for their common life. In turn, this commitment to worship empowers creative initiatives in education and ministry. Leadership also is in creative ferment. The ministry of lay persons is more profoundly grasped at the local level than ever before. Most members of Episcopal churches emphasize the goal of enhancing ethnic and cultural diversity in the church's membership and leadership. They also affirm the ordination of women to the priesthood and episcopate. Evidence appears to confirm that the face of the church's leadership is indeed changing. Along with broad shifts in leadership, Episcopalians at the local level are finding new means of being linked to one another. A variety of unofficial, informal networks and programs such as Total Ministry and Education for Ministry (EFM) afford resources and connections that enrich congregations.

Our research also highlights one particular issue: conflict. Conflict is an aspect of congregational life that figured prominently in small groups everywhere. The data demonstrated conclusively that conflict among Episcopalians defies common wisdom. While most tensions and disagreements in the church popularly are ascribed to secular, ideological polarities, the data show that the so-called "culture wars" between conservatives and liberals do not correctly define the church's primary division for most Episcopalians. Rather, the primary division is the profound disconnection most Episcopalians sense between themselves and the church's institutional channels. Typically, diocesan and national church structures and activities elicit little local interest. The people in the pews are not hostile to the wider church. Rather, they feel its programs and priorities have little bearing on the issues local congregations face. The Zacchaeus researchers were struck by the contrast between extensive local vitality and widespread local indifference to the Episcopal Church's institutional life.

The Zacchaeus Project concluded late in 1999 and was succeeded by a new phase of research. Those working on this new phase—known as the Emmaus Project in acknowledgment of the significant numbers of Episcopalians who find themselves upon the road of spiritual discovery—already have conducted interviews in hundreds of locations.[1] This research has revealed a broad pattern of change in the grassroots organization and leadership among Episcopalians. The research also reveals that these changes have moved beyond local levels and begun to challenge inherited priorities and forms of organization.

The result is that the ways in which we are connected to one another are being remade not only by the force of cultural shifts but by the initiatives of creative leaders. What the noted author Ronald Heifetz has called "adaptive leadership" is apparent in the work of many leaders in congregations and dioceses.[2] That is, increasing numbers of clergy, lay leaders, and bishops are tapping the spiritual energies of the people their congregations attract. As they do, the means and ends of their leadership change decisively: they become more engaged in questions of mission; they seek to integrate worship, outreach, and education in a dynamic sense of the church as a whole; they readily expand the leadership base of the congregation, and they view decision-making moments as opportunities to enhance clarity and consensus about the congregation's mission. This pattern of adaptive behavior suggests a fresh, thorough rebuilding of Episcopal life with a novel emphasis on the church's local identity and vocation.[3] In addition to the new trends discovered in the project's second phase, the themes found in the first continue to predominate. There remain the negative indicators of widespread disconnection from church structures and programs but also the compensatory positive indicators of new forms of connection at the grassroots level. In fact, so pervasive are these positive signs that we believe the ties that bind Episcopalians are being renewed in ways that challenge the church's inherited, institutional sense of itself.

CRITICAL ISSUES

In assessing the findings of this research, we repeatedly encountered three key issues: conflict, spirituality, and leadership. This should not be surprising. For a generation these issues have dominated discussions of the church's life. Attention to these basic issues is woven into our narrative. To understand the Episcopal Church's situation, we must address them.

CONFLICT

Conflict is the most obvious issue. Media, church conventions and councils, and scholars of religion routinely have presumed that the churches are being torn apart by intractable disputes over belief and social issues. The list of issues being hotly debated has become extensive. The Episcopal Church, like all other denominations, always has undergone challenges and tension; but beginning in the 1960s with social activism over civil rights and the Vietnam War, new strains appeared, creating unprecedented levels of fury. This new sense of crisis deepened among Episcopalians in the 1970s with revision of the Book of Common Prayer and the ordination of women. By then, it seemed clear that the Episcopal Church had developed a severe fault line: a culture war between conservatives and liberals. It was assumed that the church's leadership had embraced a progressive theological and social agenda and that this agenda was meeting widespread grassroots resistance. There was broad speculation that the church might rupture, with conservatives seeking to regroup in like-minded enclaves. Indeed, a few individuals and groups made highly publicized breaks from the church and sought to become beacons of true belief and practice. Expectantly, they and the media awaited wholesale departures, but—interestingly enough—the floodgates never opened.

Of course, by the late 1970s, a sense of decline was apparent in mainstream churches. The Episcopal Church was losing members, though these losses did not appear to be the result of factional splintering. Whatever the true reason, the significant decline in membership deepened the sense of crisis. Then the highly charged issue of homosexuality took center stage and left little room for reconciliation. Throughout the 1980s and 1990s, the feeling that Episcopalians were caught in a culture war became a foregone conclusion. Conservative groups grew louder, their leaders bewailing the seeming stranglehold "faithless liberals" held on the church's direction. Liberals clung to their progressive hopes while lamenting the damage caused by "rigid reactionaries." The two camps could agree only on the great depth of the church's crisis.

There were highly publicized clashes among the church's bishops and enough widely documented instances of clergy misconduct to further strain the church's fabric. The Episcopal Church seemed unable to escape the whirlpool of conflict in which it had become trapped. The church's experience was not unlike that of other denominations, but there was little solace in this fact. Conflict seemed to be the Episcopal Church's—and much of American religion's—primary reality.

The primary source of conflict in the church has been presumed to be an Episcopal version of the wider culture wars in American life. For years, conservative commentator Pat Buchanan has declared that Americans face a deep conflict over values. He has argued that this conflict is so profound that it represents nothing less than a waging of war between liberals and conservatives, each trying to win America's soul. Subsequently, the noted sociologist James Davison Hunter wrote a book entitled *Culture Wars: The Struggle to Define America* in which he agreed that Americans were deeply divided along ideological lines over basic values. The effect of his book was to confirm the suspicions of many Americans about the extent and nature of conflict among us.[4]

The emphasis on conflict in American religious life gained momentum and something approaching scientific respectability from the work of such influential organizations as the Alban Institute. Alban arose to provide consulting services to congregations in conflict. For decades, Alban has published books and organized conferences that offer analysis of conflicts in religious organizations. Skilled Alban consultants work with congregations across the country at pivotal moments in local church life. The need for such interventions is undeniable, but—as will be argued below—the data gathered by our research point to the emergence of new, local strategies for addressing conflict. Based on our research, belief in the primacy of conflict in religious life turns out to be neither correct nor helpful in understanding the life of Episcopal congregations.[5]

Closely allied to the view of congregational conflict as culture war is another widespread presumption: that congregations inherently become repositories of social pathology. The late Rabbi Edwin Friedman attracted a wide following with his theory that congregations resemble dysfunctional families. Friedman made a notable contribution to those who study and lead congregations. He depicted congregations in dynamic, rather than static, terms. He also posed innovative ideals of religious leadership that promised to draw congregations out of pathology and toward healthy stability. Nevertheless, Friedman reinforced the suspicion that religious organizations, notably congregations, encourage dysfunctional behavior patterns. He offered a more damning indictment of religious life than those who simply presumed its conflicted state.[6]

More recently, congregations and other types of religious organizations have been cited in the work of Harvard political scientist Robert Putnam. His book, *Bowling Alone: The Collapse and Revival of American Community*, argues that American society has become so individualistic that it is losing its historic ability to produce "social capital," which might be defined as shared forms of activity that offer social cohesion and identity. Putnam perceives a dramatic reduction of the influence of such organizations as the League of Women Voters or the Kiwanis that have afforded public means for engaging critical issues and forging social policy. Such groups have not disappeared, he notes, and in some localities retain considerable influence. But overall, they are unable to attract the level of support and assert the sort of influence they previously could muster.

In a sense, Putnam's pessimism is surprising, given his earlier writings that emphasized the resilience of democratic societies. Hints of his former hopefulness returned briefly when, after the terrorist attacks in September 2001, American public life showed itself able to return to relative normalcy quickly, and individuals demonstrated greater interest in public affairs and a greater sense of trust in one another. Ultimately he concludes that this "spike in political awareness" has not encouraged Americans "to run out and join community organizations or to show up for club meetings that they used to shun." In other words, Putnam wonders whether the reality of domestic terrorism will produce any long-term rejuvenation of American institutions.[7]

Putnam's work does not specifically treat the Episcopal Church or any particular religious group and only speaks broadly about religious life. Thus his work is unlikely to uncover the new social capital that Zacchaeus Project research has found in Episcopal congregations. None of our findings challenge his conclusion that historic forms of social capital in America are in great flux. But if Episcopal congregations in any way reflect their larger social context, our data suggest that this flux represents not the disintegration of old forms of social capital but the emergence of new forms. Thus this book, which describes the new shape of religious life among Episcopalians, represents a challenge to the pessimism of Putnam's argument but not to its basic direction. The authors grant that inherited institutional forms are in decay;

but we do not believe that the erosion of certain forms of institutional life can be equated with an overall decline of social capital. In fact, the title of this book represents a direct challenge to his pessimistic belief that America's public forms of shared meaning are in severe decline.[8]

Conflict and decline in religious and social life are so broad and complex that no book can engage them adequately. But the Zacchaeus Project findings—as gathered and interpreted here—can offer the church important corrections to prevailing assumptions about conflict and decline. The cumulative advantage of thousands of stories told to our interviewers in hundreds of local settings affords us an informed perspective that reframes the meaning of conflict in congregations, contextualizing it from the ravages of culture war into a still challenging but considerably more constructive environment. To be sure—though we cannot quantify it precisely—some Episcopalians once were troubled by revision of the Book of Common Prayer and by the ordination of women to the priesthood and the episcopate. Some now appear equally troubled by the prospect that the church might officially sanction the blessing of same-sex unions or the ordination of persons living openly in homosexual relationships. Often such particular fears reflect a deeper concern that the church's moral strictures have relaxed or that the church has surrendered its necessary loyalty to the Bible and to basic Christian doctrine.

The primary source of conflict in the Episcopal Church, however, is not distress over doctrine or revisions of worship or ministry. Rather the primary source is a widespread sense that the church's diocesan and national structures focus inadequately on mission and do not provide the resources and guidance necessary to enhance the ministry initiatives of local congregations. The primary decline many Episcopalians perceive is the loss of practical commitment to local mission. They perceive that resources and energies at the diocesan and national levels are often devoted to programs that do not honor local wisdom and do not address local needs. The result is that many people in local leadership roles simply ignore the church's official channels when they seek

the resources necessary for their common life. This sense of disconnection is the principal source of disaffection among Episcopalians.

Because the focus on building up congregational programs is
paramount in local Episcopal life, most conflict in Episcopal
churches concerns the intentions and strategies of program life.
Often conflicts over program life reflect the outlooks of different
constituencies in congregations, particularly different age groups
in churches (as evidenced in the Christ Church small group discussions examined earlier). When it comes to program life, older,
long-established leaders and younger, newer arrivals usually have
very different assumptions, priorities, leadership styles, and
strategies for finding the necessary finances.[9] However, if program life in the Episcopal Church is such a constant source of
conflict, then there is a very positive implication that should be
acknowledged: a lot of conflict about program life in the Episcopal
Church necessarily signifies that there's a lot of program life! Our
data indicate that Episcopal congregations are in the midst of
remarkable creative ferment. In this context, conflict reflects the
emergence of new patterns of activity amid older forms and priorities. Conflict is a sign that Episcopalians are in the midst of
major transitions in understanding and living the Christian faith.

The research also refutes the well-established metaphor of
the congregation as dysfunctional family. On the evidence, congregations are not inherently pathological and do not get locked
into intractable patterns of conflict. In more than three hundred
visits to congregations, researchers found virtually no places that
escaped conflict entirely, and yet most found the means necessary
to address and resolve their challenges. Interviewers heard
detailed descriptions of how the members of these congregations
discovered ways to overcome their difficulties. Based on these
accounts, our findings credit local Episcopalians with a capacity
for resilience, depth of commitment, and degree of sophistication
that many experts on religious life refuse to grant.

Clearly, some conflicts in congregations resist resolution.
Conflict may produce fear and inertia. It may incline a local
church to focus on preserving an imagined stability rather than

risking new forms of vitality. But the tendency to overemphasize the destructiveness of conflict without probing the nuances occludes the sort of perspective that is necessary to understand the paradox of local vitality and institutional crisis that defines the church's contemporary life.[10]

In emphasizing local vitality, this research joins a body of work by other writers who present a very different point of view on conflict. For example, the Zacchaeus Project's perspective is consistent with Alan Wolfe's in his book, *One Nation, After All: What Americans Really Think About God, Country, Family, Racism, Welfare, Immigration, Homosexuality, Work, The Right, The Left and Each Other*. Wolfe, who is the director of a research center on religion and American life at Boston College, conducted extensive interviews in four metropolitan areas. He discovered a deeply rooted capacity for ethical sensitivity and moral action in middle-class America. Unlike those who emphasize crisis, Wolfe found enduring forms of public purpose and, more importantly, an underlying sense of common bond. His ability to go deeply into local American life and to discover a lasting framework of social value and action encouraged us to seek similar wellsprings of shared faith among Episcopalians.[11]

Other researchers on American religious life have described the power and depth of congregational life. Since the work of the late James Hopewell, an Episcopal priest whose research led him to articulate a new appreciation for congregations, a cluster of dedicated writers and teachers has attempted to develop a new perspective on the study of congregational life. Inspired by Hopewell's focus on the structures and processes of people in congregations, a variety of new historical, social, and theological perspectives have emerged.[12] These perspectives—which include research into congregations in transition (such as changes in leadership, neighborhood demographics, or congregational size)—have found their way not only into academic studies but also into practical conversations about life in congregations.[13]

Nancy T. Ammerman and her student Nancy L. Eiesland have done important research that reveals emerging patterns of congregational adaptation. Eiesland, following Ammerman's example, describes the persistence of a sense of place even as congregations are adapting to dramatic social changes.[14] Similarly, Donald Miller has described how new congregations arise and older ones are rebuilt, physically and spiritually. Once again the creation of new patterns of religious community—rather than rampant conflict and pathology—comes forward as the principal reality in Episcopal congregations.[15]

SPIRITUALITY

Our research findings reveal that, for a significant, even pervasive, number of Episcopalians, religious life now is defined by spiritual criteria rather than institutional structures. In this regard, Episcopalians seem no different from many Americans. Countless people today are rebuilding their religious lives, forging connections with congregations, and exploring wider linkages, and behind this broad, energetic initiative are the same spiritual criteria so important to Episcopalians.

Of course, as every commentator on American religion notes, "spirituality" is as difficult to define as it is appealing. The breadth of the term suggests its ability to encompass disparate ideals and activities, although it frustrates concise definition. We must probe what the idea of "spirituality" suggests, because it embodies what the people in Episcopal pews are saying and doing. Just as conflict represents a basic thread throughout this book, so it is necessary to understand what "spirituality" means to Episcopalians today.

Part of the problem of defining spirituality is that it is a primary reference point in all religious life. Spirituality refers to the deepest possible source of meaning and to the human encounter with it. It is both content and experience, both the origin and the end of human longing, the assurance of what is fixed and the possibility inherent in change. The spiritual dimension of life includes that which is eternal and those human patterns that seek the eternal. Often depicted as breath or wind or fire or clouds, the spiritual dimension represents the point at which what is divine and what is human meet.

According to noted sociologist Wade Clark Roof, "spirituality" today means the following to most people: a source of values and meaning beyond oneself, a way of understanding, inner awareness, and personal integration. Typically, Roof and other observers believe the spiritual currents in society are predominantly individualistic. As Roof comments, "religious identities in contemporary society are fluid, multilayered, and to a considerable extent personally achieved." Religious life today features "eclecticism, or constellations of elements and themes from different faiths and traditions, put together by individuals exercising their creative agency."[16] Not surprisingly, Roof finds that individual spiritual explorations stand in stark contrast to inherited patterns of belonging to religious denominations. Today, highly personalized blends of belief and practice prevail over effective enforcement of institutionalized standards of order and orthodoxy.

However, as Roof and another noted observer, Robert Wuthnow, have discovered, individual religious identity must be "rooted to a considerable degree within community."[17] Without a communal context "it is difficult to regularize religious life around a set of practices and unifying experiences, to mobilize people around causes, or even to sustain personal religious identity." Consequently, argues Wuthnow, a widespread search for new forms of community has emerged. For example, the therapeutic small group movement indicates and exemplifies a longing for shared forms of authenticity and effectiveness. Participants seek to build a framework of interpersonal relations that encourages the true self to emerge, to be healthy, and to prompt health in others. Spirituality today represents a meeting ground on which the individual self joins with other selves.[18]

One outcome of the growth of interest in a shared spirituality has been a fresh exploration of religious tradition. This finding may be somewhat surprising, given that most forms of traditionalism tend to equate religious tradition with religious institution. Previous generations have tended to make factional use of tradition by drawing upon the past to find precedents for a particular model of leadership or governance that suited their preferred ecclesiology. For example, the Anglo-Catholicism of the late nineteenth and early twentieth centuries searched tradition to corroborate their reliance upon apostolic succession and primacy of the episcopate.

Contemporary spiritual seekers also search the past for precedents, but their search is qualitatively different: they are searching for historical sanction for spiritual community. More specifically, the current return to tradition borrows heavily from historic forms of prayer and worship, ancient teachings, and patterns of church life but does so without any factional motivation, agenda, or purpose other than to discover new kinds of social currency that then may be dedicated to the purpose of spiritual community-building.

Today's spiritual sense of journey diverges in one important aspect from the historical model. Historically, spirituality has been rooted in a sense both of inhabiting a fixed place and of being on an individual journey. Today's spiritual search begins personally and may remain intensely private but ultimately strives for a common pursuit and the formation of a group of spiritual pilgrims. Implicit in the search for spirituality is the assumption that it is a dynamic quest for a common life.[19]

Historically, the concept of community—so important to Episcopalians and to American life generally—has been understood to begin with the identification of a particular place. But today's widespread reassessment defines something more than the presumption of a particular locale. Contemporary spirituality prizes a sense of place as the basis for shared efforts to build a sense of community. As author Thomas Bender has observed, community "is a network of social relations marked by mutuality and emotional bonds." Community begins individually, with each person's experience of being known and accepted; but community is then expressed collectively in shared obligations and opportunities. Most respondents described what the experience of going to church meant to them in very spiritual and personal terms—at least initially. Interestingly, given sufficient time and attention from their listeners, most quickly modulated their story such that the most meaningful aspects of church-going were revealed as decidedly collective; furthermore, they usually referred to very specific programmatic collective experiences rather than to a more generalized, abstract sense of belonging. And so the intangible social bond of belonging thereby creates tangible social results in our church communities—social results which manifest as complicated patterns of participation rooted in particular forms of language, observance, and practice. In other words, so as to make the conceptual leap all at once, belonging creates culture.

In contemporary spirituality, community has acquired the status of communion. That is, community now describes a prized experience of mutuality. What is new in this spiritual discussion is the assumption that community cannot be inherited or presumed; it must be created. Thus, community now is associated with a dynamic experience of shared spiritual journey rather than a static ideal limited to a particular place. Chapter two gives close attention to basic shifts in the ideal of community among Episcopalians. Understanding how the meaning of the Episcopal Church as a community has changed—largely at the grassroots level—will be the key to describing basic shifts in the church's identity and vocation.[20]

Despite their appeal, concepts such as "spirituality," "community," "place," and "journey" remain too easily within the realm of the abstract. To understand their practical import and application, it is necessary to give concrete examples of how they are expressed in the lives of actual people and congregations. Our findings are consistent with the work of Craig Dykstra and Dorothy C. Bass on the "practices" of Christian faith. While a practice can be "any socially meaningful behavior," for Christians the concept of practices identifies specific activities that express the faith of Christian people over time and in particular settings. Practices are habitual forms of expression that become integral to Christian identity and vocation in specific settings, especially basic patterns of worship. Practices also include patterns of governance and forms of organization in congregations. These encompass both formal and informal ways of sustaining common life, including response to human need, teaching and nurture, defining and enacting mission, and observing pivotal moments in personal and collective life. The Zacchaeus Project's examination of life at the Episcopal Church's grassroots paid close attention to local practices, with researchers asking what they meant in context, what they represented as trends, and what they indicated for the church's future. It is important to note that these questions about the religious significance of practices were asked at a time when "religion" and "spirituality" usually were thought to stand in opposition to one another. Our research findings about practices dispute the simplistic and popular view that religion necessarily is institutional and stodgy while spirituality represents individual dynamism and freedom.[21]

In *Strength for the Journey*, Zacchaeus Project colleague Diana Bass offers important insight into the nature of spiritual journeys today. Describing her own spiritual journey over twenty years and eight Episcopal congregations, Bass stresses the centrality of practices in structuring a common life. These practices center on regular participation in worship in ways that afford encounters with ancient Christian example. Practices also include seemingly mundane aspects of sustaining the life of a faith community, such as preparing and sharing meals.[22] As she suggests, the practices of Christian life entail a sacramental sense of practical tasks. Rather than an expression of institutional adherence, spirituality for Episcopalians across the country has become rooted in the practical tasks of building local spiritual community. The people in the pews of Episcopal churches are on a spiritual search for God that takes the outward form of going about the ordinary business of creating and strengthening parish life.

LEADERSHIP

Historian George M. Thomas has observed that religious movements attempt to "construct a new social order...in their specific claims and demands."[23] Similarly, theologian H. Richard Niebuhr once noted that Protestantism in America is essentially a social movement.[24] When they have been most clear about their identity and vocation, the Protestant denominations have functioned not as religious institutions but as missionary societies. Their activities and their forms of organization have reflected a clear and practical focus on the challenge of mission. Signs of this legacy remain. The Episcopal Church is still formally known as the "Domestic and Foreign Missionary Society." This heritage, which will be discussed in more detail in chapter two, dates to the late eighteenth century when social realities compelled a dramatic reorganization of the church. With the end of the American Revolution, adherents of the colonial Church of England lost the established status they enjoyed in certain colonies and the social prestige that distinguished them in all. They also suffered from close association with the repudiated colonial power. Thus, not only did they lack sufficient organization for the drastically changing social circumstances, but there was no precedent for the challenge of reorganization they faced. More than other Protestants, Episcopalians had to forge an identity that was faithful to both their heritage and their setting.

In part, the success of the Episcopal Church's rebirth in America relied upon the way in which it appropriated democratic process in a nation that had ended established churches. Episcopalians in each state organized into dioceses which began electing their own bishops. Soon a national church structure followed. The church created a triennial, bicameral General Convention organized like the U.S. Congress. The Convention became the formal center of Episcopal governance, the basis of its coherence in the American setting. Dioceses followed with their own regular convention structure. But securing appropriate governance accounted for only a portion of the church's adaptive challenge. Governance supplied the form of the church, not its substance. The true achievement of the Episcopal Church after the American Revolution was its ability to articulate a sense of mission and to derive a form of organization that suited this challenge.

Once the demands placed upon their church by the Revolutionary War had been successfully attended to, Episcopalians began to evolve complex organizational structures similar to the other mainstream denominations. And like those other denominations, the Episcopal Church's structures became more and more centralized. Gradually the church's identity and vocation were entrusted to an elaborate, hierarchical organization. Paralleling the emergence of centralized corporate and political organizations in secular culture, the structure of the Episcopal Church seemed appropriate to the challenge of mission in its American setting. But with uncertainties about the church's institutional forms apparent from the late twentieth century on, the question of what organizational form might emerge to foster the church's mission in a new era has become central, although the historic scope of the question is not widely understood. It is crucial to ask how the institutional life of the church might be restructured in light of why people are drawn to local churches and how they participate in them. Because the process of seeking God in a local, spiritual community is becoming dominant, the ties that bind people together in shared religious identity are taking a new form. This impulse is not confined to the Episcopal Church. In fact all American organizations are in the midst of reframing their intentions and their forms. This book will consider where the churches stand in relation to the restructuring of other sorts of organizations, including for-profit ones. Clearly the churches share in the sorts of challenges all organizations face. But the distinctive aspects of religious life must also be appreciated if the churches are to do more than simply imitate secular patterns of reorganization.

This book's emphasis on this point reflects concern for the Episcopal Church's *identity* and *vocation*. These ideals typically bespeak the church's sense of its *mission*. If mission is the church's core task, vocation becomes a way of emphasizing that the church must translate its identity into practical expressions. That is, what the church does grows out of how it views itself. This narrative uses the concept of vocation in order to emphasize the contemporary challenge Episcopalians face. It will become clear that the challenges of mission are being asked locally and that the consistent result of this soul-searching is congregational vitality. It also will become clear that these same challenges are *not* being faced squarely at all levels of the church.

To grasp the ability of the church to respond to its organizational challenges requires reviewing the traditions and trends in American religious leadership. In all organizations, including the churches, leadership has become the subject of frenetic discussion. Today, there is a widespread sense that leaders can be trained for their roles. There is also a fresh appreciation for the ways in which leadership must transform or transcend inherited roles. In the last quarter of the twentieth century—prompted by the work of James MacGregor Burns and others—leadership discussions highlighted the theme of the leader as an agent of social and organizational change. This perspective has influenced the way clergy approach their work.

Leadership discussions include an emphasis upon "change" or "transformation"—two often-cited hallmarks of astute leaders. But the emphasis upon change arises more properly in the context of an emphasis upon mission. This research has demonstrated convincingly that the church's intentions and strategies are securely grounded when they focus on mission. Once the emphasis upon this understanding of mission is established—at least at the leadership level—then the appropriate set of leadership practices begins to become apparent. Such practices then enlarge the realization within the congregation by creating personal and organizational opportunities in which members begin to glimpse their collective mission.

Effective leadership in today's churches would appear to be contingent upon leaders' realization that a focus on mission *must* be primary. But their work is not yet done with this essential realization; rather the realization is only the first—albeit the essential—step in establishing the real work and the healthy life of any congregation. Charisma, creativity, the ability to effect change or transformation—all the supposed "tricks of the trade" of those who must lead and inspire others—actually become more important in this context of clarity of focus upon mission. Congruent with the burgeoning new understanding of mission in the Episcopal Church is a new emphasis upon the personality and, especially, the character of leaders today. Character in this instance means more than the responsibility leaders must demonstrate, though personal responsibility in a variety of forms is a firm requirement for all leaders. Character also refers to the sorts of traits leaders should cultivate. For instance, Daniel W. Hardy has written that Anglican approaches to theological education must become appreciative of wisdom gained in local settings. Stressing the role of a distinctively Anglican sense of identity and vocation, Hardy suggests that leaders must rely on tradition while they develop an ability to learn from and about the settings in which they serve.[25] Rather than presuming inherent pathology or the necessity of change, the leader must understand a setting at its best. Today's best leaders embody an appreciation for those they seek to serve.

In summary, this narrative will describe patterns of flux in the Episcopal Church. It would be tempting to view these currents of uncertainty as portents of destruction. But the research does not indicate that the sky is falling. There is indeed remarkable movement, but it appears to be not downward and destructive but upward from the grassroots and constructive. And all indications are that with it comes a fresh rush of the Holy Spirit, a wave of spirituality that is remaking the church. In other words, the news is good but must be named as such and understood clearly to allow its implications to bring fresh vitality to all sectors of the church. Explaining the implications of this good news is the purpose of this narrative.

STRUCTURE OF THE BOOK

The themes of conflict, spirituality, and leadership will continue as reference points throughout this story of the church's shift from religious institution to spiritual community. In chapter two, the sources of the church's current situation are examined through the lens of Episcopal history, with particular focus on the church's ever changing American identity and the evolving styles of organization and leadership that helped secure those identity changes. Conflict fills chapter three as the organizational life of the Episcopal Church begins to fail in the second half of the twentieth century. Chapter four takes a larger look at organization, on the level of both American and Episcopal life. In chapters five and six, patterns of local mission and ministry are examined. In chapter seven, we explore how Episcopalians identify, seek, and find the resources their local initiatives require. In chapter eight, we ask what the shift from institution to community implies for understanding the Christian faith and Christian tradition today and tomorrow.

How might Episcopalians grasp the possibility before them? How can they construe the true nature of their church's situation? To answer these questions, we turn to consider how the church's sense of mission in America took form.

NOTES

[1] The Emmaus Project takes its name from the New Testament account of Jesus' resurrection appearance to several of his disciples as they traveled along the road to Emmaus. See Luke 24:13–32.

[2] Ronald A. Heifetz, *Leadership Without Easy Answers* (Belknap, 1994).

[3] The structure and methods of the Zacchaeus Project and of the continuing research which we have called the Emmaus Project are described in Appendix A of this book.

[4] James Davison Hunter, *Culture Wars: The Struggle to Define America* (Basic Books, 1991).

[5] Interestingly, in a report on the state of American religious leadership, Alban juxtaposed its habitual emphasis on conflict with reference to signs of creative ferment in religious life, citing the Zacchaeus Project's evidence of renewed congregational life as exceptional to the usual sources of intractable conflict and steady decline. Of course, Alban is correct in noting the strains facing judicatories and national church structures. We acknowledge the reality and importance of these issues, but argue that congregational vitality portends a transition in the ways American religion is organized. It is also important to note that, with the publication of this report, Alban announces its intention to balance its habitual emphasis on crisis with a more formative perspective. See *The Leadership Situation Facing American Congregations: An Alban Institute Special Report* (Alban, September 2001).

[6] Edwin H. Friedman, *Generation to Generation: Family Process in Church and Synagogue* (Guilford, 1985).

[7] Robert D. Putnam, "The United State of America," *The American Prospect*, February 11, 2002, pp. 20–22.

[8] Robert D. Putnam, *Bowling Alone: The Collapse and Revival of American Community* (Simon & Schuster, 2000).

[9] See Jackson W. Carroll and Wade Clark Roof, *Bridging Divided Worlds: Generational Cultures in Congregations* (Jossey-Bass, 2002).

[10] It is worth noting that early in 2002 the market research firm Roper ASW reported the results of a survey of over 2,000 Episcopal congregation members, clergy, bishops, national leaders, and General Convention deputies. These varied constituencies agreed that the church's priorities should be "spiritual growth" and attracting youth and young adults to the church. This study reinforces the Zacchaeus finding of the importance people in Episcopal pews attach to spirituality. It is also noteworthy that the highest response to the Roper questionnaire came from bishops and national church leaders. This suggests that at least some potential respondents viewed the exercise in institutional rather than spiritual terms. See "Researching Episcopal Constituencies," Roper ASW, January 24, 2002.

[11] Alan Wolfe, *One Nation, After All: What Americans Really Think About God, Country, Family, Racism, Welfare, Immigration, Homosexuality, Work, The Right, The Left and Each Other* (Viking, 1998).

[12] James F. Hopewell, *Congregation: Stories and Structures* (Fortress, 1987). Also, James P. Wind and James W. Lewis, editors, *American Congregations: New Perspectives in the Study of Congregations*, two volumes (Chicago, 1994). Nancy T. Ammerman, et al., editors, *Studying Congregations: A New Handbook* (Abingdon, 1998).

[13] Roy M. Oswald and Robert E. Friedrich, Jr., *Discerning Your Congregation's Future: A Strategic and Spiritual Approach* (Alban, 1996), and Roy M. Oswald, *New Beginnings: A Pastorate Start Up Workbook* (Alban, 1989). Also, Carl S. Dudley and Nancy T. Ammerman, *Congregations in Transition: A Guide for Analyzing, Assessing, and Adapting in Changing Communities* (Jossey-Bass, 2002).

[14] See Nancy T. Ammerman, et al., *Congregation and Community* (Rutgers, 1997) and Nancy L. Eieseland, *A Particular Place: Urban Restructuring and Religious Ecology in a Southern Exurb* (Rutgers, 2000).

[15] Donald E. Miller, *Reinventing American Protestantism: Christianity in the New Millennium* (California, 1997).

[16] Wade Clark Roof, *Spiritual Marketplace: Baby Boomers and the Remaking of American Religion* (Princeton, 1999), p. 35.

[17] *Ibid.*, p. 39.

[18] Among Robert Wuthnow's many books, *Sharing the Journey: Support Groups and America's New Quest for Community* (Free Press, 1994) and *Acts of Compassion* (Princeton, 1991) make this point most clearly.

[19] Robert Wuthnow, *After Heaven: Spirituality in America Since the 1950s* (California, 1998). In this book Wuthnow argues that there has been a shift from the dominant American spirituality of the 1950s that focused upon belonging to wider institutions through participation in local affiliates to a broad contemporary sense of being on a journey. Zacchaeus researchers do not believe that the linkage between spirituality and a sense of place is as diminished as he argues, though we agree that the sense of place is shifting for Americans and that there is little institutional allegiance implied in it.

[20] Thomas Bender, *Community and Social Change in America* (Rutgers, 1978).

[21] Craig Dykstra and Dorothy C. Bass, "A Theological Understanding of Christian Practices," in Miroslav Volf and Dorothy C. Bass, editors, *Practicing Theology:Beliefs and Practices in Christian Life* (Eerdmans, 2001).

[22] Diana Butler Bass, *Strength for the Journey: A Pilgrimage of Faith in Community* (Jossey-Bass, 2002).

[23] George M. Thomas, *Revivalism and Cultural Change: Christianity, Nation Building and the Market in the Nineteenth-Century United States* (Chicago, 1989).

[24] H. Richard Niebuhr, *The Kingdom of God in America* (Harper, 1959).

[25] Daniel W. Hardy, *Finding The Church: The Dynamic Truth of Anglicanism* (SCM, 2001).

2

THE TIES THAT ONCE BOUND
The Power of Memory

"When I graduated from seminary there wasn't much disagreement about what we faced." In an East Coast city, the recently retired priest had been considering the direction his ministry had taken. He had cited accomplishments and challenges in his most recent parish. Then he began to savor memories of his early years. He reclined slowly in the chair, twirled his glasses methodically, and eyed a distant point out the window. After a few seconds of silent reflection he turned back from the window, gave a slight shrug, and added, "You see, it was the 1950s. We knew what the church was and what we were supposed to do. Everyone in my seminary class wanted to make the church run better. We were going to build it up and make it work better." "So, what did that mean to you and your classmates?" the interviewer wondered. The priest stroked his chin, considered the question, and replied, "Well, we were going to expand the church. You know, grow the membership, build new buildings and revamp old ones, start new churches, involve more people. It was a time of expansion. And we thought the challenge was to make the institution run better." He paused and chuckled slightly. "And we thought we knew how to do that. We knew how to be better structured, better organized." He spun slowly in his chair and looked out the window again. When he was settled, he cleared his throat and spoke slowly, "But we never imagined what we would face."

An elderly man in the Midwest also recalled the 1950s and his years as a lay leader in his parish and diocese. "On Christmas Eve it would always be so beautiful. Of course, there would be snow outside, and it would be cold. But inside, the church would be full, and everyone would be so nicely dressed. And you would know everyone! The service would be so dignified. Our rector then was a great teacher and preacher. And you would see rows of mink coats; every woman had one on."

A woman of his age group sitting near him in this small group nodded and added her own recollection. "The church would be decorated so beautifully. We all pitched in and worked on that. And you see what a beautiful church we have. Because it is Gothic, it rises like an offering to God." Her hands rose solemnly to illustrate the point as her face shone warmly. "And we didn't think we were staid or took ourselves too seriously. This has always been a welcoming church. That's who we are." "Aw hell," another elderly man interjected. "Of course we know who we are. I've heard all this talk about identity for years. We didn't have that problem. We knew who were and what this church was! We just need to get back to it. That's all!" His point made, he sat back and with a dramatic flourish folded his arms across his chest.

Though an older generation of Episcopalians is passing the mantle of church leadership to a younger, its memories and sense of itself remain clear. "We understood the places we served," observed one priest from an East Coast parish. He had retired several years before but continued to assist a large parish on a part-time basis. He also participated in the life of his local deanery and diocese. When memories of his years in ordained ministry in that diocese flowed, he could not resist comparing the present with the past. "You didn't have to show us how to be involved; we knew we had a role in the community; that was part of what we assumed we would do. You joined the Rotary Club and the school board, and you knew how to take part in them. It was part of your responsibility." Then his face darkened and his voice became somber. "These new clergy today just want to dress up and play church. They don't have any sense of their social role. They don't know how to take part in their communities. They don't even know how to run a meeting. The clergy today don't know how to lead!"

For some long-time Episcopalians, nostalgia preserves the ideal of what church should be and proves where we fall short today. Nostalgia for the church's past usually surfaces reverently, and usually sadly, also, with the sense of something precious lost, leaving a church no longer as it once was. Memories warmed by nostalgia depict a time when Episcopalians were united by a clear sense of their identity and vocation, a time when Episcopalians knew who they were and what they should be doing.

Such memories surfaced frequently in Zacchaeus Project interviews. Often beginning as mere conversation starters, then quickening into pleasant communal "campfire" stories of the sort that every close-knit group likes to tell, these memories sometimes became so intense that their power overwhelmed the tellers and their listeners. Even the small-group participants who were newer to the church and knew nothing of this supposed age of unity and clarity could understand the hurt and longing sometimes unleashed during the interviews. After all, who wouldn't want to return to a golden age? Who wouldn't long to recover those ties of fellowship that apparently were tighter than any today?

Nostalgia is in great demand, and Episcopalians have their own varieties. Not only are there older Episcopalians who remember a "golden age" in their experience of the church, there also are newer Episcopalians who never knew the golden age but long for something like its certainty and assurance. The Mitford novels written by Jan Karon speak perhaps to many Episcopalians who find the past alluring, whether they lived through it or not.

Mitford, a fictitious small town in the idyllic setting of the North Carolina mountains, is a friendly, self-assured community with a gentle pace. Father Tim is the rector of the Episcopal Church in town, and his flock loves him for his faithful presence in their lives. However, as the first novel in the series begins, Father Tim's life in Mitford is not free of longing. He is single and his loneliness is apparent. But he remains faithful to his congregation and community, and his faithfulness is rewarded. He meets and marries a local woman, finding in the church and the local community the final fulfillment of his hopes and his faithfulness. In this town and its Episcopal church, his life readily becomes whole. Father Tim becomes secure in himself because Mitford's sense of itself, and the identity of the church there, are intact. Wherever the local church's identity is rooted in an enduring social framework, Karon's novels suggest, life's challenges can be overcome and the people of that church always will find hope.[1]

The popularity of the Mitford novels reflects the hope that the basic qualities of church life can be preserved and that the church can stabilize its social settings. Karon depicts a world that many older Episcopalians hope to preserve. But it is also a world that many newer Episcopalians long for. As they envision what the church might be, these newer Episcopalians envision a church that embodies promise and purpose amid the world's doubts and struggles. In their ideal community, the religious and social frameworks meld to offer a clear sense of place. The priority of belonging is assumed, and the patterns of participation are defined.

In a number of respects, the memories of older Episcopalians and the hopes of newer ones converge. For both sorts of Episcopalians, the past suggests qualities of church life that must be renewed. For example, a woman in a Midwestern college community parish recalled the ties that once bound Episcopalians: "In South Carolina where I grew up, people lived in the same place for so long. You knew everybody. It just is not the same now." Her memories depict an intact social fabric, unlike the patchwork complexity of today. They also reveal her ideal of what the church must strive to re-create today. In similar fashion, one church member in a small town in the South declared: "We are very proud of our long history. We give thanks for what this church has provided over the years." His implication was that there are qualities of church life that must be preserved.

Occasionally, Episcopalians admit that their memories can be stumbling blocks. At another parish in the South, the members of a focus group had been describing their effort to call a new rector. As they did, they revealed a basic dilemma. "Our search for a new rector has struggled along. Many people wanted someone who would take us back to the glory of the good old days. We didn't take time to get honest about who we are now, not what we were in the past."

When Episcopalians remember the past, they describe a powerful feeling of belonging, of being known and valued in their local churches. They also describe the experience of being a part of a wider institution where local initiatives were honored. With a broad smile on his face, a retired college professor in the Midwest recalled his experience of his diocese. "There used to be a woman on our diocesan staff who knew all the churches and all the people. She would know you by name. And everybody knew her." His right hand made sweeping gestures as he spoke. "If you had a question or a problem you could call her. And she would call you right back. Everything you needed would get done."

But the sense of community they describe has diminished. Today when one asks older Episcopalians to recall the past, they often do so by contrasting the church they remember with what they experience now. Their comparisons can be biting. At one Southern parish, several members complained that "we don't know how to reach out for help or where to look. The diocesan office isn't a place where we've gotten any help. We feel cut off and alone." A nearby parish told a similar story: their search for effective models of program life led to more conversations with local Presbyterians than with their diocese. "We have drawn many useful ideas from the nearby Presbyterian church, learning from their mistakes and taking advantage of their successes to apply to similar issues we face here."

Coming from Episcopalians who once felt closely connected to their diocesan and national structures, such statements are sobering. Now many Episcopalians have concluded that diocesan staff lack appreciation for—or even awareness of—the distinctive issues their congregations face in their distinctive settings. Worse, the church's national structures and those who direct them are generally unknown to the people in congregations and appear to have no relevance to local concerns. The result is that these Episcopalians experience a profound disconnection from the structures of their own denomination and turn to fellow Christians in their vicinity who share similar challenges. Their longing to build Christian community at the local level far outweighs denominational identity. Today, increasing numbers of people who call themselves Episcopalians think of themselves primarily as members of local congregations. They are not conversant with the issues that consume the Episcopal Church's national staff; neither do they know very much about the concerns or workings of their diocese. Although they occasionally are frustrated with the Episcopal Church's institutional activities, they expend surprisingly little energy on the larger church. Instead, they direct their interest and effort toward building a local spiritual community. This basic change in allegiance and focus has become characteristic of the church's grassroots.

The sources of this disconnection vary. Sometimes it is a perception that the church's standards of belief and practice have diminished. "That the Episcopal Church hasn't set out where it stands is a key issue. The church has ridden the fence on abortion, same-sex unions, and openly gay ministry," members of one parish asserted. "Why don't the church's leaders just read their Bibles and follow God's Word," wondered members of a Southeastern parish. In some instances, church members perceive that their priorities and leadership style distance them from the wider church. "The national Episcopal Church is never considered in our thinking or planning. We are a place where teams and mutual helping are essential. Nothing in the national church remotely resembles teamwork in any sense of the word."

It is widely assumed that many members of Episcopal congregations, like members of other mainstream denominations, are disgruntled. Supposedly, the local churches are populated by intransigent conservatives who do not respect national headquarters and the dioceses because the leadership roles at this level of the church are held by irresponsible liberals. But a closer look at what Episcopalians are saying at the local level reveals another somewhat surprising reality. Most Episcopalians explain their sense of distance from institutional church structures in simple, unmistakable terms: local focus is on local mission, but the focus of other levels of the church always seems elsewhere. "The national church started off as a missionary society, to support missions," observed one lay leader who had studied the church's history closely. "They've become a bureaucracy that serves its own interests." Often, there are explicit pleas for assistance. "Help us with religious education, with outreach, with formation, with strengthening our people instead of tearing them apart with conflicts." Or, "help us with resources to learn to think theologically, instead of just politically," members of another parish pleaded.

The source of such longing is more than nostalgia. Clearly many members of Episcopal churches long for a renewed focus on mission. They believe that mission entails effective ways of encouraging new ties that bind. They perceive a desperate need for such emphasis. "Our society is undergoing rapid changes, diminishing intimacy and connectedness and increasing alienation. The church can be a major source for rebuilding community and bringing light into darkness." Though implicitly critical of the church and cynical about its fulfillment of its calling, this comment by a lay leader is notable for its sense of mission possibility, not for its despair. It is also noteworthy that her image of the church is neither nostalgic nor idealized; rather, it derives from the church's ability to adapt to its current situation.

Those readers who consider nostalgia to be a potentially unhealthy form of escapism will be heartened to learn that this idealized way of looking backward does not appear to be prevalent at the grassroots level. But that is not to say that Episcopalians have turned from their past. Many people interviewed during the Zacchaeus Project told stories from the good old days, but most of them did so for guidance, not escape; and most of them did so thoughtfully and realistically. Listening to his fellow parishioners describe their congregation's recent growth, an older man who had been a church member for many years suddenly spoke. His memories put the church's recent vitality in helpful perspective. "I've been a member here for forty years. When I joined, this was a strong church. A few years later the whole diocese went High Church. Remember all that stuff? All those events happened at the same time—the Prayer Book and the ordination of women. At that time, many people left this parish. It was even rumored that the diocese might close us down. Then we got another rector. He instituted good worship and good preaching. Then the parish grew again. We went up. Not all at once, but steadily. Now we attract a young group, and we have a young woman as our rector."

This man's account is typical in its balanced view of the struggles that changed the church's former fabric. His way of relying upon the past suggests that, for Episcopalians, memories of a time of clarity in the church inform their view of its mission today. As this man spoke, several of the newer members of his congregation—people who had not experienced the church of a generation ago—nodded vigorously, apparently compelled by his memories. When questioned, they agreed that his view of the past was instructive without being overly idealized. One person commented that such candor is helpful when the congregation faces new challenges and that the newer members value examples of how an older generation of leaders responded to the task of mission. He added that they find confidence for the future in knowing that the congregation survived even dire situations. The survival of the community no longer is at stake; but they have come to understand that they must focus on mission when they hear the experiences of the past. Images from the past serve the church of today well when they provide not only ideals of church life but incentive to attend to mission.

In one Western parish, where the focus clearly is on mission, membership had more than doubled in five years, and parishioners spoke enthusiastically of their "Spirit-led" vision of what the church could and should be. One woman—a newer member—spoke of the "huge hunger in my own life and of my contemporaries who want God." She and others like her were "starving for their church life, their spiritual life, to inform their whole lives. So that their work and life is integrated with their faith." She believed that, in her parish, she and others like her have been able to find what they were seeking: "a sense of purpose, an openness and honesty and dedication to trying to be the hands and heart and feet and body of Christ in the world. It is pretty amazing!"

As this woman spoke, the quality of common life she described began to recall the depth of faith and community and the profound sense of belonging that older Episcopalians so often spoke of and so nostalgically longed for. But the difference between the older and newer generations soon became clear. When asked about the church beyond their parish, these church members expressed a view that earlier generations of Episcopalians would not have recognized. "I don't think people really know anything about the Episcopal Church," one noted. The renewed vitality of their congregation that created such close ties within their community did not seem to be re-creating the ties that once bound Episcopalians to the church's wider structures. Their loyalty is almost exclusively to their congregation and to the demands of mission in their locality. They do not see themselves as members of the current wider religious institution.[2]

Neither does the emerging Episcopal experience of community place much reliance upon inherited institutional structures or historic social patterns. For example, certain new patterns of lay leadership—as will be described in more detail later in this book—demonstrate remarkable scope, authority, and initiative. The division of labor that once separated what clergy did from what laity did is largely gone. Today's members of Episcopal churches understand the church as the fruit of active, local initiative entailing the mutual efforts of clergy and laity. The church is not the result of clergy ministry alone; neither does it come about by the passive loyalty of lay people to remote authority figures or institutional structures that, supposedly, do the real work of the church. But it is important to note that the people who occupy Episcopal pews today are not overweening in their ownership of their communities; neither are they cynical or rebellious when it comes to church institutions and authorities. Rather, they seek effective, practical expressions of Christian faith and community that arise as a result of their shared spiritual journey. It is perhaps the sustaining strength of this shared spiritual journey that explains the depth and breadth of modern lay initiative. And it is the nature of shared spiritual journey that also best explains why—despite the grassroots rejection of many constructs of the past—we have not seen a wholesale jettisoning of our heritage. Simply put, today's Episcopalians rely upon the church's past for apt models of Christian life and community. To this end, even the newest Episcopalians do not inherently reject the local church's past or the wider church's extended history. Rather they approach the past with curiosity, and they assess it from an entirely new perspective that dictates new criteria of Christian life. They seek to uncover the spiritual sources of the church's past forms of vitality. Thus, the past offers appealing images of possibility for building the church of today.

Understanding that the church has changed profoundly, members are using aspects of the past as guides to rebuilding identity and vocation at the local level and beyond. But as they do so, confusion often results. For instance, many Episcopalians now believe that the church requires a clearer focus on mission, and yet—judging by what they told us—they also seem to see more, rather than fewer, paths to mission. For many, mission arises when the church's life is properly grounded in Scripture and tradition. To heighten the church's focus on mission, many other Episcopalians call for younger clergy; still others call for innovative worship or teaching. Some want an unapologetic restoration of authority and structure; others hope to recapture what they believe is a spiritual purity that once prevailed. In one way or another, most Episcopalians seek to rebuild the church, and they view its past as the best resource. Thus, Episcopalians in varied ways idealize the past. They long for the clarity of its apparent focus on mission and for the organizational resolve that pursued it. The hope of restoring ties that once bound the church is a belief that aspects of the past must shape its future.

Clearly, Episcopalians have a complicated relationship with their heritage. Equally complicated is how their heritage will affect their collective future. The paradox of local vitality and a fragmented institution—a paradox that also exists on broader religious and secular levels in America culture—adds additional levels of complexity to the discussion, with different segments of the church making use of their heritage in ways that are not merely different but often antithetical.

A much more detailed examination of the Episcopal past definitely seems in order, especially within the new light shed by data gathered during the Zacchaeus Project interviews. But which aspects of the past can best serve as guides for the church today? Above all, we must ask, is the past a reliable guide? Was there really a time when the Episcopal Church was clear about its identity and vocation? Which aspects of the past can be reclaimed and how might they be revived? Are the ties that once bound Episcopalians gone forever? Will Episcopal vitality simply be a local vitality? Can Episcopalians create a new sense of Christian identity and vocation that preserves the best of their past while addressing the challenges of the present?

Like all religious groups, the Episcopal Church has faced previous circumstances that tested its ability to sustain its identity while reconsidering its vocation. We must review the Episcopal legacy in order to understand how the church has responded to past challenges. We will discover that, when it has done well, the Episcopal Church has emerged from challenge with effective mission. As we consider how renewal of the church occurred previously, we can discover how a local impetus for mission is moving ahead now and what this portends for the church. When we review the past, we will see that what is at stake is the church's future.

UNPRECEDENTED CHALLENGES

THE LIMITS OF ESTABLISHMENT

Since its arrival in North America, Anglicanism has encountered a series of unprecedented challenges. The first challenge was adaptation of the church to the colonial circumstances of North America. For the first time, the church faced circumstances that undercut the assumptions that came with being England's established church. From 1607 on, when Anglicanism landed with the first settlers at Jamestown, Virginia, until the American Revolution, the church aspired to replicate the reality of the English establishment—and to a limited extent it did. Legally confirmed as the colony's official church, Anglicanism in Virginia appeared to continue English precedent. Organized like the English parish system, the church embodied the moderate rationalism of the Enlightenment era that developed within the Church of England. From their style of church architecture to their patterns of worship and governance, Virginians emphasized that a divinely inspired order united earth and heaven. The basis of this order lay partly in the assumption that religious belief accorded with reason. In this view of order, it was expected that the established church as a social institution embodied divine truth in socially useful form. That is, rationally grounded moral laws determined social duties and justified the institution that enforced them. This message—and the church that embodied it—took deep root in Virginia soil. At its peak, the church in Virginia combined both a profound expression of English precedent and a spiritual sense of being at home in America. A sense of social and spiritual coherence seemed in place. Religious establishment proved substantive and seemed secure in this stable, well-ordered world.[3]

While Virginia represented the largest and most influential branch of Anglicanism yet formed in the colonies, circumstances eventually permitted the creation of Anglican establishments elsewhere. The church achieved establishment status in Georgia, South Carolina, North Carolina, and Maryland. Given the fact of religious pluralism, it was not possible to replicate religious establishment in the same way in the other colonies. Elsewhere, the presence of substantial numbers of non-Anglicans made it politically inexpedient to consider the imposition of an Anglican establishment. Nevertheless, even in colonies where they were not, in fact, the established church, the Anglicans continued to act like an establishment. Typically, the church's leaders presumed a central role in developing key ministries and forms of social influence in colonial society. But in such circumstances—as in New York and Pennsylvania, for example—the church's role in society was exercised in largely unofficial ways. Even without the security of religious establishment, colonial Anglicans believed they could preserve the church's historic social role in the American environment. They assumed that the church must involve itself in the culture in order to minister to it. This ministry required the critical moral perspective that could only be developed from within society. The church required proximity to the principal sources of political and social influence in its social settings, not distance from them. In the absence of establishment, the church could derive advantage from its identification with the English throne and local culture. From the church's earliest American years, many of its leaders believed that the church's ability to muster social influence defined its place and its role.

But colonial Anglicanism was inherently anomalous. The church had to adapt its governance to a discrepancy between the ideal of establishment and the context of American realities. The church had no resident bishop, and at no time did an English bishop visit. No way of training clergy emerged, and the church's organization beyond the parish level remained rudimentary. For Virginia Anglicans, oversight rested with local vestries, an early precedent of local and lay initiative that served the disestablished church well after the Revolution. Unfortunately, local and lay initiative worked less well with institutional hierarchy; and so a tension was created early on in the church's history, with local initiative that was foundational in one sense and yet at odds with some aspects of church governance. Given this tension, it is not surprising that the emphasis on lay initiative was not always welcomed by clergy (much less by bishops). There were times when clergy seemed to be at the mercy of powerful lay leaders who left them little room for authority in local matters. Nevertheless, this system of lay initiative afforded colonial Anglicans deep roots in Virginia society, and the church functioned impressively because of them. The American environment required adaptations in the church, and Virginia Anglicans made adjustments that appeared to ensure their identity and vocation.

The most apparent adjustment concerned the church's colonial governance. Though accountable to the Bishop of London, Anglicans in Virginia and in some other colonies relied upon the office of commissary, created by Henry Compton, Bishop of London to administer the church's affairs.[4] There was no suggestion that the commissary was a substitute for oversight by bishops, though commissaries typically performed similar administrative duties. Commissaries were charged with supervising the colony's clergy and ensuring proper forms of worship and teaching. They performed well and consistently. Virginia's James Blair gained distinction, as did Thomas Bray in Maryland and Alexander Garden in South Carolina.[5]

The office of commissary represented an accommodation of the church's structures to the colonial setting. In those colonies where Anglicans could create something like the English establishment, the commissary was an effective means of oversight. But in those parts of the colonies where establishment could not be extended, how would the church gain a presence, much less grow? Fortunately, an English spiritual awakening provided the basis for Anglicans to develop an effective means of mission. By the early eighteenth century, widespread interest in deepening popular piety had born tangible fruit in England. Not only was there a wave of informal small groups devoted to prayer and study of the Scriptures, but a new interest in the social impact of Christian faith had surfaced. Organized more formally, groups of spiritually awakened laity and clergy who dedicated themselves to combating vice and poverty and to promoting the Gospel began to appear. Their influence soon spread to colonial North America where their combination of faith and social witness set an important example. The example of these groups not only encouraged colonial Anglicans to consider themselves a missionary church but gave them a tangible example of how to become one.

THE BEGINNING OF MISSION

The most noteworthy of these groups were the Society for Promoting Christian Knowledge (SPCK), founded in 1698, and the Society for the Propagation of the Gospel in Foreign Parts (SPG), created in 1701. Both organizations emphasized a devotional piety rooted in sacramental worship as well as innovative approaches to Christian mission. They differed in the ways they approached mission. The SPCK embraced education as central to the church's mission. SPCK initiatives to build libraries that would make basic Christian education more readily available to the public soon extended to the American colonies. More than education alone, the SPG emphasized mission and approached its work with unusual breadth. For instance, the SPG believed the church must expand into new mission fields, extending their missionary reach to African Americans and Native Americans. Thomas Bray, who had become Commissary for Maryland in 1696, was a principal organizer of these societies and personally encouraged their development in North America. His promotional work ensured that the Colonial church would have a practical basis for mission in America.

The founding of the SPG and the SPCK created what has remained to this day an enduring pattern of Anglican life. Innovative approaches to mission often originate as renewal-minded initiatives outside the church's central, institutional channels. Mission for Anglicans often entails appreciative adaptation of the church to its cultural setting in ways that afford it social influence. In colonial America, the result was that Anglicans understood their mission to entail not only an effort to build the church's membership in areas where it was not the religious establishment but to convert socially prominent persons and groups to Anglicanism. In this way, Anglicans of the disestablished church retained a social footing similar to the position they had held as an established church. To adapt to the colonial setting in this way, Thomas Bray and a few other leading Anglicans in North America took an important new cue from the SPCK and SPG. They began to understand themselves more as participants in a spiritual community and less as members of the established church. Imbued with this ideal, Bray saw mission as the core of the church's task, and he pursued this ideal by emphasizing the role of education and the need for missionary clergy. As a result, in 1702, the SPG dispatched George Keith to begin mission work in North America.[6]

A former Quaker, Keith was the SPG's first American missionary. New England drew his special interest. There he and subsequent Anglican missionaries faced a Puritan establishment that originated in opposition to the Church of England. Nevertheless, the church made inroads among the educated and mercantile classes. It promoted itself as an historic form of church order with a piety rooted in tradition, a governance based on reasoned discourse, and a learned and pastoral ministry. On this basis, the church steadily secured its place in New England. By 1775, the church had twenty-two parishes in Massachusetts.[7] This experience suggested the future shape of the church's challenge and the strategy it would have to adopt. Unable to rely upon the fact of religious establishment in nearly half of the American colonies, the church had to re-create itself as a missionary body. Well before the American Revolution, the church had begun to recognize that it would have to understand itself as a missionary body. In turn, to become a missionary body, it found that it would have to organize itself in novel ways and attempt to attract different audiences.

Led by the SPG, some colonial Anglicans sensed that mission represented the possibility of extending the church's scope beyond the bounds of establishment. In parts of colonial North America such as New England, it was apparent that the church could exist only when mission was embraced as its central task. In a few other places, interest in mission went even further and, as stated earlier, led to the beginnings of the church's work among Native Americans and African Americans. But these steps were inconsequential, suggesting that most colonial Anglicans had a limited scope when it came to mission; they could not fully envision the vast mission potential of America, because such a vision lay beyond the locus of English society. As subsequent events would demonstrate, this restricted outlook could have been a fatal constriction of the church's sense of the Gospel and of itself. The North American environment would demand ongoing forms of adaptation of the church as it faced successive waves of social change. When the church viewed itself as a missionary body, it proved capable of successful adaptation to these waves of change.

The Evangelical Challenge

The social challenges of the colonial North American environment included the rise of new forms of religious life that acquired popular appeal and further undercut Anglican assumptions about the feasibility of religious establishment. The most important of the religious challenges came from the broad spectrum of groups known as Evangelicals that would become influential and numerous. From the beginning, Evangelicalism represented a serious threat to Anglicanism's establishmentarian assumptions. Evangelicals combined an ability to offer a dynamic image of Christian belief with an energetic commitment to mission and a disregard for the presumptions of existing churches. This became apparent in 1740, when a leading English Evangelical, George Whitefield, made the first of his seven trips to the American colonies. Like his contemporaries, John and Charles Wesley, Whitefield had experienced the "new birth," a decisive awakening to a vivid faith. With them, he joined the "Holy Club" of pious Oxford students and concluded from this experience that the church must be renewed as a dynamic, spiritual body. Ordained in the Church of England, like John Wesley, Whitefield joined him in proclaiming the possibility of release from sin and spiritual regeneration for all. But Wesley put his energy into building a network of local religious groups. He did not intend for this network to break with the Church of England. Instead, his intention was that this network would function as a spiritual leaven that would enliven the Church of England at home and overseas. Though accused of a socially dangerous form of religious "enthusiasm," Wesley was instinctively conservative, and he pointedly urged his adherents to live as loyal subjects of the king. He never intended for Methodism to be linked with new patterns of social ministry and political activism in Britain and America. Late in life, Wesley finally offered *de facto* acknowledgment that his work had created a separate denomination when he authorized the ordinations of Thomas Coke and Francis Asbury for positions of oversight in the growing Methodist movement of North America. Even Coke, in the early 1790s, approached the new Episcopal Bishop of Pennsylvania, William White, about joining the American Methodist movement to the Episcopal Church. But events (and the wishes of Methodism's followers and some of its leaders) stood in the way of reunion. At his death, Wesley continued to affirm that he was a loyal priest of the Church of England. But by 1800, Methodism was a distinctive religious organization in England and America.

Unlike Wesley, Whitefield never intended to create a religious organization of any sort, not even a network of sympathetic followers within the Church of England. Whereas Wesley emphasized the creation of a religious community, Whitefield's emphasis was on his personal, evangelistic ministry. Instead of creating a network of new congregations, he intended for the message he proclaimed to have direct, public impact in a way that transcended the usual medium of formal church services. In fact, criticizing the churches for laxity, Whitefield proposed that the Holy Spirit must be experienced directly, not through reliance on outward forms of worship and practice based in the tenets of religious institutions. Relentlessly, in local churches and in mass meetings, he propounded his call for a new, spiritual birth in his hearers and made little effort to join them together in the sort of connection of groups of believers that John Wesley fostered.

Whitefield attracted such a following that he became a well-known public figure. Consistently opposed by local Anglican commissaries, he divided clergy over his message, his methods, and his powerful personality. To some, Whitefield presented the true Gospel and the possibility of spiritual rebirth that the church required; to others, he embodied the dangers of demagoguery and disorder. But he was impossible to ignore, and he left a notable legacy. Whitefield encouraged direct, personal, spiritual experience and a suspicion of religious institutions. He inaugurated the American tendency toward reform by grassroots spiritual movements led by charismatic leaders. He encouraged Americans to believe that the form of religious organizations mattered less than their efficacy in producing spiritual and social results. Together with Jonathan Edwards and other American religious reformers, Whitefield created the wave of revival known as the Great Awakening. As a result, American religion became suffused with the Evangelical emphasis on "new birth" as well as Whitefield's emphasis on public, rather than the institutional, aspects of religion.[8] Evangelicalism has represented a continuous challenge to the Episcopal Church to be an adaptive, spiritually vibrant, missionary body within American life.

The Awakening brought momentary benefits for the few sympathetic Anglican clergy and parishes who attempted to integrate its ideals. Local bursts of Evangelical energy encouraged the momentary growth of sympathetic Anglican congregations. Where Evangelical energies appeared among Anglicans, there were fresh mission initiatives that included attention to the religious needs of African Americans. The programs that emerged were limited to a few efforts to preach the Gospel to slaves. Nothing beyond their conversion to Christianity was envisioned, and even these efforts proved local, sporadic, and ultimately of limited success. In the long run, Anglican missions to African Americans in North America did not endure during the colonial era.[9] On the whole, therefore, the Awakening loosed social forces for which the church was ill prepared (to the extent that Anglicans of the time even deigned to believe they *should* be prepared). Fully absorbing the Awakening's influence, Baptists and Presbyterians became much more defined by it. In Southern colonies, where Anglican establishments were prominent, Evangelicals mobilized to seek religious equality. With the American Revolution, their hopes were fulfilled. In the wake of the Revolution, Anglicanism was nearly swept away. Not only was the church disestablished, but in New England it lost most of its clergy, many of whom were Loyalists who fled back to England. Even in Virginia, the church lacked the infrastructure that would permit its survival in this new environment. By one account, the church after the Revolution "closely resembled an executor settling the bankrupt estate of the old Anglican establishment [rather] than the heir of a rich and vital religious tradition."[10] The church of the English throne faced the agonizing challenge of adapting to drastically altered circumstances if it was to survive in the new United States. More than two hundred years later, the church still struggles to adapt to constant change.

THE IMPACT OF REVOLUTION

The Great Awakening set several important precedents. Of course, it was the first instance of a wave of Evangelical religious renewal to sweep North America. The Awakening set much of the lasting tone of American religion. For instance, it defined American religion as being rooted in personal experience, and it demonstrated that religious groups exerted major forms of public influence. Although the constitutional separation of church and state after the Revolution meant the end of the Anglican and Puritan religious establishments, unofficially religion would remain central to American life. The basis of religious life shifted to voluntary adherence, which meant all religious groups would be forced to attract and hold members, to create their own organizational structures, and to muster their own resources. To meet these challenges, religious groups were compelled to reconsider their identity and vocation, and to restructure their organizations to match the social environment. American religious groups faced the challenge of creating effective forms of mission, often confronting lingering public suspicion of religious institutions as they did.

The voluntary religious environment especially challenged Episcopalians. Because of disestablishment and the consequent collapse of their historic identity, their colonial forms of governance were rendered meaningless. The process of creating the Episcopal Church required building organizational structure at the state level, where the first diocesan conventions were organized soon after political independence. In 1780, Maryland began to hold diocesan conventions, and Episcopalians in other states soon followed suit. In 1784, the bishop-elect of Connecticut, Samuel Seabury, was consecrated in Scotland as the first bishop in the Episcopal Church; more bishops soon followed. The first General Convention, held in 1785, marked the real beginning of national organization. By 1792, the Episcopal Church had a functioning national structure and a Book of Common Prayer.

The Episcopal Church seemed to have survived the loss of its colonial status. Its nascent structure seemed an ideal adaptation to the new, democratic environment. The episcopate, the church's principal office, and the Prayer Book had become indigenous. In the new nation the church appeared able to continue its appeal to educated, influential people and thus to perpetuate an unofficial sense of being the religious arm of the social establishment. But the Episcopal Church required a further adaptation; to rely solely upon precedent would have doomed the church. More than organizational changes, it needed to be able to articulate its identity and vocation in a religious environment that was becoming increasingly dynamic. To do so, it would have to shed inherited assumptions and reconfigure itself as a spiritual community.

More than political independence compelled the Episcopal Church to reconsider its identity and vocation. The colonial church had not responded well to George Whitefield and the first wave of Evangelicalism in the mid-eighteenth century. Early in the nineteenth century, a new phase of the challenge from Evangelical religion arose. Evangelicalism surged to such an extent that it secured a lasting influence on American religion. In the thirty years after the Revolution, membership in the Baptist Church increased tenfold. Between 1820 and 1830 membership in the Methodist Church doubled. In less than half a century, Baptists and Methodists grew to such an extent that they constituted two-thirds of American Protestants.[11]

Evangelicalism's impact on the Episcopal Church was significant and deserves examination. Simply put, Evangelical Christianity grew because it harnessed the populist, democratic currents of the new nation. In part, this achievement reflected the example of the movement's energetic leadership. The work of Methodist revivalist Lorenzo Dow and organizer Francis Asbury shaped a generation of leaders including Richard Allen, founder of the African Methodist Church, Barton Stone of the Christian Church, Joseph Smith, founder of the Mormons, and William Miller, who inspired the Adventist Church. Evangelicalism rapidly splintered into a broad spectrum of groups, but a consistent style of populist, democratic leadership defined them as Evangelical.[12]

Consistently these leaders understood and responded to popular perceptions and aspirations. Because they realized that churches relied upon popular assent, Evangelical leaders succeeded spectacularly. Seeing the deep longing of many Americans for a sense of place in a nation whose frontier was expanding, Evangelical leaders linked the Gospel to a promise of personal destiny and declared that Christianity was a liberating, equalizing social force, a compelling innovation in the American democratic experiment. When Evangelical preachers announced the possibility of salvation, their hearers understood it as incentive to take religious and social initiative. Evangelicalism became noted for its capacity to mobilize large numbers of people for social, as well as religious, purposes. The emergence of effective opposition to slavery by the middle of the nineteenth century owed much of its force to the Evangelical ability to galvanize grassroots moral sentiment.

But effective leadership was only one aspect of Evangelicalism's achievement. The new leaders and their followers proved innovative and adaptable in their organizational style. Relying on roving, local preachers, Methodism profoundly influenced American frontier life, encouraging the growth of frontier communities by knitting together otherwise isolated settlers into worshiping congregations. As communities took shape on the frontier, Methodists often promoted the creation of schools and later helped to build civic infrastructure, especially local government. For Methodists, such practical initiatives had a deeply religious basis and ultimately a religious intention.

Like all Evangelicals, the Methodist view of religious experience centered on the decisive moment of personal salvation, or being "born again." Awakened to faith in Jesus Christ, the new believer was drawn into the challenge of continuing growth in holiness, or sanctification, a core doctrine for Methodists. This process unfolded in the context of the local congregation, where a vigorous style of worship and ministry was a necessary adaptation, given the constant challenges of life on the frontier. Methodists retained an intensely local focus; but they linked congregations into regional networks that were secured by roving preachers and later by regularized oversight from district superintendents and bishops. The Methodist manner of forming networks by focusing on mission as the basis of local congregational experience established an American religious precedent. It defined the manner in which Christianity could successfully evangelize in the new nation. Local congregational life was honored while being drawn into an extended organizational framework. Recognizing the priority of local initiative, this organizational framework ensured that congregations received the resources for mission they required. In the process, congregations exerted an enormous social and moral influence on their localities. The expansion of Methodism and of other frontier Evangelical churches created a vast "organizing process." Evangelical religion played a major role in shaping the fabric of American life. It has continued to play that role to a profound extent.

The success of the Methodist organizational approach to evangelism became quickly apparent to the leaders of other denominations. Given the breadth of Evangelical experience, the influence of the Methodist style of organization spread broadly and even encouraged ecumenical networks that cooperated on various aspects of mission. Even such leaders of mainstream religious life as Lyman Beecher and Timothy Dwight, who were suspicious of Evangelicalism, sensed the opportunity that Methodism's form of organization suggested. While they criticized the emotionalism of religious revivals, they recognized that popular piety was a means of organizing effective new forms of mission. The result was that the mainstream denominations sought to emulate Methodism's organizational style and focus on mission. Consequently there arose a vast array of organizations—many of them ecumenical—that focused on specific forms and aspects of mission. Often fostered and led by committees of lay persons, these networks encouraged the growth of Sunday schools, literacy training, knowledge of the Bible, and urban and frontier evangelism.[13] These networks gave rise to denominational agencies that fostered an institutional approach to mission. But their achievement went beyond fostering the rise of denominational structures. By their witness, these networks illustrated that mission in America requires a focus on the local and practical dimensions of religious life in ways that are organizationally flexible.

THE BASIS OF EPISCOPAL MISSION

We have seen that, when American circumstances forced the Episcopal Church to reorganize, it began to see itself anew as a missionary body. The confluence of functioning in new ways and emphasizing mission was most apparent at local levels where there were numerous instances of new forms of initiative. A detailed account of how mission functioned locally was left by Henry Caswall, who emigrated from England in 1828 to serve the church as it grew westward. Though he eventually was ordained and became a rector in Indiana, Caswall began his ministry in American as a layman, traveling throughout Ohio, helping to build Kenyon College and to expand the number of congregations in the Diocese of Ohio. The impressions he recorded remain revealing. Early in 1831, he visited Chillicothe where the local rector welcomed him warmly. There he noted that "the Episcopal Church contains many of the wealthier and more refined families." But he worried that the church "has not established itself in the preference of the great mass of the religious people, who are principally ... Methodists, Presbyterians, and Baptists." Later he made similar observations of Cincinnati. The implication was that the Episcopal Church appeared to be losing ground to denominations that were growing because of Evangelical energies.

But there were signs of Episcopal growth in Ohio, and the way in which it was occurring was striking to Caswall. He commented that there were "about fifty Episcopal churches in Ohio," yet he was undisturbed that "as not more than fifteen or sixteen clergymen are at present in the state, lay readers have been eminently successful in keeping the feeble flocks together."[14] Caswall seemed to revel in the fact that the church's growth did not rely exclusively upon the initiative of clergy. He was not critical of clergy—indeed he attested to the efficacy of ordination by becoming a deacon in 1831 and a priest a year later—but he retained his emphasis on initiatives at the church's local levels and his esteem for the lay role in such initiatives. His basis for this emphasis was clear. There were times, Caswall noted, when the church's English heritage and reliance upon oversight by bishops aroused suspicions. Americans, he found, instinctively relied upon local initiative, upon their own ability to work together in building their communities. When local laity were prominent in Episcopal congregations, the church's mission gained the credibility it required.

Thus, when he was assigned to Portsmouth, Ohio, as a cleric, he noted proudly in his diary that lay initiative had been decisive in the growth of this congregation. Caswall's account cited the example of a man named Samuel Gunn, who had guided the Episcopal Church's presence in his town. With only occasional clergy visiting to lead worship, Gunn had shepherded the congregation as its lay reader. Compensated partly by the diocese and partly by the national church, Caswall arrived to bring clerical guidance; but he did so by honoring Gunn and building upon his work. When the elderly lay leader died, Caswall clearly was moved. Gunn "had been a friend to all," he recorded, and "had long been regarded as an example of uprightness and integrity."[15]

Caswall's experiences illustrate that, although his denomination never grew at the rate or extent of Evangelical churches, the Episcopal Church did experience periods of growth. The manner of this growth is instructive. Church leaders—then and now—have succeeded at building the church when they have honored local initiative and the people who have embodied it. Church leaders have also succeeded when they have been more devoted to the innovations required by local mission and less wed to perpetuating inherited institutional patterns.

The influence of growth at the local level decisively reshaped the church's view of itself in its American setting. The church declared, in 1820, that its official name should reflect its focus on mission, and the Episcopal Church became known as the Domestic and Foreign Missionary Society. This step implied that the church's mission was more than a series of local initiatives and that the national church should approach mission—on behalf of the local churches—in a coordinated way. Prior to 1820, whenever the church had grown, it had relied upon what one historian has called "the rugged individualism of a few exceptional pioneers."[16] Bishops such as Philander Chase in Ohio and James Hervey Otey in Tennessee had been catalysts for the founding of churches and the creation of rudimentary diocesan structures. They had worked effectively but somewhat in isolation.

Then, in 1835, the church's General Convention took a major step toward more effective and coordinated emphasis on mission. It did so by committing to provide support for local mission. It also did so by creating the role of missionary bishop. For the first time, the church would consecrate bishops for service as mission leaders in frontier areas. They would precede and initiate, rather than follow, the church's growth in new areas. Shortly thereafter, Jackson Kemper was chosen as the first such bishop. His years of dedicated service helped to launch the church in the westward territories and to guide its development there. Following the example of clergy-lay cooperation in Ohio and elsewhere, Kemper conducted his ministry in ways that supported local initiatives. Like a roving Methodist preacher, he fostered and coordinated local leaders. From Missouri and Indiana, he worked his way through Kansas, Nebraska, Wisconsin, and Iowa. He also made initial visits in deep areas of the South, setting the stage for Leonidas Polk, who, in 1838, became both the second missionary bishop and the first Bishop of Louisiana. The church's mission now integrated the work of bishops with the enhancement of local ministries. As bishops engaged the realities of their localities, the idea of the Domestic and Foreign Missionary Society gained substance. Mission entailed the coordination of local, diocesan, and national initiative.

INHERENT TENSION

Episcopalians seemed to have developed a consensus on the necessity of mission and on the means of advancing it. In fact, a troubling tension had appeared between the way in which some Episcopalians intended to adapt the church's life to the demands of the American social environment and the way in which others intended to preserve distinctive marks of the church's identity. It is necessary to describe the tension at this point in the narrative because it has continually been at the center of Episcopal discussions of mission, with a contemporary version of this tension still pervading the church today. To adequately explain the origin and development of this tension we return momentarily to the Episcopal Church's organization following the Revolution.

As the church faced the unprecedented demands of political independence and the separation of church and state, church leaders understood its identity and vocation in two ways. Some leaders believed that the necessity of mission required that the church adapt its forms to the new American circumstances. Accordingly, in 1782, William White, later the first Bishop of Pennsylvania, published a plea for the church in each state to govern itself by conventions, and the church as a whole by a General Convention. For White and other Episcopal leaders in the mid-Atlantic region, the church's identity derived from its ability to adopt representative government. They believed that, by this adaptation to its context, the church positioned itself for success in mission.[17]

Episcopalians in New England and New York disagreed. Missionaries of the SPG had been influential in forming the church in New England and New York. There the church's identity was based less on its adaptability to its setting than on its distinctive forms of worship and ministry. In practice, this meant that Episcopalians in the Northeast saw the episcopate, rather than democratic process or local initiative, as the key to Episcopal identity and the basis of Episcopal vocation. It was no coincidence that Connecticut took the initiative, after the newly organized church was shorn of English authority, to send the first Episcopalian off to Scotland to be consecrated bishop. The means of selecting bishops had changed with the rise of new political circumstances, but the centrality of the office had not diminished for New Englanders and New Yorkers; the episcopate remained the church's center. For a large segment of the church, this conviction would remain prominent.

Thus, there was an inherent tension in the Episcopal understanding of mission. Did the success of the church's mission rely upon the adaptability of the church's forms to accord with prevailing American styles of organization? Or, did the church's mission require its faithfulness to the historic marks of its identity and vocation? On the surface, that tension seemed resolved as the church determined to focus on mission in the early nineteenth century. On the one hand, the General Convention represented the church's reliance upon democratic patterns of decision making, an obvious adaptation to American life. On the other hand, the prominent role of bishops as the Episcopal Church spread westward suggested the continuing distinctiveness of Episcopal identity and vocation amid the novelty of American circumstances.

But the tension between an adaptable identity and a distinctive one was not lost. It was apparent in the hardening lines of church parties early in the nineteen century. Guided by the examples of William White and Bishop William Meade of Virginia, Evangelical Christians increased in numbers on the East Coast and in parts of the Midwest. Unlike Evangelicals of the Baptist or Methodist sorts, Evangelical Episcopalians placed less emphasis on a dramatic, personal experience of "new birth" but stressed the priority of personal faith, the authority of the Bible, and the historic forms of Episcopal worship and ministry. They also emphasized the necessity of translating personal faith into practical, ecumenical efforts to encourage educational work among poor people and the use of education as a means of extending the church's moral influence in society.

For Evangelical Episcopalians, the clergy role emphasized preaching, teaching, and pastoral care. Yet Evangelical Episcopal clergy understood that their role did not overshadow the role of lay leadership. In the Evangelical outlook, the church's governance and its mission required shared initiative. This conviction extended to ecumenical affairs. Evangelical Episcopal leaders such as Stephen Tyng urged the church to cooperate in broadly Protestant initiatives such as Sunday schools and thereby set the stage for the Episcopal Church's participation in later ecumenical discussions. The appeal of these steps signaled the rise of the Evangelical group in the church. Until it was reshaped by the newer Evangelical emphasis of the Charismatic Movement in the late twentieth century, this party maintained a clear identity and exerted major influence in the Episcopal Church.

Just as Evangelical Episcopalians emerged in a distinct way early in the nineteenth century, so a High Church party also took shape. From 1811 to 1830 Bishop John Henry Hobart of New York provided an example that did much to develop the High Church party in the Episcopal Church. He viewed the creation of new congregations as a priority of the church in New York, and he believed such initiative uniquely befitted the office of bishop. Reflecting his belief in the uniqueness of Episcopal tradition, he frowned upon Episcopalians who participated in ecumenical mission ventures, viewing such cooperation as a distraction from the Episcopal Church's expansion. For Hobart, the church's unique identity informed his emphasis upon mission.[18] Thus, as the century progressed, a tension between adaptation and distinctiveness was apparent in the Episcopal Church and reflected deep differences over the church's basic convictions.

The influence of the High Church party deepened as the nineteenth century progressed. By the middle of the century, a broad segment of the High Church party had fallen under the influence of England's Oxford Movement. For these Episcopalians, the recovery of ancient, often elaborate liturgical practices were established as a core element in the church's identity and the key to its mission. Known as "Anglo-Catholics" and as "Ritualists," these reinvigorated High Church party members offered an influential witness to the centrality of worship and its ancient origins. Finding geographic bases in portions of the Northeast and Midwest, Anglo-Catholicism asserted a widespread influence that ultimately left an indelible imprint on the entire church.[19]

By the end of the twentieth century, the influence of Anglo-Catholicism on the church's life was apparent. Episcopalians in overwhelming numbers would affirm that the Eucharist is the center of the church's worship and that worship is the core of the church's identity. They also would argue that worship—by which they usually meant the Eucharist—is the defining aspect of clergy leadership, given that only priests or bishops may fulfill this crucial role. Anglo-Catholicism, following its English sources, also would encourage the church's embrace of poor and oppressed persons. As sensitivity to the plight of suffering people deepened, many Anglo-Catholic Episcopalians would adopt a critical view of American life and would launch a variety of social ministries that would become the most influential expressions of an activist form of witness by Episcopalians.[20] Thus, the Anglo-Catholic platform did more than set the stage for Prayer Book and Hymnal revision in the twentieth century. Just as Evangelical Episcopalians enhanced the church's educational and pastoral ministries, so Anglo-Catholics inspired attention to the ancient sources of worship and greater reverence and consistency in performing it. While citing this witness, we also note that their identity as a group, like that of the older Evangelical party, became diluted by the late twentieth century as Episcopalians adopted increasingly idiosyncratic local blends of the church's traditions.

For well over a century, Evangelical and High Church Episcopalians exerted tremendous influence in the church. But even at the height of their influence, neither party alone could direct the Episcopal Church's life nor dictate its approach to mission. Yet when their ideals melded, mission received life-giving impetus. Even in the first half of the nineteenth century, there were hints of the creative possibilities of joining these two supposedly opposed church parties. One historian has cited William Augustus Muhlenberg, who died in 1877, as "the prototypical evangelical catholic." In the Catholic mold, Muhlenberg, who served the Church of the Holy Communion in New York, introduced weekly celebrations of the Eucharist and one of the first vested boy's choirs; in the Evangelical mold, he focused on seeking personal salvation and, more importantly for our purposes, defined the church as the institution devoted to this end. In his view, the church must join the personal spiritual journey to the church's ritual worship that expresses its faithfulness to Christian tradition.[21]

Unfortunately, such creative melding of Anglo-Catholic and Evangelical ideals did not always occur. These church parties— Anglo-Catholics, Evangelicals, and others—sometimes facilitated mission by combining the distinctive strengths of their witness and other times frustrated it by creating tensions within the church because of those same differences. The source of such tensions lay in disagreement about the church's relation to American life: should the church adapt, or should it cultivate its distinctiveness?

It is significant that, whenever the church's mission has gone forward successfully, varied groups within the church have accommodated and cooperated with one another; and the church's institutional processes and structures have been adapted to permit a focus on mission under changed circumstances. Even in its colonial establishment form, the Episcopal Church has never been homogeneous. It has always encompassed a series of interest groups whose ideals of Christian life are somewhat different, amid the fabric of congregations linked regionally into dioceses and drawn together by national organization. When they speak of a former coherence, long-time Episcopalians do not imply a reverence for homogeneity. Instead they refer to the church's former capacity to join disparate ideals into common mission. They suggest that the church once was able to manage the tension between the urge to adapt to American life and the impulse to be distinct from it. They long for the adaptive capability to create some new form of consensus that will advance mission in a new era. That the Episcopal Church achieved the balance necessary for mission for over a century was remarkable. That the institutional framework that fostered this approach is now widely seen to be irrelevant represents a significant, historic crisis.

FAITH IN ORGANIZATION

By the middle of the nineteenth century, the Episcopal Church had achieved a clear focus on mission in its life. It is worth noting that this emphasis on mission took a particuar organizational form. The church had become a loosely knit, decentralized organization that united a variety of parties, agencies, and interest groups that reflected local and regional points of emphasis regarding worship, belief, and pastoral oversight. As previously described, the church's mission at times relied upon the initiatives of solitary individuals, both laity and clergy. Even the establishment of parishes sometimes began this way, with one dedicated individual acting as chaplain to a few families in one area. If the congregation grew, it did so as additional families moved to the area and declared their preference for the Episcopal Church. As the congregation grew, its life could become complex and the demands on its leaders elaborate. For instance, in the 1840s, the rector of St. Andrew's Church, Meriden, Connecticut, was expected to preach two sermons "at least forty-five minutes long, preside over Sunday School at noon, and later have a Bible class and Evening Prayer."[22] Local Episcopal leaders were accustomed to working long hours in their roles. Clergy were expected to visit their flock regularly and to participate in the community's social and public affairs. But in most respects, the pattern of clergy work and church life was informal and personal. Clergy and lay leaders guided the congregation on the basis of the social patterns that were characteristic of their social setting. In general, the church reflected the mores of its localities, and those mores seemed intact and immoveable. The style of church life and leadership retained the quality of a chaplaincy.

As congregations grew, they naturally were drawn into the life of the wider church. Typically, a diocese grew as bishops and their representatives involved local clergy and lay leaders and their congregations in the workings of the diocese. Through visits from diocesan leaders and participation in annual conventions and clergy gatherings, a connection to the diocese was secured. At the same time congregations also began to participate in independent groups representing High Church or Evangelical tenets. Through participation in these church parties, congregations often found opportunities for engaging in mission or education work with other Episcopalians who shared their distinctive approach to church life. Although such connections would make it appear that congregations were elaborately linked beyond themselves, such ties were loosely knit, leaving more than adequate room for local initiative and forms of expression. Thus, before the Civil War, the church was defined more by local and regional life and an informal leadership style than by its national character.

But in the second half of the nineteenth century, a major change occurred in the life of the Episcopal Church; from a loosely knit, decentralized organization, the Episcopal Church developed elaborate, centralized institutional structures and procedures. This trend mirrored that of corporate America, which also began to build elaborate, centralized structures during the second half of the nineteenth century. It also reflected the direction of mainstream Protestant life, in which increased reliance upon organization during the later decades of the nineteenth century created the lasting perception that religious life and "religious institutions" were synonymous.

For Episcopalians, the turn toward institutional identity arose alongside a broad consensus emerged about the most effective means of advancing the church's mission. The achievement of a coherent framework that inspired widespread allegiance did not eradicate the basic tension in Episcopal life between adapting the church to American culture and assuring the church's distinctive identity. However, for over a century the church's national structures subsumed tensions that arose in the church's life. Through its institutional structures and the elaborate procedures, the church found an effective approach to mission that provided Episcopalians with a powerful sense of belonging. We now explore this institutional approach to mission and the sense of belonging it provided.

After the Civil War, it was apparent that a new emphasis on mission was the church's main theme. A new commitment to mission surfaced in the Episcopal Church's work among African Americans. An awareness of this imperative had fueled limited evangelism of the slave population even before their emancipation. In the war's wake, the church's General Convention authorized various programs, including the creation of colleges for freed slaves. Education and social ministries multiplied rapidly, and an effort to increase the number of ordained and lay African-American leaders in the Episcopal Church gained momentum. As these ministries emerged, they gained formal structure. In a variety of dioceses, African-American ministries came under the guidance of archdeacons appointed to supervise the work. Later, there would be suffragan bishops, some of whom were African-American. Significantly, the focus of this work would shift toward congregational development.[23] As it did, there was a sense that ministries to African Americans were works of the entire church. This was a new idea.

The Episcopal Church's work among African Americans offered an influential example. By the late nineteenth century new missions to Chinese, Japanese, and Native Americans had begun. Proliferating alongside these new ethnic ministries were many other specialized ministries. For example, an array of women's organizations, offering ministries run by women, appeared. These included the Girls' Friendly Society, the Church Periodical Club, the Daughters of the King, and the United Thank Offering. Various organizations for men also appeared, ranging from the Order of the Holy Cross, a monastic order that launched social ministries, to the Brotherhood of St. Andrew, a lay organization that provided social services to men. Other groups provided ministries and services based on the specialized needs of individuals (such as deaf persons) or groups of individuals (temperance initiatives, factory workers, and slum dwellers).

In each case, there was an interesting blend of old mission emphasis and new mission style. Typically, these initiatives involved a small number of people who launched a ministry and guided it until it became sustainable. At that point it acquired formal direction, such as oversight by archdeacons, and built close ties with church structures. This was a new pattern of ministry development. The localism and regionalism that had defined the Episcopal Church was replaced by a sense of national mission that could best be embodied in an elaborate institution. As the church sought a comprehensive approach to mission and became national in its scope, it evolved structures and procedures to match. The church became a complex institution.

What must be emphasized first is that this change arose as Episcopalians began to act as a church in mission. It is also important to stress that the core of mission lay in patterns of evangelism that built up local congregations. Throughout the rise of ministries designed to extend the church's work, the theme of building up communities of believers was paramount.

Not only were new congregations formed, but leaders were groomed for them. The depth of commitment to this task was evident when a Virginia priest, O. A. Kinsolving, preached at the diocese's centennial observance in 1885. He noted that the Revolutionary War had weakened the confidence and health of many parishes of the diocese and that the recent Civil War had brought great destruction to their buildings and properties; but he added that, "while many of those old sanctuaries have been disused or deserted or destroyed, others have arisen in their places more favorably located, and better suited for the use of the present congregations.... It is indeed a source of gratification and encouragement that since the close of the late war there have been more churches built in the Diocese than within the same period during the preceding years of its history."[24]

Virginia was not alone in its mission focus on congregational development. As a direct result of a new conception of the church as community, new congregations sprang up across America and existing congregations extended themselves to people previously untouched by the Episcopal Church. The resulting swift growth in membership and the new comprehensive understanding of mission gave the Episcopal Church refurbished visibility in American society.

Just as the extent of the church's work began to change and grow, so did the ways in which that work was organized. In the "age of corporations," the church faced an increasingly diverse society and envisioned a more elaborate role for itself. The local church intensified its work "for the relief of the poor in its own neighborhood" by organizing "guilds" to visit, feed, and clothe. Parish organizations functioned according to meetings that ran programs with formal budgets. Space for meetings was required, and most congregations soon had "parish houses" which could host a wide range of events and programs. In the Diocese of New York, there was something of a parish house movement in which parishes sponsored plays, cooking classes, and health clinics. In 1908, Bishop David Greer realized that new churches in the Bronx could not often afford such facilities and built Bronx

Church House for the borough churches to share.[25] With the new emphasis on the congregation's program life, the "minister's function has been transformed. He is no longer the preacher, pastor, and shepherd of a flock, but the general manager of a complex and complicated organization." Thus the "minister of today is a new kind of creature, never before known in the Church's history."[26]

Old patterns of decision making and administration based on personal relations with a few trusted and influential persons did not fade quickly. Such patterns continued to characterize much of the church's life at the congregational level and beyond. When he became Bishop of New York in 1887, Henry C. Potter did little to create a diocesan staff. "His loyal secretary-cum-chaplain, George F. Nelson, superintended what little office work Potter's style required. James Pott was treasurer of the diocese for forty years until his death in 1905; when money was short, Pott simply appealed to rich acquaintances."[27] But with the rapid growth and diversification of New York's population, the need for new churches and specialized ministries became unavoidable. Potter's would be the last New York episcopate that could operate on such a small scale. Connecticut began to plan for a central diocesan office and an official episcopal residence when Chauncy Brewster became bishop in 1899. It took until 1915 to secure a home and until 1919 for Christ Church Cathedral to offer space in its parish house for what had become a growing diocesan staff, but Connecticut continued to move toward a more elaborate diocesan structure.[28] This trend was not restricted to Connecticut and New York. In parishes and dioceses across the country, more formal procedures were running the church's increasingly elaborate organization.

It was apparent that more elaborate patterns of congregational life were changing what clergy did and that new specialized ministries outside historical norms were appearing. In the early twentieth century, Episcopalians in Richmond, Virginia, created the role of city missioner. The cleric who held this position "traveled widely, visiting the sick, aiding the needy, distributing Bibles and food, and holding religious services. In addition to hospitals, jails, factories, the Confederate Home, and the state penitentiary, he stopped at individual houses." R. Cary Montague gained renown in this role. He organized ecumenical worship services in a large theater. He was a faithful, welcome visitor to disadvantaged people. He spoke on behalf of all people in need and urged the church's redemptive response to them. For Montague, ministry entailed advocacy and activity. He became one of a new generation of clergy for whom the church's words must be matched by deeds that would confront social ills.[29]

THE INTENTION OF MISSION AND ORGANIZATION

The Episcopal Church's success in this time of rapid expansion lay in its ability to offer a clear, compelling, theological foundation for institutionalization. The ideal that forged the church's new identity and vocation was that of the "national church." As adopted by the Episcopal Church, the national church ideal actually had two quite different natures: a church that had become national by virtue of its new sense of responsibility and new understanding of the proper scope and extent of mission; and a church that had become national by virtue of assuming its rightful place as the modern successor to the English ideal of religious establishment. The differences were considerable between "*a* national church" (the Episcopal Church as one—though not necessarily the only—religious group to have undergone a transformation in its understanding of mission) and "*the* national church" (the Episcopal Church singled out for a special destiny); and yet the two ideals conflated easily in the minds of many Episcopalians, so much so that they quickly became indistinguishable.

Not a specific goal or set of programs, the national church ideal was one to which the actual life of the church should point. "The mission of the Episcopal Church was...social regeneration through Christian moral truths and American democracy. The Episcopal Church would be the leaven that raises the United States...to new heights of goodness and virtue."[30] The national church ideal became the means by which Episcopalians balanced their effort to adapt creatively to American life with their requirement to retain a distinctive identity and vocation. The Episcopal Church crafted both an increasingly sacramental sense of itself, and a set of structures that resembled the emerging form of corporate America. Under the national church ideal, Episcopalians could gather a wide variety of particular mission initiatives. The ideal of becoming the national church inspired the conviction that the church must function expansively and effectively; it must address the most gripping national issues in light of the Gospel. It must redeem social life by the impact of its programs. Under the influence of the national church ideal, Episcopalians began to think of the church as more than the bearer of a message: the Episcopal Church's intention was to embody the kingdom of God, and to call for society to be transformed in its image.

Although a variety of Episcopalians contributed to developing and popularizing the idea of the national church, the most prominent source was William Reed Huntington. His popular books, The Church Idea (1870) and A National Church (1899) offered an intellectual grounding for the ideal, and his effective lobbying for the ideal in church circles helped to secure its acceptance. Huntington believed that the Episcopal Church was uniquely positioned to minister to American society in ways that would promote effective social improvement and ecumenical union through faithfulness to ancient Christian patterns of worship and ministry. He did not originate this idea, but his manner of promoting it meant that he became a uniquely influential synthesizer of the Episcopal Church's religious identity and social role.

In the fashion of his era (as exemplified by his English and Canadian counterparts, W. H. Fremantle and Herbert Symonds), Huntington also believed that, in order to be fully effective, the church must work with other denominations. Huntington's intent was not the scrupulously careful, legalistic ecumenism that gained momentum in the latter half of the twentieth century. His intent was a much broader consensus on the defining tenets of the Christian faith, the recognition of which—he believed—necessarily would propel the major American denominations into new forms of cooperation. However, the first step toward recognizing those marks of identity that all mainline Christians had in common was for the various denominations to understand themselves separately; in the case of his own denomination, he recognized these essential defining marks of identity: the Holy Scriptures, the Nicene Creed, the historic episcopate, and the sacraments of Baptism and the Eucharist. Although the rush toward broad interdenominational consensus and cooperative social action that he anticipated did not occur, Huntington *did* unintentionally provide a means for Episcopalians and Anglicans around the world to better understand their distinctive identity as Christians.

Huntington's ideal of remaking America by the standard of the kingdom of God compelled Episcopalians to undertake many of the ministries and programmatic social services discussed earlier. The national church ideal forged a close linkage between the church's internal processes and the advance of God's kingdom. The ideal formed by this linkage became more powerful in the mind of the church than other possible ideals, such as the salvation of individual souls or the growth of the church's membership. In turn, the pursuit of this ideal seemed to require a closer, more elaborate coordination of national, diocesan, and local church life. As a result, the church's national, institutional programs began to bear the weight of Episcopal identity and vocation. Confident of their mandate to build the kingdom of God, Episcopalians expanded their program life and the organizational structures necessary to support them from the late nineteenth century on.

An important instance was the creation of the Episcopal Church's Pension Fund. Though the church had organized funds in the late nineteenth century for the relief of clergy and their widows and orphans, by the early twentieth century the inadequacies of these provisions were apparent to some. Bishop William Lawrence of Massachusetts was particularly concerned about "slipshod business practices in the Church," including the support of clergy. He embarked on a campaign to create a pension fund and managed to enlist the active support of financier J. Pierpont Morgan, among other notable Episcopalians. To Lawrence, the church must in all respects function in accordance with the finest professional standards, and he managed to impress this idea on the General Convention of 1913. To carry the idea to fruition, he commented, it was necessary to "have a knowledge of the conditions and a statement of the facts." Lay leaders of the church must be presented the subject "in such a way as to make it clear to a businessman that there is any method or plan so well worth his consideration as to prompt him to invest a large sum."[31]

The establishment of the Pension Fund exemplified the new, institutional view of mission. The church was seeking efficiency through a programmatic, professional approach. Staff would be hired and particular social situations would be analyzed and addressed using the best knowledge that could be amassed. Committees of the General Convention would carry the church's work forward. Their activities required budgets developed and managed by clusters of appropriately trained people. With impetus provided by the national church ideal, the church moved deeply into a new sense of itself.

Other mainline Protestant denominations also were moving toward centralized, bureaucratic organizational structures. Like the Episcopal Church, they sought to expand the scope of their ministries and to make them more efficient. Like the Episcopal Church, they created specialized departments and hired professional staff to direct them. Increasingly, mission occurred in programmatic form. It might be tempting to conclude that the churches were simply imitating corporate life as business developed along similar lines. In fact, there were obvious parallels; the growth of elaborate organizations reflected a general drive for efficiency in American life. But religious institutions also were motivated by powerful theological motives. For Episcopalians, the need for efficiency reflected their focus on mission in pursuit of the ideal of the kingdom of God.[32]

As Protestants continued to specialize and professionalize, Episcopalians distinguished themselves in their commitment to the ideal of the national and corporate church model. By the dedication, talent, and money available to it nationally, the church seemed poised for major impact on the nation's most gripping social questions. And because the Episcopal Church's identity and vocation seemed to fit so clearly and easily into the national and corporate church ideal—aided and abetted by a heritage that included official established status—Episcopalians gained public attention and influence out of proportion to their relatively small numbers.

The Episcopal Church's clarity of intention allowed the church's mission to go forward in bold and very particular ways that continued to raise the church's profile in America. One notable example was the Episcopal Church's efforts to establish religious schools. By the early twentieth century, there was a dramatic increase in private or "preparatory" schools generally in America. Even in the late nineteenth century (in an early demonstration of the developing national ideal), the Episcopal Church had expanded widely into the field of education; in the even more education-minded early twentieth—by which time the national church ideal had grown stronger still—it almost was inevitable that Episcopalians would rush into an arena of American life as central as the education of their children. In 1920, the Diocese of Virginia alone purchased two Richmond boarding schools as a demonstration of their dedication to Episcopal education: St. Catherine's School for girls and St. Christopher's for boys. Similar Episcopal schools all across the country combined college preparatory study with religious instruction in a manner that created a distinct ethos, an environment in which worship and study inculcated patterns of faithfulness and social service.[33] These educational efforts were further supported by the long heritage of English religious schools and universities. Many Episcopal schools were closely patterned after these schools—Oxford and Cambridge Universities especially.

It is significant that, as Episcopalians built an elaborate institutional base that addressed almost every aspect of American
society, they also increased their emphasis on worship. By the
beginning of the twentieth century, for example, most churches
in the Diocese of Connecticut had begun to rely upon vested
choirs and elaborate mechanical organs to provide music for worship.[34] A revival of Gothic-style architecture had influenced
church design, and the fruits of liturgical revival were widely
apparent. Generally, worship was more carefully designed and
conducted with greater formality than Episcopal worship of a
century earlier. Significant variations were also apparent. There
were, of course, High Church and Low Church parties, each
dominating the church in certain parts of the country, but there
also was a remarkable variety of local and regional styles of Episcopal life, with each congregation seeming to possess its own idiosyncratic approach to being Episcopalian. Within the framework
of national organization and the national church ideal, there was
room for variety. In fact, Episcopalians would readily cite their
variety as emblematic of their achievement. The truth of their
expression of the Gospel seemed to lie in an ability to build
common mission out of many local affirmations of faith.

Of course, there were limits to the church's capacity to
embrace diversity. Late in the nineteenth century, a group of
Episcopalians left the church out of a concern that its worship
and theology were becoming too "Roman."[35] The rise and continued life of the tiny Reformed Episcopal Church seemed an
unfortunate aberration. By the early 1900s, however, there were
signs of other conflicts to come. When Walter Russell Bowie,
editor of one of the Episcopal Church's most influential newspapers,
The Southern Churchman, began to take a consistently liberal
stance on social issues and interpretations of the Bible, controversy erupted, with conservative clergy and laity challenging
Bowie in print. It was not easily resolved, even after Bowie
resigned as editor in 1924. Leading a conservative counterattack,
a Richmond, Virginia, layman, Langbourne Williams, purchased
majority control of the paper, in 1927, and instituted an editor

who reflected his theological taste. In its new guise, *The Southern Churchman* ardently defended the Bible's literal truth against radical clergy and intellectuals who would challenge it.[36] The liberals were far from routed, however (for example, in a few places, the 1920s saw hints that the accustomed roles of women and minorities in the church were being challenged). But more significant than the determination of which group had gained ideological ascendancy at any given moment is the observation that a noisy new level of discourse had arisen within the church—the discourse of discord.

Relatively few Episcopalians at the time saw these developments as any real reason for alarm. Few if any could have recognized them as intimations of the even greater discord to follow later in the century. The links between local congregations and their diocesan and national structures were secure enough to keep factionalism in check. Furthermore, the church was confident in its ability to produce leaders of the stature of Henry Knox Sherrill, whose tenure as Presiding Bishop from 1947 to 1958 ushered in a period of unity in mission that represented a high point in the church's experience. It was Sherrill who declared that "often the Church has great convictions about little things; instead, the Church must have great convictions about great things." In his ministry, Sherrill embodied what he proclaimed. His varied responsibilities reflected the depth of both his religious vision and his social vision. In addition to Presiding Bishop of the Episcopal Church, Sherrill served as President of Corporation, Yale University's governing body, and founding President of the National Council of Churches.

It is telling that, when he reflected on his work, Sherrill compared his role to that of the head of a multinational corporation.[37] Under his influence and the guidance of other dedicated local and national leaders, the Episcopal Church had become an institution that elicited broad and deep loyalty. The tensions among Episcopalians, especially the tension between the urge to adapt to American culture and the longing to be distinct, seemed resolved.

But tensions would reappear. Religious institutions would discover that the idea of spiritual community in America could not be presumed but would have to be explored and articulated anew. In each generation, the church would have to revise its self-understanding as a Christian community, by recovering a primary emphasis on mission and reorganizing itself accordingly. Not surprisingly, this need to rediscover Episcopal identity and vocation created discontents within the church.

Notes

[1] See Jan Karon, *At Home in Mitford* (Viking, 1996) and successive titles in the Mitford series.

[2] Robert Wuthnow, *After Heaven: Spirituality in America Since the 1950s* (University of California, 1998)

[3] Rhys Isaac, *The Transformation of Virginia, 1740–1790* (University of North Carolina, 1982).

[4] Robert Prichard, *A History of the Episcopal Church* (Morehouse, 1999), p. 27.

[5] John Frederick Woolverton, *Colonial Anglicanism in North America* (Wayne State University, 1984). Following Woolverton's example, we refer to the colonial church as the Church of England, and the post-Revolution church as the Episcopal Church.

[6] Daniel O'Connor, *Three Centuries of Mission: The United Society for the Propagation of the Gospel 1701–2000* (Continuum, 2000).

[7] Woolverton, p. 118, p. 123.

[8] Harry S. Stout, *The Divine Dramatist: George Whitefield and the Rise of Modern Evangelicalism* (Eerdmans, 1991).

[9] Prichard, p. 59.

[10] Nathan O. Hatch, *The Democratization of American Christianity* (Yale, 1989), p. 60.

[11] *Ibid.*, p. 3.

[12] *Ibid.*, p. 13.

[3] Donald G. Matthews, "The Second Great Awakening as an Organizing Process, 1780–1830" *American Quarterly*, 1969 (21: 1), pp. 23–43. Roger Finke and Rodney Stark have updated the argument that the Evangelical message and style of organization were geared to successfully evangelizing the new American frontier. See Finke and Stark, *The Churching of America 1776–1990: Winners and Losers in Our Religious Economy* (Rutgers, 1992).

[14] Henry Caswall, *America and the American Church*. Religion in America Series. (Arno, 1969), p. 55f.

[15] *Ibid.*, p. 103.

[16] Prichard, p. 126.

[17] White's *The Case of the Episcopal Churches in the United States Considered* is discussed by Prichard, p. 84.

[18] Robert Bruce Mullin, *Episcopal Vision/American Reality: High Church Theology and Social Thought in Evangelical America* (Yale, 1986).

[19] George E. DeMille, *The Catholic Movement in the American Episcopal Church* (Church Historical, 1941).

[20] Paul T. Phillips, *A Kingdom on Earth: Anglo-American Social Christianity, 1880–1940* (Pennsylvania State University, 1996).

[21] Prichard, p. 150f.

[22] Nelson Rollin Burr, *The Story of the Diocese of Connecticut* (Church Missions Publishing, 1962), p. 241.

[23] Three colleges for African Americans were founded in the second half of the nineteenth century: St. Augustine's in Raleigh, North Carolina (1867), St. Paul's in Lawrenceville, Virginia (1882), and Voorhees in Denmark, South Carolina (1897), as well as a seminary for African Americans, the Bishop Payne Divinity School in Petersburg, Virginia (1878), as described in Prichard, p. 181.

[24] *Addresses and Historical Papers Before the Centennial Council of the Protestant Episcopal Church in the Diocese of Virginia* (Thomas Whittaker, 1885).

[25] James Elliott Lindsley, *This Planted Vine: A Narrative History of the Episcopal Diocese of New York* (Harper & Row, 1984), p. 252.

[26] S. D. McConnell, *History of the American Episcopal Church* (Thomas Whittaker, 1890), p. 430ff.

[27] Lindsley, p. 232.

[28] Burr, p. 202.

[29] Samuel C. Shepherd, *Avenues of Faith: Shaping the Urban Religious Culture of Richmond, Virginia 1900–1929* (University of Alabama, 2001), p. 57, 165.

[30] Ian T. Douglas, *Fling Out The Banner!: The National Church Ideal and the Foreign Mission of the Episcopal Church* (Church Hymnal Corporation, 1996), p. 90.

[31] Harold C. Martin, *"Outlasting marble and brass:" The History of the Church Pension Fund* (Church Hymnal Corporation, 1986), p. 3, 66.

[32] Peter Dobkin Hall, "Religion and the Organizational Revolution in the United States," in N. J. Demerath et al., eds., *Sacred Companies: Organizational Aspects of Religion and Religious Aspects of Organizations* (Oxford, 1998), pp. 99–115. See Milton J. Coalter, John M. Mulder, and Louis B. Weeks, eds., *The Organizational Revolution: Presbyterians and American Denominationalism* (Westminster/John Knox, 1992).

[33] Shepherd, p. 70ff.

[34] Burr, pp. 238ff.

[35] Allen C. Guelzo, *For The Union of Evangelical Christendom: The Irony of the Reformed Episcopalians* (Pennylvania State University, 1994).

[36] Shepherd, pp. 268–276.

[37] Noted in an unpublished booklet by Ian T. Douglas, "The Times and Timeliness of Henry Knox Sherrill," Episcopal Church Foundation, 1999.

3

CONFLICT, CULTURE, AND INSTITUTION
The Many Forms of Episcopal Conflict

M any Episcopalians believe that conflict is the church's greatest challenge. As we interviewed members of Episcopal churches across the country, accounts of conflict surfaced readily. Far from glossing over the conflicts they had faced in their churches, our respondents were eager to speak. We heard about the past and the present, about national issues and local ones, about questions that have been addressed and questions that have proven intractable. The sources or subject matter of Episcopal conflict, past and present, as recounted by hundreds of Episcopalians all across the country, ranged broadly—if somewhat predictably—across these and many other topics: core values of Anglican faith, Prayer Book revision, ordination of women, homosexuality, local leadership, the challenges of diversity, lack of Christian education materials, lack of national or diocesan support and leadership. The forms and natures of Episcopal conflict also ranged broadly; these, however, proved more surprising than did the sources of Episcopal conflict.

Given the received wisdom about conflict in the Episcopal Church, our researchers fully expected to find instances of conflict in the culture-war mold of conservative-versus-liberal. And there were indeed many such predictable instances, especially among Episcopalians who recalled the turbulent decades of change toward the end of the twentieth century. But there was also every imaginable variation upon this model of political polarity, and some of them go very much against our preconceptions. For example, some stories of conflict about the period of turbulent change revealed not the conservative Episcopalians of conventional wisdom, just *careful* Episcopalians! Here were people easily mislabeled as conservative but who in fact turned out to object surprisingly little to the tendencies of change in the Episcopal church; rather it was the reckless *rate* of change that they objected to, and the painful cultural whiplash that many communities experienced as a result. Then there were stories from very liberal congregations who had reacted quite otherwise to liberal initiatives that seemed legitimate in the abstract but naïve, wrongheaded, or simply impractical in practice. As will be illustrated in some of the conflict stories to follow, local practice plays havoc with conventional understandings of political polarities.

In the data gathered by our researchers, conflict often manifested itself as two "adversaries" squaring off to represent two diametrically opposed viewpoints. But the political polarity discussed above was only one of many forms of adversarial conflict. A polarity that might be described as local-versus-institutional also was prominent, with the "adversary" in this instance being national or diocesan staff who would not or could not offer assistance for local initiatives. There also were permutations of this model, one of which retained the marked divide between the wider and the local church but did so without the adversarial component; in this less charged understanding of conflict, the local communities clearly were unhappy with their disconnection from the diocesan or national level, but they were somewhat resigned to it and assigned less blame than did other Episcopalians, believing that some distance between "us" and "them" simply was an inevitable fact of human and institutional natures. Sometimes both polarities—political and institutional—were at work simultaneously, creating a highly charged conflict, with the national or diocesan staff usually cast as aloof liberals and parishioners in the pews as hands-on, down-to-earth conservatives.

The generational divide represents another important polarity at work in Episcopal churches. As illustrated by the stories in chapter one, generational gaps were sometimes sources of solace and stability to communities, with elders contributing wisdom and perspective and younger people adding energy and enthusiasm. Other times the distance between the generations stretched the ties that bound them almost to the breaking point—especially between older cradle Episcopalians and younger converts who had very different religious roots and consequently very different visions of the future. The generational polarity sometimes seemed particularly likely to combine with other polarities in the church, thereby creating highly charged superimpositions that created tensions on several simultaneous fronts. For example, the older generation sometimes aligned with the conservative end of the political spectrum and the younger generation with liberal. Or, the older generation adopted an establishment perspective that aligned with the institutional church and a very pronounced style of Anglicanism; meanwhile, the younger generation focused on local concerns and seemed almost interdenominational in their approach to worship and community.

These are just a few permutations of polarized conflict in the church; many others were observed. But it is important to stress that conflict, as expressed in hundreds of interviews, was not always as schematic and clearly defined, with divisions drawn, blame assigned, and culprits identified. The concerns and sentiments expressed did not always array themselves neatly along any recognizable political, sociological, or theological continuum. Our researchers frequently encountered amorphous concerns about the present or the future or even memories of the troubled past that resembled anxiety more than conflict—as conflict usually is defined. In their stories they talked of such things as struggling to find meaningful Christian education materials for the children in their congregation; they seemed less focused on whether or how the diocese or national church had failed them in this search and more focused on using local networking—often among other denominations in the area—to locate the best resources. Such "adversary-less" struggles may have generated less tension than did the more polarized conflicts but, then again, these less clearly articulated conflicts also may have generated less focused efforts and less potentially constructive energy than did the more clearly defined issues. In the final analysis, this more amorphous form of conflict may be the more prevalent, but it also is much harder to pinpoint and examine.

The stories that follow exemplify all of the above categories and forms of conflict (sometimes a single story may exemplify several all at once). They are arranged more or less according to the subject matter of the conflict, but this is largely a concession to the medium of transmission—telling a complicated, multidimensional story in linear book form. In actuality these stories as told in small groups around the country spilled forth in an almost musical fugue, with element piling after element—evolving one from the other in ways not always obvious. For example, a discussion of a congregation's struggle with the ordination of women might easily segue into a discussion of the challenges of ethnic or cultural diversity within the congregation. By topic, these juxtapositions make little sense; experientially they make all the sense in the world, because both these developments represented seismic changes in some communities— changes that tested them to their very limits.

THE IMPACT OF CHANGE WITHIN AMERICAN CULTURE

Societal Change

Episcopalians perceive that American culture is changing rapidly and in unexpected ways. "Change, incredible change over the course of our lifetimes," one Episcopalian noted. "And it is continuing."

Since the 1950s, there have been a variety of shifts in American life. Four in particular are often cited: communication, transportation, mobility, and accessibility. First, the forms of technology available for communication have become more complex and more elaborate. Second, transportation has become exponentially more efficient and extensive. Third, more people relocate more times over the course of their lives than ever before. Lastly, the 1950s began an age of accessibility in America, in which not only were communication and travel better but more Americans had the education and the financial resources to take full advantage of them.

The pace and complexity of American life have increased markedly over the past half century. But even more apparent is the increased variety in American life. Ethnic and racial diversity—once a social reality only in a few, large metropolitan areas—has become a reality in almost all parts of the country. With ethnic diversity has come religious diversity—a proliferation of religions once identified with other areas of the world. For example, there are now more than twice as many Muslims in America as there are Episcopalians. There have been dramatic increases in the numbers and public visibility of Hindus and Buddhists. At the same time, interest in non-Christian religions and the growth of non-traditional forms of religious life have become defining features of American life.

For Americans in general, the remarkable variety of people who now call themselves American raises urgent new questions. What common vision unites us? Is such pluralism the fulfillment of the American dream or an unwieldy source of social tension? For Episcopalians in particular, the proliferation of non-Western and non-traditional religious groups has created a grassroots desire for greater clarity of identity—especially with regard to beliefs and practices.

Questions about identity acquire force when two unsettling trends in American life are added to the overall uncertainty of American life. First, there is a general sense that the bonds of American civic life have loosened. Not only have large numbers of Americans withdrawn from active participation in mainline churches, but they are less active in service clubs and political groups. Apparently many Americans believe "it makes little difference whether they engage in civic activities or not." There are hints that many "regard their neighbors as inherently untrustworthy," and that "many Americans are turning their backs on the general welfare and pursuing their own interests as singlemindedly as possible."[1] As a result, according to Robert Wuthnow, all historic American institutions are now "porous." That is, people increasingly participate selectively and loosely, frequently shifting loyalties as readily as they shift their geographic locales. To accommodate this reality, many institutions have "loosely confederated structures" that "also shape the ways in which individual Americans live and relate to one another, dictating greater flexibility and limited commitment." To frame a question as Wuthnow might ask it: is America breaking apart and coming together in a new way? If so, is our social fabric weaker or stronger? Or is it simply different?[2]

Second, as we have encountered among Episcopalians, many Americans value the unprecedented variety of life today but are troubled by our loosening connections. Along with signs of weaker allegiance to institutions, many Americans perceive diminished religious commitment and moral fiber. Since the Vietnam War, a variety of missteps by all public institutions and those who lead them has created a sense of "disenchantment." Revelations of corporate and personal wrongdoing have eroded optimism and created an aura of suspicion about all public figures. Even religious leaders have not proven immune from abuse of power and of people whom they should be faithfully serving. Once presumed, trust now has to be built by those who would accept public responsibility of any sort. Perhaps at no time since the revolution that created this country have so many Americans been so reluctant to trust and to participate.[3]

Church members grasp that cultural shifts impact their congregations directly and cannot be avoided. They also realize that they must devise effective ways to understand and to respond to major cultural shifts. "We can't let social change drag us down; instead of responding to social changes, the church should be guiding social change." One of the main challenges Episcopal congregations face, and one of their greatest sources of conflict, arises from seeking ways to live the Christian faith and develop Episcopal life in the midst of extensive cultural change. The anguished questions of one lay person express a concern we have heard throughout the church: "How can we know what holds, what ought to stay the same? How can we keep a balance? How can we be open to change, but keep that which ought to hold fast?"

RELIGIOUS CHANGE

Religious life in America generally has changed in ways that parallel social changes. Just as trust in American institutions and leaders generally has eroded, so has trust in religious institutions and those who lead them. As described in a previous chapter, Episcopalians consistently enpress feelings of detachment and suspicion toward wider church structures. Even when conflict in Episcopal congregations clearly has a local source, the efforts of leaders to define their authority and their role may reflect a general confusion about Episcopal identity and vocation. Efforts by diocesan staff to intervene in congregational conflicts play to mixed reviews. As often as not, the initiatives of diocesan or national staff are interpreted locally as more of a commitment to preserving institutional structures than to appreciating and addressing local realities.

It is difficult to specify how this instinct for institutional survival became dominant. The church's structures arose out of a consensus that mission required a more organized approach. But as centralized authority, formal procedures, and hierarchical structures evolved, their original intent suffered. Their well-intentioned efforts to adapt institutional structures to new realities or to instill new fervor for mission never achieved the hoped-for results. In some instances, momentary bursts of fresh purpose flared then faded. In some localities, benefits could be cited for a time. But elaborate and partially successful efforts at renewal, such as Venture in Mission or the Decade of Evangelism, ultimately looked more like institutional engineering than engagement with the realities and needs of most congregations. In fairness, the Episcopal Church's leaders faced challenges they never could have envisioned. They understood their role to be that of formulating institutional responses in an era that was questioning the very worth of all institutions. Episcopal Church leaders sensed the seriousness of trying to keep pace with cultural change without losing religious identity in it.[4] But given their assumptions about the nature of their religious institution and their role in it, they appeared inflexible—unwilling (or perhaps unable) to grasp the shape of the social crisis they faced. Nor could they realize that the future of American religious life would require a different approach to leadership, belief, and organization. As one writer has explained it, the historic American religious groups, including the Episcopal Church, have steadily lost their "mastery" and their "mandate."[5]

Religious life in America also exhibits the same mobility seen in secular America. Thus, Utah is no longer the only place to find Mormons, and Roman Catholics are no longer present in large numbers only in urban, industrial areas. Evangelicals and Fundamentalists do not find strongholds only in the South, and Asian religions are no longer confined to a few areas of the West and Northeast.[6] America is not only religiously pluralistic to an amazing degree but pluralism is apparent in every section of the country.[7]

Religious pluralism has created some interesting conversations about identity among Episcopalians. At one parish in the Southeast—where there always have been significant expressions of conservative Christianity—the new strains of Fundamentalism that are sweeping the country have challenged Episcopalians as never before. "We are just overshadowed by the Fundamentalist churches around here. They have clear and simple answers to everything, and that is attractive to people who feel confused. Then you read about yet another conflict at the meetings of our national church and have to walk out to face your neighbors who ask why you belong to this church. Those political polarizations are weakening us, while churches with neat answers to every-thing are expanding rapidly. I wish we could find ways to express our beliefs faithfully without demanding that everyone agree with everything we say. Our difficulties with that make me worry about our survival."

The ambivalence and hesitation of many of our respondents about such matters were evident. As one put it, "Even after that so-called 'Decade of Evangelism' many of us are still awkward about inviting people to church, actively reaching out, getting newcomers involved, and keeping programs going. There's a lot of church-shopping going on out there, and people are hungry. But we don't want to seem pushy and may be so reserved I'm afraid we don't make them welcome. We do have a strong sense of community in this congregation, but somehow I wonder if that makes it difficult for a visitor to break into the circle. How can we become more effective as evangelists?"

THE IMPACT OF CHANGE IN
THE EPISCOPAL CHURCH

Over the past generation, the Episcopal Church has come through one challenge after another. Tensions over social issues and activist stances by leaders in the 1960s gave way to battles over liturgical revision and the ordination of women to the priesthood and episcopate in the 1970s and 1980s. In the 1990s, conservative revulsion at liberal advocacy of welcoming—and even ordaining—gay persons further charged the church's atmos-phere. To many, the church began to resemble a cluster of ideo-logical enclaves, and the initiative seemed to swung to whatever group that voiced the loudest outrage. The perception that many grassroots members of Episcopal churches were offended and preparing to revolt has pervaded recent decades.

Any claim that Episcopalians work well together would seem to deny these ideological differences and battles. This is not so. There are indeed serious differences, but there also are many instances of success at local levels in addressing them. For the majority of Episcopalians we interviewed, the key to navigating through the differences is a sense of identity that begins with a firm commitment to worship as outlined in the Book of Common Prayer; for others it begins with being inclusive and affirming different views and cultures, embracing diversity rather than ignoring it. Respondents frequently referred to the worship and cultural breadth of the Anglican Communion as their model. The seismic shifts in congregational relationships can occur "successfully but not without stress arising from having to live into new behaviors," reflected one wise parish elder. As we consider several major transitions in the church's life, we will discover the strengths Episcopalians can use to face further challenges ahead.

And yet the church somehow managed to come through each of these challenges, so much so that the once divisive tensions over ordaining women and changing the Book of Common Prayer are seen nowadays as remote by many—the concerns of a previous and proactive at work than simply waiting for a generation or so until these controversies lose their potency. Far from being stymied by such conflicts—as would have happened had Episcopalians tried merely to go *around* their disagreements or get *over* their frustrations—Episcopalians appear to be finding an invigorating new sense of identity and vocation in the very midst of controversy and turmoil. A broader perspective seems required if we truly are to understand the nature of conflict in the Episcopal Church. There remain plenty of acute differences in belief and in overall approach to Christian faith, and several of these will be examined below.

TENSIONS OVER BELIEF

Episcopalians consistently express broad allegiance to the church's traditions, although they may differ over appropriate interpretations and expressions of them. They also broadly endorse the central role of worship in the church's life, although there may be differences over particular styles of liturgy and music. One senses a capacity for flexibility among Episcopalians that only becomes rigidity when they perceive that irrational, uninformed financial and program expectations are forced on them by external authorities. For this reason, some members of

Episcopal churches both affirm the church as an ideal and issue loud protests against it based on their perceptions of the beliefs and priorities of some church leaders.

One form such protests take is to demand greater doctrinal specificity. "It is good to be in a place bound together by tradition, a root that goes way back. That is what brought me here," a woman in a Northeastern congregation said. "But there is something missing. It seems like we don't have any doctrinal clarity in our denomination. I don't know if this is accurate or not, but I hear it a lot, and it is a very hot issue for many people. We need some sort of doctrinal center to what we're doing."

A member of a focus group in a Sunbelt congregation put the matter more sharply, "We really are Evangelical and try to stay focused on the Scripture. God's word shows us what we are supposed to do, not the bishop. The Bible says we are to preach the Gospel, bring in the lost, reach the unreached. However, the diocese and the national church are going about all sorts of things that have little or nothing to do with Christ's Great Commission for us. They have just wandered off into apostasy."

It is difficult to gauge the extent to which such perceptions exist across our church, but the frustration is apparent in many places we visited. For some who share this outlook, the sense of doctrinal confusion gives rise to a fear that the church may split. From others, for whom the doctrinal confusion has reached the level of apostasy, there sometimes is heard a desire for such a schism. At the other end of the theological spectrum are some who worry that the push for doctrinal specificity brings with it the danger of limiting the church's welcoming inclusiveness to all. Somewhere in the middle are those Episcopalians who see the same debate from an entirely different perspective; for them the real problem in the Episcopal Church is a crisis in leadership, not a crisis in doctrine (their perspective—and the views of other Episcopalians concerned with leadership within the church—will be examined in further detail below).

Probably the most polarizing topic within the doctrinal debate today is the issue of whether or not to accept into leadership positions those persons with homosexual orientation. This matter is seen by some as just the visible edge of a much deeper, systemic problem. They define the problem as the drift of the Episcopal Church away from its core values: historic Anglican roots in faithfulness to the Bible, respect for the church's traditions, and unquestioning obedience to God's commandments and moral standards. They consider their opposition to the acceptance of homosexual persons as church leaders to be a mandate; and correcting the church's drift, they often argue, is the necessary step the church must take if it is to be faithful and to grow.

At the other end of the spectrum are those who argue with equal ardor that this issue is the place where the extent of God's love for all people can—and must—be affirmed and realized. They see the debate about sexuality as an opportunity to come to understand better what is meant by belief and to discover what it means to practice the Christian faith in community. For this group, the word "inclusion" carries the weight of the Gospel's intention almost as much as the word "justice," which makes full acceptance of homosexual persons a prominent priority in their lives in the church.

In between these two positions are many Episcopalians whose positions are not so easily characterized. Indeed, the issue of full acceptance of homosexuals sometimes seems almost ancillary. Some see the whole issue as yet another failure of church leadership. Perhaps hardest to categorize is the large group of Episcopalians for whom the issue primarily represents yet another vexing and draining controversy in a now decades-long line of such controversies. Within this group there are some people who are *for* full acceptance, some who are *against*; even so, their most defining characteristic is their discouragement. One elderly respondent (who probably fits into this group's "opposed" contingent) said wearily: "Back in my generation, we argued about race and whether women should be priests. But now that we just seem to have dealt with those issues, up comes this new problem of sexual orientation that really pushes my buttons all over again!" Representing the other contingent of this category of Epsicopalians is someone from a parish in the South who reported that:

several years ago, the city's Gay Men's Chorus approached our church for permission to use our choir room one night per week for their practice. There was a long controversy about that, with much discussion. After a year, the vestry finally concluded that we would allow them to use the space. But we were so tired of the controversy that we just dropped the issue, instead of taking advantage of the opportunity to get beyond the question of using our space to face the underlying problem of how to relate to gay and lesbian people. We were tired and stopped trying.

But in many instances, the presence of gay people in a congregation is not a stumbling block. We found a number of cases where Episcopalians understand the presence of gay people as an instance of diversity in the congregation and try to address the issue constructively. One woman expressed her hope that her congregation could find some resources to deal with explosive issues productively. "We have begun to face and deal with some types of diversity, but we still have a long way to go. We've gotten past the tokenism of the past, but we still don't draw upon the richness of our many differences." She continued, "Some differences seem to paralyze us. Surely there are some places where changes such as this have been dealt with effectively. I wish we could find some way to learn from them, draw upon their experiences and resources, learn how to build on our strengths and move forward instead of staying stuck as we are."

While some in the Episcopal Church appear to have settled into hard and fast camps on the specific issue of homosexuality and on broader questions of sexual morality, a different reality prevailed in the majority of congregations we visited. In place after place, these difficult questions were not the staple of daily life. When such questions came up, as they did with some frequency, usually there were members of local congregations who were trying to find ways to engage the issues thoughtfully, as an expression of their commitment to Christ and to one another. Here is an example of one such dialogue in one local group:

"I don't care what the bishop says. I'm clear on this issue. It's wrong, and he's wrong. That's all there is to it, and I don't care what anyone says."

"But you *have* to care! This issue could destroy our whole church."

"Well, if that's what the church is about, you can just count me out. My spiritual growth is the issue, not that one."

"But don't you see how you and I move forward in our spiritual growth is tied to the question of how we deal with people who are different from us? When some of our brothers and sisters are excluded from the table, we all are hurt."

A third person joined in, "Look, it took us quite a while to accept women as priests. Can you imagine how past attitudes of rejection affected them? It was destructive to men, too. So now we are talking about whether people whose sexual behavior differs from ours are humans. The question is, 'can any person become a baptized believer?'"

"How can we think about our own spiritual growth when we are rejecting some people in God's name? It just doesn't work like that. You can't be loving and rejecting at the same time!"

"Oh, yes I can! I accept the person but not the behavior. Jesus said, 'go and sin no more.'"

"So how did you apply that thinking to women who wanted to be priests?"

"That's an entirely different matter."

"Well, if we can't find a solution right here in this little group, it really shouldn't surprise anybody that huge national meetings haven't resolved it. I don't think they ever will do so until we begin building some agreements locally. We should be patient and continue working on the matter instead of burying our heads in the sand and hoping it will all go away."

This exchange not only illustrates the challenge of addressing this particular tension, but it also underscores the centrality of the congregation in our church's life. Creative ways to facilitate new links and exchanges of information among congregations—without trying to control such occasions—are being explored in a surprising number of Episcopal congregations.

CHANGES IN EPISCOPAL WORSHIP

The sometimes heated debate over homosexuality recalls us to another traumatic change in our relatively recent past: the revision of the Book of Common Prayer of 1979 and the subsequent period of extraordinary change in Episcopal worship. For those who participated in our focus groups, acceptance of the Prayer Book revision of 1979 is presumed. That is not to say there were no lingering feelings of pain from the transition, but it seems important to state that we met no one who viewed that battle of over two decades ago as unfinished. In fact, given the large number of newer Episcopalians in the church today, many people we encountered were unaware that there had been recent changes in liturgy that caused such turmoil. Simply put, these vital changes through which the church has gone now appear accepted by the overwhelming majority of Episcopalians.

There is another bridge that many Episcopalians believe they have crossed successfully: the preponderance of women in ordained positions of leadership. Since women were first officially ordained in January of 1977, their numbers have risen to well over twenty percent of all Episcopal clergy and even higher proportions in our seminaries.

At every stop in our study, we met women in leadership roles, and seldom did any of these describe tensions or questions arising over whether or not they should be occupying these roles. This is certainly not to claim that there are no Episcopalians who retain hesitations about women in positions of leadership and that no glass ceiling on women's advancement exists. Rather, we simply observe that our respondents seemed to presume equality between the sexes regarding leadership roles in the church.

"Remember all that stuff twenty-five years ago? Remember the events that happened about the same time? There was changing the Prayer Book and ordination of women. Many of the older members left here then. It was even rumored that the diocese was talking about closing this church. Then we got a good rector who instituted good worship and good preaching. It was an old style Anglican Sunday morning. The parish began growing again—not all at once, but steadily. Now we have a young woman as our rector, and we're attracting a lot more young people."

"That's right," nodded another in this group. "It's hard to believe that we were in such a difficult situation once, because things are going so well now. And the future looks rosy too. We really are on a roll!"

THE CHALLENGE OF DIVERSITY

Historically, the Episcopal Church has sought to embrace social, as well as theological, diversity. The ideal that a congregation's mission begins not with its membership roll but with its geographic vicinity—as in the Church of England's parochial system—is still widely held among Episcopalians. This understanding of mission entails an affirmation of the social patterns and groupings of localities and then working to incorporate them into congregational life. In the present circumstance, this historic ideal is challenged by forms of diversity ranging from differences in age and ethnicity to differences in views about social justice. This remarkable range of diversity has created forms of conflict in Episcopal congregations that are not necessarily adversarial or even controversial in the usual sense of that word, yet it is conflicts such as these that perhaps represent the greatest challenge to the church in the twentieth century.

Many of our congregations report success with such challenges. Others report setbacks and failures. All congregations report some sort of conflict related to the challenges of diversity, but as the stories that follow will illustrate, most are undeterred from their search for shared purpose and spiritual community.

DIVERSITY IN WORSHIP AND MINISTRY

At one urban Episcopal church, the reality of diverse interests required different forms of music. "Some want traditional Anglican music, while others want more contemporary music. Others want music for kids. There are different kinds of audiences here, and

we try to accommodate them as best we can." In another congregation, a member explained, "Our worship services are different,
and they appeal to different people. There was some awkward-
ness in the Christmas services. They were not of a single piece
but were three very different services."

As they come together in sacramental worship tailored to the
stylistic preferences of groups, most Episcopalians are accepting
of a very wide range of theological views. The historic Anglican
emphasis on the parish as a geographic region of responsibility is
seen in this perspective. Anyone in the region is welcome,
regardless of views. Many respondents said they had come to this
church from other denominations that demanded acceptance of
a specific list of beliefs in order to belong. Their unanswered
questions and unresolved doubts were treated quite differently in
the Episcopal Church; they were accepted and treated as the
doorways to growth.

"The Episcopal Church focuses on nurturing your spiritual
growth and on formation, rather than upon insistence on certain
answers." said one typical respondent. "I was never before
encouraged to raise any questions or doubts, and it was only
when I came here that anyone suggested those were the very
things I needed to struggle with. That process has been my source
of deepening faith."

At a Southeastern congregation, the church's openness to
different points of view was affirmed with great conviction.

> I find so many other churches are not nearly as open as is
> the Episcopal Church in all facets. That's why I'm here. I
> was raised in a church where it was always, 'you don't do
> this, you don't do that.' Now I don't want anyone telling
> me what to do or not do, and they don't try that here.
> Instead, they inspire me to think about what I should do and
> offer me ways to do the right thing and guidelines to make
> my decisions by. That's what I like about this church. I can
> come here to worship with others, and I have principles to
> stimulate my thinking, rather than a list of simple rules and
> neat little answers to everything. That's why I like it here.

We have found repeated instances of the importance Episcopalians place on diversity. Theologically and practically, diversity

has become one of the church's foremost ideals.

Such realizations bring healing in many congregations, but others continue to struggle with the challenges. One member told this story of struggle: "We are closing out our food pantry because we haven't been able to reconcile the interests of the people who run it with the interests of many others in the congregation. The people running the pantry insisted on doing things just as they wanted, and they definitely did not welcome the suggestions of others for changes. It can be upsetting when a few people get together with totally rigid views and exclude others, but sometimes that happens."

"You can't be hypersensitive in a church," added another. "Being a Christian and loving others involves making lots of compromises, and that is extremely hard for some folks."

At a rural mission site in the Midwest, a similar sentiment emerged. "It's the failure to get consensus on the small, insignificant things in church life that can lead to disasters later. Someone donated a picture, and the priest just hung it on the wall in the sanctuary. Immediately, a few people became critical of what she had done and demanded it be taken down." Clearly, churches are places where differing personal priorities are not easily merged into a collective sense of faith and purpose.

GENERATIONAL DIVERSITY

With some frequency, Episcopalians list differences among generations as one of their most significant challenges and most frequent sources of congregational failure. But the presence of increasing numbers of young people in many Episcopal churches remains a source of hope, even as tensions about it are usually apparent. In describing their congregation at worship, the participants in a focus group in the Southeast inadvertently revealed the presence of fault lines among their varied age groups. "Yes, there's a big generation spread in church; you are over here with teenagers who are moving ahead and the middle group who are OK with it; and then the older group who are more traditional who are seeing things happen they don't like."

In the Southwest, one congregation described the difficulty of proceeding with a renovation which had become a necessity as the congregation grew but which unexpectedly brought tension anyway. "There were deep divisions here that encompassed people with a long history and people who were quite new." It was apparent that most of the congregation's new members were younger adults, the majority of whom were married and had young children. They looked to this congregation for facilities that would permit expanded Sunday school and youth programs geared to their families. But the congregation's older, long-standing members had passed the phase of raising children. They did not share the urgency of creating larger facilities. Many of these older members were on fixed incomes. While they cautiously welcomed growth, they resisted the demand for renovation as an unwelcome financial burden being forced on them by acquisitive newcomers. They fretted that these new members were changing the character of a congregation they had worked for decades to build. To older members, the accomplishments of the past and the close-knit relationships that had made them possible seemed in danger of being swept aside by the impatient newcomers with fast-paced lifestyles. For the new members, on the other hand, the congregation's relevance rested in its ability to adapt to new patterns of family life and the stress these new patterns necessarily brought.

A similar set of opportunities and demands can be found in many Episcopal congregations. A lay leader in one Southeastern congregation put it this way: "There are so many young families with children coming in. That is markedly changing the composition of our membership. Most of them are from other denominations and have absolutely no background in Episcopal traditions and practices. Clearly they see something they value. How do we teach them about the meaning of those traditions yet remain open to change and innovation?" A Western lay leader took a less optimistic view of this trend: "The Episcopal group is dying away nationwide because new generations are not in tune with Episcopal traditions."

In the Midwest, a parish staff member ruefully admitted that "the youth group has been a disappointment. We don't have one right now. It just hasn't come together. We are trying to regroup, but it is not a priority of the congregation." A young adult in the West despaired that "we are not meeting where our kids are at and so they go elsewhere....We as a church typically don't credit them for being smarter than we think they are. They like to talk about God, but are typically afraid to, not to mention that they feel they will not be heard by adults."

In another congregation, a lay leader commented that "over a third of our members are new and young, but we still have a solid core of elders, even though that number is declining now. We have 118 people over the age of seventy. In the past, there was an underlying feeling of being separate. The younger group had a strong sense of involvement in social justice issues, while the older group tended to be suspicious of what the newer ones wanted. Our success has been getting more people involved, talking with each other and pulling together. Now there is a broad base of support on our most important issues. We're increasing the sense of belonging together, of 'we-ness.'" This sense of renewed cohesion was cited by respondents in many congregations.

One Western parish reported that "at one time, we didn't have many small children; now we're drawing them, and we want them to feel a part of the church. We decided to place a children's rug and toys in front of the pews in the nave during the service. It has been popular with a lot of people, but there is a lot of energy around whether or not this is working. Some see it as a disturbance. It is still going on, and we are trying to make it work." So much divisive energy surrounded the children's rug that the group repeatedly diverted from the interviewer's questions to return to it. Rather than squelch these diversions, our interviewers took careful note, finding their tenor and their direction striking. The comments that surfaced began as expressions of frustration with one another and with the situation but evolved into proposals of compromise and fresh consensus. This glimpse into the life of one congregation taught us to view even the most severe and protracted instances of conflict as dynamic processes in which the participants usually try to move toward genuine forms of resolution.

One large Midwestern congregation had done considerable work to attract new members and to develop outreach and service ministries in the neighborhood. Along with some instances of impressive success, there were noticeable tensions. "A few years ago, for example, we started a baseball program for the kids in the neighborhood, most of whom had nothing to do with the church. When a baseball went through one of our stained glass windows, some people in the congregation began complaining that the kids' program was just wrong for us. One man insisted he didn't see why we ever put in the baseball diamond. Another said that if the kids were going to be on our property, they should wear appropriate clothes. Yet another chimed in with, 'just [having them here] isn't enough. There's a big breakdown with these kids in society, and having some of them play baseball in our lot isn't going to change that.' Another younger woman came back with, 'Wait, it's tough to have youth programs today. There will be ups and downs. These kids have lots of pressures and strains. They need a lot of guidance and training. That requires trust, and building trust takes a lot of time.'"

RACIAL, ETHNIC, AND CULTURAL DIVERSITY

On the West Coast, a congregation was deeply proud of the extensive diversity of its membership, including age, race and ethnicity, and sexual orientation, all held together by a powerful sense of shared experience and purpose. "We take parish camping trips, and people will sometimes look over at us and say, 'now just what brought that curious group together?' It is our love and enjoyment of one another."

"I guess you could say that diversity is our identity here," said another respondent in this group. "When it works, it's wonderful; but when it doesn't, it's painful."

At times, the extent of a congregation's diversity makes the fact of its success astounding. "We have over twenty zip codes represented among our members. Yet our worship has never been more vital. This parish, which had been a sleeping giant, has really come to life. We had to struggle to build connections with each other, but we found that we were stronger than we thought. Now we know we're not so fragile and not going to fall apart. If a situation comes up, we know we can handle it."

A congregation adjacent to a large public university recognized that diversity is both an ideal and a challenge. "We are accepting of a very wide range of beliefs. There is no litmus test for acceptability—everybody is welcome. However, that diversity is sometimes a mixed blessing. It can provoke conflicts in the short run. You just have to hang in there and find the common ground. Most of the time, the result is far better than what those in initial agreement could have done by themselves."

While most Episcopalians are hopeful about bridging cultural differences, they are under no illusions about the extent of this challenge. Finding the balance between being broadly inclusive, including the diversity in the congregation's vicinity, and finding unity and coherent identity can be difficult.

"This was a predominantly white church," a participant in another focus group recalled. Then "we ended up being ninety-five percent black." To achieve true diversity in the parish, varied forms of worship have been tried. "We have been able to attract a number of Anglos to our church, and we want to build on this to reinvigorate us into that realm of ethnic diversity reflective of the population based in the city."

In an Eastern city, the merger of a predominantly black congregation with a predominantly white one has not been easy—even with the best of intentions from both groups. One lay leader from the black congregation spoke candidly about her experience of the merger, during which warm words about diversity sometimes were followed by lukewarm actions. "You know the hypocrisy of Christianity: we are going to bring you in but we are going to keep you separate. You know we were not truly under the umbrella of brotherhood and sisterhood."

One congregation, whose members are mostly African-American, resisted calling itself a "black church." One leader there said, "If we are going to be Episcopalians, then we are going to be one of the family of Episcopalians, regardless of anybody's color or race." Another participant in this discussion added, "Don't you see that we have a chance to live out something that not many churches do? Not many churches are as integrated as we are. I don't mean just racially, but also socially and economically. The leadership of this parish is truly integrated. The one thing we *all* have in common is that we all are Episcopalians."

In one West Coast location, a lay leader observed that "because of the changes in our neighborhood, we now have a lot of Cambodians. So we developed a Cambodian outreach; we have a Cambodian youth group." In the Southwest, a lay person commented that "the strictly Anglo-American is a minority in our school system. Blacks and Hispanics are the major population and the Episcopal Church has reached out to that area, and we have been totally unsuccessful."

Several other West Coast congregations noted the reconciliation of cultural differences as a significant challenge. "The core of our sense of call is to integrate the cultures of this area into our worship services," one urban group noted. Their sense of challenge reflected the staggering variety of nationalities in their region and their ongoing efforts to design culture-specific worship for as many as possible. "We are seeing more demographic changes in the community. There has been a rapid increase in the Korean population, and they don't seem to be familiar with liturgical worship. How to make everyone feel welcome when the community is so very diverse is an ongoing challenge for us."

Language differences can be a particularly challenging conflict in multicultural communities. "Our bilingual services sometimes just feel artificial," said a lay leader in another West Coast parish. "Why are we all here? Is it just for show? It seems so formulaic some days. The music is hard for people from another culture, although we do include two songs in Spanish for another large group in the congregation."

In the urban Northeast, a focus group including people from several nearby congregations easily identified cultural divides as a significant challenge for their churches. "We are in a new era with more people of color and with being more extensively involved in neighborhood issues. Such a groundswell is a grace. But there are difficult differences around race and class and sexuality. We recognize these issues and our need for mediation and reconciliation."

In another group, a woman recounted a surprising experience: "I remember being in a women's aerobics class at the Y. It was a racially mixed class, and I don't know when it hit me that everyone in the room was an Episcopalian. I remember being so excited when I realized that. We're all Episcopalians here! That was the common thread linking all these different people together."

LEADERSHIP CONFLICTS

One of the central issues Episcopal congregations face is the matter of leadership. Many congregations seek help in dealing with difficult issues such as setting priorities and nurturing common faith, yet they distrust what the church's official leaders offer. In the words of one respondent, "I really wish somebody would finally put the basics of faith into order for everyone but do so without sacrificing the rich and creative differences we bring. We want to be engaged with and own our own programs, but we find our time and energy stretched beyond our limits. We want to welcome others, but we find some of them beyond our tolerance and threatening our core commitments."

Another put the matter this way: "Developing stronger lay leadership is a major need here. We want to be more effective leaders in the church and the world, but where is the preparation? I don't think we're just supposed to be junior priests. We do have different roles. But how do I practice my faith in my job, where power and authority are such issues? How do I practice my faith in my neighborhood and even right here in church programs? What do you do when a volunteer drops the ball? I hope there will be some resources to help us become better leaders."

Learning how to be effective leaders in voluntary organizations is a challenge, especially to those with strong business backgrounds and demanding careers. People who have come through difficult experiences in congregations agree that they should place inclusiveness and community over efficiency, even if important decisions have to be postponed. However, they wonder by what authority they should proceed. They realize that their approach to situations in the local congregation is likely to be different from what they would presume in their businesses or professions. They have sensed the important difference between informal influence and formal authority. But they are not always clear on which approach best matches particular situations. How to make such judgments and apply the appropriate leadership style to specific demands are examples of how the church might help them to grow as leaders.

"We are so busy here that we are just exhausted, and then we aren't sure how to work together effectively in our ministries," said one woman. "Everyone works full-time in demanding jobs, and only the retired people have much time and energy to put into church projects. I try to think of my job as a ministry, but often it's just busy work. By the end of the day, I don't have anything left to give. There are so many needs, but you can't respond to them all. How should we set priorities? How do we become good leaders and effective ministers? We really need help with these issues."

Many respondents expressed uncertainties about the reliability of church offices and the lack of clarity about such basic distinctions as the differences in responsibilities between lay and ordained persons. These tensions become more severe as uncertainty about how to conceptualize and address these issues becomes apparent. "I think our whole church is experiencing a tension between a hierarchical decision-making structure and a more democratic or collegial approach. We haven't found our balance between these ideals," one lay person concluded.

"Us" Versus "Them"

Amid the varieties of conflict and responses to conflict among Episcopalians, one theme stands out: the historic ideal of the national church has largely disintegrated. As a result, local congregations are looking not to denominational or institutional models of leadership in order to find their way forward as Christian communities but rather to larger and older Christian traditions; they also are looking to the dictates of the contemporary search for spirituality. Denominational identity and loyalty to institutional structures that once were abundantly evident no longer can be presumed. "I've learned to trust God, not the bishop," a lay person reported. "It's not the end of the world if you disagree. This congregation is like a big family. You hold your ground and don't run away."

In our mailed survey of congregational lay leaders, respondents were found to be less positive about their relationships with their dioceses than were participants in the interviews and focus groups. This suggests that the in-person findings on this issue may underestimate the extent of dissatisfaction among Episcopalians with their wider church structures and officers. Both the survey and the interviews produced some quite negative responses about the national church.

While most respondents in local congregations saw themselves as growing in strength, they saw the linkages between them and the wider church as ineffectual and growing weaker. There were some expressions of longing for more effective connections with the wider church, but few held any hope for bridging the chasm. Instead of looking to the official sources for ideas, help, or resources to address their needs, most of the people we interviewed told of drawing upon informal networks, often reaching well outside Episcopal sources. They perceive the national church as having drifted apart and its office-holders serving mainly their own bureaucratic inertia in the hope of institutional survival, rather than coming together around common purposes that actually support and serve local congregations. A broad range of Episcopalians see bridging these gaps as hopeless and pointless, while even those who want change do not believe they have enough influence to make change happen.

But what is striking to us is the extent to which the leaders of Episcopal churches believe they require linkages beyond their congregations to facilitate local mission. It became increasingly evident to our interviewers and researchers that much time and energy is spent by local leaders reaching out to structures of the larger church in search of the resources and guidance they believe their congregations require; even more evident is the disappointment they feel when their efforts are fruitless. In most cases, they eventually look locally to other churches or they look widely, usually outside the Episcopal Church, for the means of building their congregations. Their search usually is not conducted in rancor or driven by ideology. Instead, they simply seek responsive, effective sources for programs and guidance in order to advance their mission.

Our data argue that, despite their strong local focus and a marked self-sufficiency, Episcopal congregations consistently look outward. We found little or no evidence to support the criticism heard in some quarters of the church that our local congregations have turned inward and care only about their own members. Instead, we found abundant signs that Episcopalians look beyond their congregations not only for resources but also for opportunities to join in networks of mutual support and mission. Despite their obvious ambivalence about the church's hierarchy, many respondents hoped ways could be found to draw the many parts of the church together into more productive partnerships. The resilience of this hope should be a major source of encouragement for the Episcopal Church's professional leaders. But the tenor of this hope should also alert the church's leaders that a new style of cooperation is now required. For the church's mission to advance, there must be a new, horizontal sense of being a spiritual community, not the older, vertical sense of being a religious institution. And if systematic churchwide changes are to have validity at the local level, the experiences and wisdom of numerous local leaders must be tapped before intended changes are implemented.

CONFLICTS OVER CHRISTIAN EDUCATION

We now turn to a more detailed look at how the conflicts that arise from reaching outward for resources get played out within the local community. As stated previously, the area of congregational life sometimes referred to as "program" is often fraught with conflict; also established earlier was the supposition that program conflict frequently has a marked generational component. Now three corollaries should be added: first, for most of the Zacchaeus Project respondents, "program" usually boiled down to one principal congregational activity—Christian education; second, conflicts having to do with program (i.e., Christian education) may be generational in origin, but they invariably were acted out at the level of leadership; third, conversations about Christian education easily modulated into "us-them" dichotomies of local congregations versus the national church or the diocese, except that in this context another level of the larger church—the seminaries—played a conspicuous role. With regard to this final point, there was a widespread perception of a lack of connection between congregations and seminaries that included— but extended beyond—the matter of religious education. Respondents in both groups expressed regret that no one on the other side seemed to hear their needs, draw on their strengths, convey an adequate response, or seek partnership.

In a number of congregations, respondents expressed concerns about the quality of resources for Christian education. They cited lack of materials and failures of delivery by wider church offices, including seminaries. Even more agonizing than the lack of materials is the sense that there is a lack of leadership for Christian education. They perceive gaps in clergy skills in this important area, and the multiple demands on clergy and lay leaders' time are further distractions from this basic responsibility.

"The diocese isn't doing anything about outreach, about Christian education, about the links with the seminaries, or much of anything else I can see. Neither are the national offices. I'm afraid we're becoming Congregationalist in our approach and losing our rich Anglican heritage. But when there's nothing going on at the top, who is going to address these things with us here?" In the face of such varied cultural challenges, the local church faces a significant challenge. It must be "the point of continuity in a rapidly changing society, a place where you come home to acceptance and affirmation."

"I know it is a hard thing, but you have to address education on very basic things, not always just talking about social issues. Liturgy and the Bible are what we need first. You have to have ways to teach them to children and adults, too," said one respondent.

Another in this group added, "The age group between ten and twelve is crucial. "You have to begin in childhood. We need to be able to discuss the issues of these children in terms of Christian faith."

"Well, it's really the same for adults," added another, as heads nodded in agreement. "In-depth study is needed. Some of our people don't understand why we're passing the peace. Some don't understand the basics of the Bible. But where are the curriculum materials?"

In another congregation, a respondent put the matter in a way that echoed many others: "I think the seminaries just don't understand what we really need, both for our children's religious education or for preparing priests to deal with the realities of parish life."

At one Southwestern congregation, one leader explained that the widely used *Journey to Adulthood* curriculum "will take a lot of work for us to adapt it to our needs. Our Christian education director brought it in, and it looks good, but it requires so many mentors. We couldn't find them, so it didn't happen as we hoped."

For the record, it should be stated here that seminary leaders and students who were interviewed also were troubled by their weak ties to congregations and frustrated by what they saw as outmoded and dubious practices of the diocesan structures, especially diocesan Commissions on Ministry. "The diocesan COMs never seem to ask what congregations need in the way of priestly competencies," one seminarian ventured. "Those committees seem to me to be largely composed of older people who want new priests to conform to their old image of the church. They have little in the way of either theological or practical understanding of the priesthood, and they have little awareness of the future needs of the church at any level."

A faculty member endorsed this view and added, "Well, I try to get invited to diocesan meetings whenever possible, but it's difficult when you sense you're not really wanted. I don't know how to get the doors open wide enough to join in the conversations." The sense of being excluded from the church's structures and leaders, while facing institutional expectations that are holdovers from a bygone era, fueled frustrations expressed by many seminary respondents.

Many congregational leaders would agree. They seek but cannot find effective partnerships that will result in both better religious education materials for parishes and better preparation for priests. They look outside for educational materials from other denominations. They support their priests in seeking continuing education for the practical demands of their roles. But such resources and opportunities are often perceived to be independent of official channels.

As one leader put it, "How can it be that private Episcopal schools provide such top-flight education, while our church's Christian education materials are so horrible?"

"We borrow from other churches whatever is successful. We use Cursillo, and we use Alpha," was a refrain that was frequently heard. But Alpha and Cursillo, though popular and widely thought of as Episcopal programs, did not originate as products of the church structure. Rather, these programs for enlivening Christian faith arose unofficially outside the church's offices. Alpha began in a parish of the Church of England, and Cursillo began in the Roman Catholic Church in Spain. The Episcopal popularity of these offerings reflects a consensus about what resources best respond to the challenge of adult faith formation. Other respondents have mentioned a variety of "unofficial" curricula, notably EFM (Education for Ministry) and DOCC (Disciples of Christ in Community), both launched and managed by the University of the South.

One respondent captured the sentiments of many when he explained the reliance on these programs. Noting that such programs address voids in Christian education curricula for all age groups, he added that "we don't do well with our youth," he said. "Sometimes we complain about the quality of seminary graduates we see, but religious vocations are begun or neglected right here in the congregation. I wish there were good resources to help us improve our Christian education program here. What we got from the diocese was just way out of date and useless. We're trying out some materials we got from another denomination now. I have no idea how they may or may not relate to what the diocese is looking for in the way of postulants. I hope we can find some ways to improve in this area, but it will take all of us working together and not just going on separately in our own sites." Although this respondent did not give high marks to diocesan initiatives, a few praised the efforts of their dioceses, but then sharply excepted these from similar national church efforts, which they did not value.

TENSIONS BETWEEN CLERGY AND LAITY

Tensions having to do with leadership do not simply pit the local congregation against wider church structures. All too often, Episcopal congregations report conflicts with their own clergy. Most often these conflicts concern leadership. "The issues were about our rector's commitment to doing the job here," a lay person reported, and she proceeded to describe the unfolding of severe conflict in her parish. "Lots of things were being left undone. The vestry felt powerless, and our frustration was building, building with no outlet. The vestry...got a mediator.... He came down, and the parish divided along lines. There was a large meeting one Sunday. It was a bloodbath. It was wrenching."

It was painfully apparent to members of one Southern parish that the situation was deteriorating. "Our transition between priests about four years ago was a very difficult time for us. The former rector had been here for over twenty years and was really losing it. Staff morale was in the tank, and assistant priests came and went before we learned their names. People were working at cross-purposes and stabbing each other in the back. It was a real mess, and we didn't know how to get out of it."

Even the departure of an ineffective rector does not always resolve conflict. In another parish, after the rector's retirement, "the bishop sent an interim. He was into control with a capital C, and that triggered so many problems among us. It got into a polarization between the vestry and the interim priest on everything. We really struggled to learn about and practice effective leadership, but he seemed to block every effort."

Members of one parish admitted that a few years ago they had faced the anguish of discovering the rector's pattern of sexual abuse. The subject did not surface easily; even years after, the memories were vivid, and there were tears. One man admitted that his son had been a victim. The group described feelings of shock, of being "beleaguered, left out, and alone." For a while they were "in denial and hiding." At the time, they saw themselves as a "broken family" who only "wanted to survive." Compounding the pain, their bishop at that time did little to aid them. The interim rector seemed to defend his accused predecessor. For a long time, the diocese offered little assistance. The experience of little pastoral support for healing and a new beginning left the parish with "an anti-clerical culture" that was exacerbated by several interim rectors. The result was that these parishioners no longer "blindly trust" clergy. "No more pedestals," they stressed. But when one man said, "My faith is not in you" to the new rector, he replied, "Good!" Church members took this as a sign of a new day, one in which they are more self-reliant. They report that they are more confident of God's presence with them and more skilled in lay ministry than before. Now they are "owners of the parish" and believe they must be proactive with clergy and the diocese. They also believe their healing is continuing, and they believe the diocese has learned from the experience.

The members of one parish—saddled with a particularly ineffective rector—detailed the conflict that resulted from the heavy-handed actions of a forceful lay leader who stepped in to fill the leadership vacuum. One couple, they noted, was "unhappy about the policies of the national church." Referring to them as "the large pledge," the group described how this couple "had some Evangelical speakers come" who were "very fundamentalist." They "would pay for them," and at first "we would try to support it," but "it wasn't the personality of this church." An alternative Sunday evening service became the center of this couple's campaign. The "slaying the spirit stuff—that was all led by one family. Then they began to question and correct and cajole: 'you're not as Christ-like as you should be,' or 'you're not as caring,' and they didn't want any instruction from the priest in the church. They were self-guided, and the tradition wasn't there for them."

The couple in question also began a campaign to send a letter saying the parish would "withhold our pledge to the national church." But "the amount we sent wouldn't have been a drop in the bucket." One focus group participant then added: "I think they were so used to getting their way that they couldn't believe we were not going to sign this letter and send it up there. But I wasn't about to sign that letter." Nevertheless, the tension persisted until a new rector came. "He took a stand," and the church's leadership began to find out "what it means to be an Episcopalian. And we realized that our strength lies in that, it lies in the tradition. And that when we start forgetting that tradition, we lose our identity, and we do become factional and start bickering amongst each other."

TELLING AND LISTENING

Episcopalians demonstrate substantive capacities for drawing upon their faith and traditions to cope with significant differences, changes, and crises. Among the many places we visited and people interviewed, it was rare to find a place where there had been no experience of stress. Yet there was clear evidence of abilities to face and overcome difficult situations. The basis for successfully addressing challenges in congregational life includes a willingness to face and discuss issues openly.

"There is a healthy dialogue here. You know you're listened to and heard here. We have a lot of diversity, but by respectful attention, we have kept our young people engaged and haven't alienated the traditionalists among us," reported the members of an urban congregation.

Another congregation, trying to decide if additional worship services were necessary, expressed a similar opinion. "We try to talk the issues through. We try to maintain an open mind about whatever issue comes up and discuss it with the advocates and the doubters. I think more people recognize the value of listening and dialogue and are getting on board early in the process. The whole area of active communication is key to growth."

In a similar vein, many respondents used such phrases as "hang in there together," and "just wrestle with it," and concurred that it is "OK to disagree." The common perception is that successfully dealing with any difficult issue requires a group process in which two-way communication is essential. We have been encouraged to find energetic laity and clergy whose leadership promotes healthy patterns of communication. We have also been impressed that some bishops and diocesan staff members make the resolution of conflict a priority and address conflict in practical and flexible ways. While these leaders too often act in isolation from each other, they contribute to our conviction that Episcopalians increasingly are capable of effective attention to divisive issues.

The need for such skills is apparent. It is clear that some of the tensions we face have become sharply defined and even polarizing. Energetic advocates on either side of divisive issues have emerged and eagerly stump for their preferred solutions. However, many Episcopalians, especially at the local level, see that pushing a preferred solution too hard tends to generate more resistance than persuasion. Instead of political or legislative approaches, local congregations frequently develop expertise at hearing one another's stories of faith. Keeping explosive issues in the context of a shared faith journey offers a possible direction for reconciliation and renewed vigor. Rather than depicting God's kingdom in terms of rules or resolutions, our respondents frequently noted that Jesus dealt with questions about faith and practice by telling parables. These stories reached beneath divisive abstractions to touch the hearts of his listeners. That example suggests a useful approach for dealing with our current tensions.

Our research has made use of such an approach. As participants told their stories of faith, many realized anew the depth of their faith commitment and the perspective it affords them on particular challenges. Differences in views often turned to shared conclusions that were richer than any one person could have anticipated. Groups were able to reflect creatively on the power that arises from the experience of telling and listening to each other's stories. In the course of such experiences, some grasped that they could extend this process into the lives of their congregations and with those outside these communities. As they told their stories, a clearer sense of being on a shared journey of affirmation and discovery emerged.

To return to an earlier discussion, older Episcopalians might begin their stories in the troubled decades of the late twentieth century, talking of conflicts that seemed remote and indeed moot to newer members. Yet when allowed the opportunity to tell their stories exactly as they needed to tell them, older Episcopalians usually homed in on the present and on current local concerns relatively quickly, applying lessons of the past that often were unexpected revelations to the newer or younger Episcopalians. Over and over again, our interviewers observed that, when stories were allowed to go whither they would—even back into the past to dig up memories and injuries that others might have wanted to remain buried—the results were meaningful to the group overall. And as the interviewers watched and listened as these stories that were removed in one way or another from the other stories in the room—either by the passage of years or enmity or differing beliefs—most tended quite naturally toward the present rather than the past, toward resolution of some kind rather than dissolution. However, polarities and disagreement did not necessarily disappear .

If our church can be said to have ties that hold us together, it is the power of the story—of mutual commitment and shared faith. Our findings clearly show that Episcopalians have differences. But we can address our differences fruitfully by joining qualities of a shared process and patient listening to each other in our mutual experience of worshiping a God who accepts and loves all of us. The source of our commitment to one another is this sense of sharing a spiritual journey in which there are abundant resources to address tensions and accommodate differences.

The single most surprising and remarkable impression left upon our researchers by the hundreds of stories they gathered is that, in the final analysis, the form that conflict most often takes in the Episcopal Church seems more energizing than anxious, more collegial than adversarial, more hopeful than despairing. Prevailing wisdom will deny that conflict has right uses, but our data would suggest otherwise. Perhaps our high school English teachers were onto something when they lectured us that any novel or short story needs some kind of conflict, without which there would be no development, without which there would be no need to read said novel or short story. While we will stop short of saying that we *need* conflict in order to activate our Christian lives together, there may be an important lesson here. Conflict left as conflict of the culture-wars variety can only harm, but conflict listened to and engaged with and learned from never harms—although it usually *does* hurt. But somewhere during all the listening to, engaging with, learning from, and indeed hurting, conflict undergoes a remarkable transformation. Conflict becomes *story*. And stories heal.

NOTES

[1] Robert Wuthnow, *Loose Connections: Joining Together in America's Fragmented Communities* (Harvard, 1998), p. 3.

[2] Ibid., p. 5f.

[3] Amanda Porterfield, *The Transformation of American Religion: The Story of a Late Twentieth-Century Awakening* (Oxford, 2001). Francis Fukuyama, *Trust* (Free Press, 1995).

[4] Jackson W. Carroll and Wade Clark Roof, eds., *Beyond Establishment: Protestant Identity in a Post-Protestant Age* (Westminster/John Knox, 1993), p. 17.

[5] Leonard I. Sweet, "The Modernization of Protestant Religion in America," in David W. Lotz, Donald W. Shriver, Jr., and John F. Wilson, eds., *Altered Landscapes: Christianity in America, 1935–1985* (Eerdmans, 1989), p. 27.

[6] Martin E. Marty, "Introduction: Religion in America, 1935–1985," in David W. Lotz, Donald W. Shriver, Jr., and John F. Wilson, eds., *Altered Landscapes: Christianity in America, 1935–1985* (Eerdmans, 1989), pp. 1–18.

[7] Diana L. Eck, *A New Religious America: How a "Christian Country" Has Become the World's Most Religiously Diverse Nation* (Harper, 2001).

4

THE TURN TO THE GRASSROOTS
Beyond Program

In theory—and apparently in practice in many Episcopal congregations around the country—mission is the core of the church's life. Mission embodies the church's identity and vocation. It is the church's basic intention in all of its activities. But what does mission mean for Episcopalians? Late in the twentieth century, in the midst of furious controversies, the Episcopal Church resolved to pay fresh attention to mission. After major retrenchments in its historic foreign and domestic mission work, the church seemed to require a new focus on mission. Such a new focus—seemingly—would unite it and supply the fresh clarity its identity and vocation required. But the manner of the church hierarchy's approach to reviving mission was revealing. The church's bold new initiative took the form of an institutional program. The General Convention of 1970 authorized a campaign to raise $100 million for mission. By 1985, more than eighty-five dioceses had raised more than $170 million, and the program, named "Venture in Mission," was underway.

Venture in Mission generated enthusiasm for mission in a number of dioceses. The program appeared to offer a timely combination of diocesan and national church initiatives with important opportunities to benefit local community and congregational programs. The success of Venture in Mission can be attested to by the fact that, in many dioceses, the fundraising continued beyond the initial phase. In fact, most dioceses reported success, and Presiding Bishop John Allin called Venture in Mission an opportunity for "new commitment to the mission of this church."[1]

Venture in Mission succeeded far more than most of the church's major program initiatives in the late twentieth century. Some initiatives—such as the General Convention "Special Program," which funneled mission funds to highly politicized organizations—proved extremely controversial.[2] In contrast, Venture in Mission sought to side-step controversy and rally the church for mission. It did so by returning control of mission programs and mission funds to regional and local initiative. But in retrospect, the impact seems to have been incomplete. Something other than a major centralized, institutional program was needed to build the church's mission, even if the object of that centralized program was—somewhat paradoxically—decentralization. And in response to that need, a new approach already was developing at the grassroots level of the church.

In the Northeast, a group of Episcopalians from different congregations compared how their parishes viewed the resources offered by the diocese and national church. "I do not sense we need support from the diocesan office for program or helping with our every-member canvass," one person asserted. "We have a different role," another agreed. "We work with the diocese a lot," one person countered, suggesting a different sort of experience. But "we are not drawing on them for our programs; they are drawing on us," another injected. Yet another person elaborated, "Generally speaking, of the types of people at the diocesan office, they are a different type of individual than those at the parish. I think the diocese needs *us* to help with *their* programs." His message had a sarcastic bite as he suggested that his fellow parishioners could do a better job of running the diocese than its current staff.

As he continued, it was abundantly clear that he viewed his diocesan leaders as incompetent. "From the bishop on down, most of those people are a little different than [those who are] very successful at a church level. They tend to be bureaucrats." For several minutes, the discussion centered on the relevance or irrelevance of diocesan and national programs to local church life. Then, as if closing the door to a dusty attic, the group returned to comparing life in the various parishes they represented.

Most of the people who now identify themselves as active Episcopalians have little awareness of what functions the diocesan and national levels of the church perform. The church's structures appear to be a series of programs bearing little relation to life in most congregations and run by people who seem unwilling or incapable of understanding the perspectives of local leaders and devising sensitive responses to them. Of course, sooner or later, there are contacts between local congregations and the church's wider structures. We frequently heard local church leaders describe these contacts in strikingly consistent ways. Typically, a bishop from the diocese visits the congregation, and there is a momentary burst of good will toward the diocese. Now seen less as an inanimate program structure, the diocese acquires a human face. Lay people still have little sense of what the diocese does, but they usually feel drawn to the bishop. Occasionally, a diocesan staff person visits to offer resources or to promote another program. Or, a congregation in search of a new rector seeks diocesan guidance and works to apply diocesan guidelines to their local situation. Said one respondent from a congregation going through a very difficult transition, "The diocese has been very helpful in so many ways as we moved from being a mission to a parish. They used us as a showcase, and our priest has made good connections through the bishop's office and staff."

Periodically, a few congregational leaders attend a diocesan event, usually a diocesan convention. These leaders have been chosen to represent their congregation, and they do so proudly. Often, good feelings about the diocese result. There are contacts with leaders of other congregations. Each congregation's representatives return home and announce that the diocese seems abuzz with meetings, events, and programs. The purpose of this flurry is not always clear, but the level of activity can be impressive. Diocesan staff members have announced their readiness to serve, and the congregation's leaders may take appreciative notice. The diocesan newspaper flashes hopeful updates of events, speakers, and workshops. Amid laments from the diocese that not enough people participate in events or programs they offer, a few more of the congregation's lay leaders may attend. Occasionally, one or another program will tap the acute needs of some churches, and the diocese will gain local stature.

But for most laity, the diocese and the national church will remain invisible. And for diocesan staff, there will be a nagging sense that their efforts benefit too few of the church's people. Somehow the energies of dedicated people in the church's structures do not galvanize many in the congregations. Worse, the national church seems utterly removed from local life, until a controversy, lawsuit, or crisis of misconduct at a local parish level somewhere in the country reaches the media and demands that national leaders respond. The interests, approaches, and loyalties of most Episcopalians simply do not extend to the church's official structures. And the efforts of lay and ordained diocesan and national staff members often have only a limited ability to enhance widespread comprehension of what they do. In frustration, many professional diocesan and national workers remark that most Episcopalians do not look beyond their own congregations. However, many *do* look beyond their own pews, but—as examined in the previous chapter—congregations are more likely to look to neighboring congregations or to semi-official or unofficial nondenominational networks than to their own institutional structures. As mission shifts from the church's historic institutional channels to local, semi-official, and unofficial patterns of originating and extending the church's life, it is becoming something different from the sorts of programs such channels once generated. The benefits of this shift are apparent, though in somewhat paradoxical ways, when one considers membership and financial data on the Episcopal Church. A popular view holds that the Episcopal Church and all mainline denominations are slowly losing membership and will eventually disappear.

At first blush, the facts support this idea. Between 1967 and 1997, the Episcopal Church suffered a thirty-six percent membership loss, returning its membership to where it stood in 1947 at 2.2 million members. This membership loss is often cited as a sign of the church's overall stagnation. But during the same period when the Episcopal Church was losing members, its attendance was increasing by more than thirty percent. Surely this figure reflects a more complex set of realities than the membership data of the period can provide. One such reality is that patterns of belonging to churches were changing during the thirty-year period in question. People were no less ready to participate; in fact they were more so. But they were less ready to "join" the Episcopal Church in the traditional sense of the word (a reality that also applied to most other historic American religious groups).

As membership dropped from 1967 to 1997, financial giving to the church more than outpaced inflation, a trend consistent with the paradoxical attendance figures of the period. In fact, between 1991 and 1997, the financial assets of all Episcopal churches combined grew from $1.1 billion to $2.8 billion. While the financial and attendance data we are able to present remain incomplete and merit closer analysis than we can provide here, they suggest a reality of ferment and transition rather than a time of gradual decline. And they support our study's overall thesis that the Episcopal Church is in the midst of a transition in which an older style of belonging is in decline while a new style is emerging. In other words, the emphasis on decline misses the other half of the church's picture.

While this data can easily seem abstract, the findings reflect an historic shift in the Episcopal Church. The data reveal the rise of a new period of vitality among Episcopalians and suggest its source. Taken together, these figures represent the more than 7,000 Episcopal congregations and the people who look to them for guidance and inspiration in their Christian lives. Given the flux in the church's life at its national level, our findings compel us to take a fresh look at the church's local levels, where new forms of initiative and growth have taken hold. From this local point of view, the real shift in the church can be appreciated clearly. That is, patterns of local life are changing extensively, moving from heavy reliance upon the church's national organization and its program initiatives to an emphasis on the congregation as a collection of intimate groups grounding people in the Christian faith, providing spiritual support, and encouraging a variety of opportunities for growth, service, and mission.

So vital have become the mission initiatives of grassroots church leaders that congregations have begun to extend beyond themselves. Indeed, new patterns of linking and being linked allow local initiatives to reach beyond the official structures of the larger church, even as, in some cases, they are emulating the outward initiatives of those structures. So successful are some of these local efforts that their reach now extends overseas. These local initiatives take many forms: prayer groups, retreats, service projects, conferences where informal networks begin and extend, special campaigns, and long-range plans. The ambitious scope and rich variety of these initiatives represent profound shifts in the life of the church.

The leadership style whereby such initiatives have come to pass—especially with regard to "division of labor" within congregations—represents yet another profound shift within the Episcopal Church. In the past, Episcopalians tended to divide the church's concerns into two broad spheres—the spiritual and the temporal—with the clergy solely responsible for the spiritual and the laity charged with maintaining the temporal. Of course, the church's polity has always allowed for local initiative, and the circumstances of American religion encouraged it. But a clear sense of denominational identity sustained the church well into the twentieth century. It is that emphasis on denominational identity and the key role of the church's institutional structures at the national level that has changed decisively. Most Episcopalians today link the church's life and leadership to an overall sense of local spiritual community rather than to particular functions reserved for formally defined offices, particularly those at the church's metropolitan and national levels. They are seeking to determine whether the people who occupy those historic offices, especially that of the bishop, can be trusted as spiritual guides for their congregations.

Of course, one might assume that this shift represents a loss of the church's historic identity and vocation. If there is conflict and the church's leadership seems torn over the appropriate means and ends of Christian life, isn't there institutional paralysis and confusion rather than clarity? Isn't such a drastic shift evidence of a need for basic clarification about what clergy should be doing and what responsibilities properly belong to laity? And doesn't the reality of such questions strengthen the assumption that the national church is in decline and that its decline portends the breakup in some way or other of the Episcopal Church? Doesn't the Episcopal Church require clarity about itself at all levels in order to achieve new and lasting vitality? How can it achieve such clarity if its formal structures receive scant respect?

In fact, the national church's achievement in clarity of purpose and structure was never as complete as nostalgia sometimes depicts it. Although much revered in many quarters of the church, the national church ideal at its peak was still far from realized. There were always regional variations in the church's life. And we have noted the rise and influence of the High and Low Church parties. But the most obvious expression of the national church's unrealized vision was the development of the church's life in the West.

In the western part of the United States, the mainline denominations did not enjoy the long history of clearly defined roles within society that characterized other regions of the country. The vast distances and fierce independence of the people who settled the region worked against the mainline denominations' ability to create the sort of institutional framework that was achieved elsewhere. From the earliest days of settlers moving westward, the sense of freedom and individuality combined with an emerging spirituality based in the natural world to produce a widespread experience of "spiritual sustenance that has made institutional religion quite irrelevant."[3] Because clergy were few, congregations had to share, but the vast distances that separated congregations spread the clergy very thin; and so congregations soon learned to rely more on their own abilities than on institutional structures.

Furthermore, there was little social pressure to be loyal to a religious institution. From the earliest years of settlement, the West epitomized the part of the country where people felt free to choose, free to style their beliefs and lives as they saw fit. As a result, loyalty to denominations there was weaker than elsewhere in the country. During the 1950s—the peak of loyalty to mainline denominations—churches in the West struggled to build the sorts of structures and loyalties seen in other areas.[4] But the Episcopal Church simply was not able to grow on the basis of the kind of institutional loyalty that was presumed in the eastern and central areas of the country. Denominational growth was set back even further by the surprisingly rapid growth of the population and its dizzying diversity. The region's growth far outpaced the church's ability to respond, given the relatively small resources that had been allocated to this enormous task.

As we have suggested, the ideal of the national church, which served as the basis of Episcopal identity and vocation well into the twentieth century, had its limitations. It proved more compelling in some parts of the country than in others, and it relied upon the effectiveness of the church as a centralized institution. The erosion of the national church ideal and the exhaustion of the church's former institutional aspirations resulted in conflict and decline. But, paradoxically, the church is growing. New patterns of local initiative that defy perceptions of conflict and disarray at the national level have taken hold. To understand what these patterns are, we must step away from national-level generalizations about church life and look more closely at what is taking place among Episcopalians at the church's grassroots.

THE BASIS OF INITIATIVE

A HEARTLAND PARISH

In the heartland of the United States, there is an old, downtown Episcopal church in a small city. Its 8 and 10 A.M. Sunday liturgies are well attended, with the early service following the more traditional Rite I liturgy, and the later service usually being Rite II. When eight of the parish's members gathered to describe their life, their responses revealed many of the trends that are reshaping Episcopal churches in all parts of the country.

Asked to describe a recent success in their church, these Episcopalians quickly noted a capital campaign. Across the country a number of congregations report recent or anticipated capital funds drives, and this church's experience sounded like many others we have heard. "We raised more than we had anticipated," one person emphasized, "and pledges went up, too." Then he detailed the results. "We were able to fix up some long-needed repairs, plus do some things we wanted, including making the entire building handicapped-accessible, renovating all the Sunday school classrooms, installing new heating and air conditioning throughout the building, putting in an elevator, creating a library and study room, etc." But buildings were not ends in themselves, even with the high degree of success they experienced. "We have also really moved forward on our ministries to people, with teams to visit the sick and those in the hospital, providing the money so a young woman could get the medical care she needed, and expanding our support to a number of outreach projects in this city."

Although they rejoiced at their successes, the members of this parish vividly recalled how much they had had to overcome in order to grow. One recalled, "All this is especially important to us because, just before our current rector came, we went through a terrible period." The current rector has been with them for nine years, they explained, but the memories of a difficult time in the congregation's life remained vivid for some. They did not dwell on details of the past but conveyed enough of what happened to explain the power of their healing and new direction. One member remembered: "The bad time was about the former priest. He was an alcoholic and really made a mess of things.... Some folks sided with him, and others opposed him. The polarization just tore us apart. Finally, the vestry went to the bishop and asked for his help. The bishop talked with him and persuaded him to go.... The whole process just left us in ruins."

Another member added: "It took a while for us to heal and come back together. The fact that we now can really see growth and a strong sense of community here is evidence that we have overcome that bad time in our past. We feel good about where we are. The Lord has brought us out of bondage and into the light."

How did the parish start upon the path of renewal? "The up-side is that there was no one to do anything if we didn't take responsibility and do it. We learned a great deal about leadership and initiative. The supply priests didn't try to 'solve' everything for us but suggested ways we could do it ourselves. That was difficult but invaluable for our growth." One senses in this conversation that the parish's leaders found the means of resolving their issues and moving ahead—and that they did so enthusiastically. One also senses that the experience they gained stands them in good stead for future challenges.

IDENTITY AND BELONGING

This story—about a congregation that discovered new self-sufficiency, but only after a time of trial during which members feel helpless and alone—will resonate with many Episcopalians who have pushed through hard times in their parishes and emerged the better for the experience. Self-sufficiency is not merely a transfer of loyalty from the denomination to the local level as a result of disappointment or pique with the church's structures. Rather, in a profound way and for positive reasons, Episcopalians are shifting from thinking of themselves as members of an institution to cultivating a sense of common purpose and mutual support on a shared journey of spiritual growth. A lay leader in the Northeast conveyed a sense of how Episcopalians are coming together in new, common endeavors. "The development of relationships that are significant was the best evidence of our success. I saw it in terms of growth in group cohesion as well as individual growth and in many opportunities that come with that growth," she explained.

Members of a church in a Southern state proudly described their recent success at working together in a capital fund drive. "We greatly needed money to repair this old building and expand our parking area. There are so many people coming in that we've long since outgrown our capacity." The gratifying result was that "we far exceeded the consultant's advice and even our own goal. We don't have a lot of wealthy families, so we didn't follow the rule that you have to get the bulk of the money up front from a few people. Ours was just the opposite—the bulk of the money came from many small contributors. As the contributions came in, we saw many people sharing a vision of our future. The whole process was a time of great growth in faith and seeing it in action. We grew in our readiness to trust God and each other."

When asked what accounted for the successes they had realized, these lay leaders stressed that working together in healthy, mutually supportive ways was paramount. "We really listened to one another, respected our differences, and worked to conclusions better than I ever expected. We hung in there and worked through tough problems. Now there's a deep sense of connectedness and energy among us." Without knowing all the stages, our interviewers sensed that the leaders of this congregation had learned a new style of shared leadership. And when they described their success, it was this fact that stood out above all others: success had come because these local leaders had proven their ability to learn from their experience and to adapt their style of leadership and the life of their congregation to the circumstances they faced. Our research has revealed that numerous local Episcopal leaders, both lay and ordained, are succeeding because of their willingness to learn and to adapt. When they do, success comes in a variety of ways.

"Our youth group is probably the most powerful source of inspiration for everyone in the congregation," related another leader. "We are now planning our sixth year of a summer mission program in Philadelphia. In support of that, the congregation has several major fundraising events during the year. Preparing for the mission, supporting it, and hearing from the adults and young people when they come back are all major parts of our community." In this instance, the example of a youth program inspires other church members and their particular programs. Success in one area often has a catalytic effect on the whole of a congregation's life.

Typically, we found, the experience of coming together arises in the midst of a shared sense of congregational activity, as is often the case when Episcopalians envision ways to revitalize their local communities. In only a few years, the lay leader of an urban ministry program based in one local Episcopal congregation had inspired and encouraged lay leaders from several other churches, suburban as well as urban, to begin their own educational projects. These educational projects served as a way to alert lay people to local needs and to equip them to respond. And in the process of applying themselves practically to a project, participants experienced considerable spiritual growth. Yet despite the extent of this success, this leader was reluctant to take personal credit for the success. "The reason I see it as a success is because it isn't based solely on the efforts of one individual. It has been a process-oriented program development, involving gathering a lot of information and resources from outside our committee, including many men and women from all around the community and crossing racial and class lines." The program had begun with a small group but steadily expanded to include an elaborate network of volunteers from many congregations. The rector of the sponsoring church knew about and approved the program but was only peripherally involved in any of the activities. Yet this rector had the wisdom to recognize and make room for the work of a capable lay leader.

Extraordinary local initiatives such as this urban ministry are not unusual in the Episcopal Church, and yet we rarely acknowledge their truly visionary natures, perhaps because we tend to equate "visionary" with the lonely individualism expected of ascetic, isolated prophets, at one extreme, or presiding bishops, at the other. Many local leaders we encountered did indeed display highly individualized visions of ministry, yet the realization of their visions was always firmly established within local identity, a sense of belonging, and the practicalities of living together in community. The extraordinary nature of what they accomplished together was subsumed in an even more extraordinary experience of belonging.

In a downtown parish in the Midwest, parishioners proudly described an interdenominational program to feed and house homeless persons that their church had helped to found. As the group discussed what had sustained their participation for nearly two decades, they discovered a common factor that few of them had previously realized: the same older husband-and-wife team had recruited, trained, encouraged, and involved each of them in the program. When the group probed further, they also realized that this couple had secured most of the resources that the program initially had required. From the leadership of these two people, an entire program grew, was sustained, and became an integral part of the larger congregational identity.

As one church member in the Northeast noted, being part of his parish meant "meeting a practical goal and the sense of good feeling that came with that." The sense of belonging even overrides private, individual good feelings. "We're people who love each other more than getting our own way in decisions," one lay leader revealed. "We are called to pray, to be open to one another. The parish as a community is more important than any building," emphasized another. The ideal of local life for Episcopalians has become one of sharing and practicality. Episcopalians not only idealize a sense of dynamic belonging, they offer abundant evidence that they are seeking and finding it. Many such stories gathered by our researchers defy conventional wisdom about the private and individualistic aspect of American religion.

In some cases, the sense of community deepens into something like a family at its best. "We are like an extended family here. Each one helps the other when there's a need. That brings us closer together. That's how Christians are supposed to be." This comment from a Southern parish leader is especially revealing. Far from suggesting that the ties binding Episcopalians have weakened, this quotation, added to the others above, suggests that Episcopalians are capable of building—and experiencing—close ties. In fact, our findings suggest that the highest aspiration of Episcopal congregations is to achieve such a degree of closeness. Interestingly, Episcopalians view such closeness in dynamic, rather than static, terms. That is, belonging to Episcopal churches is increasingly viewed as a shared and shifting process. The intention of this process is to build the congregation as a spiritual community rather than to enhance its loyalties to the structures of a religious institution.

CHANGE AND COHESION

Change in the life of the community can interfere with or undermine such dynamic cohesion. The proper management of transitions in congregational life is crucial. "We recently brought in an interim priest. Our rector had been with us for fourteen years, so this was really a big change. For a while there, we were rudderless without a rector. The congregation now recognizes how the interim priest brought us through the change and built strength here," explained one respondent. This instance, like many we have encountered, reveals the pivotal role played by clergy. While lay initiative is necessary to make particular programs run and to set an example of teamwork, the clergy must set an overall tone for congregational life and inspire a vision that defines its direction.

In another diocese, one respondent described a similar experience:

> Our former rector had been with us for thirty years. After he retired, the search process took a lot longer than we thought it would, and we became discouraged. Eventually we called a new priest, and now it's a totally new congregation. People who previously had been unsure of themselves now have much greater confidence. We're doing the job of the church much better and know much will happen in the future. We're growing by leaps and bounds, and there are much better links with community groups, too.

Members of one church in a Western state told of having discovered the horrible reality of their rector's sexual misconduct. Compounding their problem was the gradual discovery that the priest had been sowing dissension among lay leaders since shortly before the first allegations surfaced. After a prompt response from the bishop and a thorough investigation, the priest was removed from the parish. But this step was only the first of many in dealing with this painful discovery. With little reservoir of trust and the fresh challenge of dealing with enormous pain, the congregation nevertheless went to work. They had realized that the problem in their midst was more than the conduct of one unhealthy individual. As a congregation, they had allowed a destructive individual to function unchallenged until the situation became intolerable. Their challenge was not only to replace their rector but to build their congregation's leadership culture anew. The old way of making and implementing decisions had to be replaced. No longer could a few people make decisions in secret. Now, there had to be a broad base of decision making and an open, public process by which all the members could know and participate in guiding the congregation's life.

While this new direction seemed the only alternative to most members of the congregation, a few left. Others were disgruntled but remained. A few of these were present at the small group session, and one of them mumbled that the rector had not been treated fairly; one or two others revealed that they knew something had to be done, but they felt that the change had been too drastic; several others joined in to complain about the unpleasant new mood that was pervading the congregation. But most of the congregation's members committed themselves to rebuilding the congregation for the future. Step by step, they climbed out of their hurt and despair. Now with a new rector and the completion of a successful building project, their sense of "pulling together" was apparent. "The building is more than a structure. It reflects a new spirit of cooperation here. We discovered a new sense of being together. After all the tensions we had to overcome, we now enjoy harmony, sharing, and mutual respect," said one member.

Another person in this group said, "We now see ourselves as the *Episcopal* Church in this town." She emphasized the word "Episcopal" to convey that the lay leaders of this congregation had reached a new sense of what it means to be Episcopalians. She continued, "We're a community of people searching together, sharing a journey together. There's a deep sense of shared owner- ship we feel about this place. We see ourselves as a gathering place for the whole community, a place for reconciliation and acceptance. I really like that little sign out front that says, 'The Episcopal Church Welcomes You.'"

Failed programs often prompt the kind of sudden change that can prompt greater congregational cohesion. At one congrega- tion, it was the unexpected failure of their favorite fundraising event that brought change and, eventually, a stronger identity and sense of belonging. "We had successful rummage sales for several years, but that time the weather was lousy and almost nobody showed up. We felt defeated, because we had put so much time into getting it ready. After a few weeks of trying to avoid the subject, we began talking. We knew we needed some- thing better to pull us together and allow us to support our com- munity service projects. We refused to let the defeat drag us under." Indeed, the vitality we sense among Episcopalians often has as much to do with failures and finding the means to address and move beyond them as it does with having various programs run smoothly and conclude successfully.

PLACE AND JOURNEY

From the earliest days of the Church of England, Anglicans have located their spiritual roots in living the Christian life in a particular locality, where the sinews of community and ministry were presumed to be unchanging. Today, however, there are increasing numbers of Episcopalians who understand the spiritual life not as inhabiting a fixed location but as a journey. Often those who prefer the metaphor of the journey coexist in the same congregation with those who adhere to the older ideal of inhabiting a given place. It is our conclusion that the image of the journey gradually is becoming ascendant, though often the point of the journey for many members of Episcopal congregations is to build a new sense of spiritual community in their locality.

In ways that transcended ideological divides, our respondents stressed that their faith has drawn them into traveling together in a shared spiritual quest that is not dependent on clergy presence. One West Coast respondent who served on her vestry said, "I am sure we are being led on this journey. There is a guiding light. I wondered why God put me here, and I tried to listen to people around me. Our vestry grew clearer about the spiritual basis for our efforts together, and the results have confirmed that. We are further along the road now than we were several years ago. There are more young people here now, greater vitality, and a stronger bond of support as we move along together."

In a small Southern town, we heard the story of a small congregation that was only five years old and had no building. Because they met in space rented weekly from the local Y, their church's furnishings had to be unloaded and set up every Sunday, then taken back down and stored after the service. One Sunday, when the Y's janitor forgot to leave the building open, services had to be held in the parking lot. Despite the sense of impermanence, this congregation's sense of identity and shared purpose were strong. "God is leading us on this journey together," several emphasized. These respondents eagerly affirmed their sense of being Episcopalian. "Those old Anglican ideas of tradition, reason, and Scripture are really vital for us. They have enabled us to hold together and grow. We are God's people in this town. The church is *us*, the people of God traveling through life together, not a building."

In another small town halfway across the country, a new Episcopal congregation shared a similar perspective. Their community began eight years ago and had grown to more than one hundred members. In their brief history, they had worshiped in several schools and a warehouse. They had a strong sense of themselves as sharing a journey together, whatever the physical structures they used. "For me, what's important isn't the building but the togetherness of the group as we move forward. We still love and support each other after all the locations we've come through," said one. Through this journey, they shared a commitment to the Christian faith and to supporting one another. The religious backgrounds of the members were diverse, and some said they were not certain what being an Episcopalian really meant and wished their diocese and national leaders would help them understand that better. Meanwhile, they cited the centrality of the liturgy, partnerships with other churches in service to the community, and freedom to grow as clues to their identity.

Instances of the revitalization of older congregations also abound. A small church in a Northeastern suburb found that an all-member retreat enhanced efforts to overcome age divisions and become more cohesive across generations. Another congregation located in a poorer section of a large city raised several hundred thousand dollars to repair its sanctuary and expand service projects in the neighborhood. Numerous other examples confirmed that older congregations were discovering new vitality and growth.

Clearly, many Episcopalians at the grassroots are working together well. One congregation named their recent call of the first female rector in the diocese as their example of success. "We had been a passive, unchallenging group for many years, unwilling to take any risks, but now we are enthusiastic, energetic, and optimistic. We have a fresh sense of ownership and shared leadership. Going through the search for a new rector together stimulated new life here. We discovered we were capable of far more than we had known."

Members of another congregation cited the fortieth anniversary celebration as a pivotal experience:

It was a week-long celebration. Each group or program in the church made a banner to represent its ministry. We collected pictures, stories, and memories from folks who had been here in the past but had moved elsewhere. There were tables with exhibits all around the common room. The whole parish came together for several dinners, and people told stories about challenges we had come through together. We were without a priest then, but that didn't stop us at all. We worked together and had a really great time. We saw how much we had come through and how many successes we had had. That gave everybody a lot of encouragement and energy.

FAITH AND MINISTRY

Almost every congregation we visited exhibited the principle that all believers are ministers. From soup kitchens to schools, from organizing worship services in nearby nursing homes to building a clinic in a remote South American village, Episcopalians express their faith by engaging as volunteers in outreach and community service programs. Likewise, they serve in public leadership positions, from local school boards to the U.S. congress, and they describe all these roles as forms of ministry.

In the words of one respondent:

> The Gospel just transforms your life. After a while, you want to share God's love with others, whether they come to this church or not, and whether you use words or actions. As I reflected on how God loves my own hurt parts, I began wanting to respond to others who were hurting or in need. When I was invited to help with the shelter project, I was hesitant at first, since I'd never done anything like that. But as soon as I began, I knew that was where I was supposed to be. The inward journey and the outward journey are linked parts of a whole life.

Outreach efforts do not necessarily carry the expectation that recipients will attend worship. However, this is the hope—and perhaps even the motivation—of some. Episcopalians also hope that their ministries to the larger community will attract new members in other ways as well. Such ministries necessarily heighten a congregation's visibility, which can result in visits by neighbors ranging from the merely curious to those who have been deeply moved by the congregation's witness of commitment to their larger communities. Neighborhood social activists who are pulled into the local church's orbit because they want to serve as program volunteers are another potential source of new members.

In a number of cases these hopes for increased membership have been justified. Referring to a period of increased ministry to the local community, one respondent said, "During that five-year period, we went from twenty-five percent of our congregation being newcomers to about forty percent, and the majority of those were from the vicinity."

Almost every congregation we visited, including small ones, described a variety of community service projects they had initiated and sustained. Larger congregations often took the lead in drawing other churches together for cooperative efforts, from homeless shelters and soup kitchens to schools and employment training programs. But even small Episcopal churches sought ways to minister. We were also struck by the emphasis that most members of Episcopal churches placed on hands-on involvement. More than giving money, Episcopalians in our study wanted to do something beneficial. "We are here to love and serve those in need, in whatever form that takes," explained one respondent whose words represent the sentiments expressed by many. In the words of another, "We are Christ's presence right here in this old part of town. We are energized by God's love for us and want to pass that along to others in need, so we have developed several social service projects in the neighborhood. Our outreach programs have attracted other churches in town to join in."

At yet another church, respondents explained, "This congregation is known as the 'doers' in town because of our many community service projects. When the mayor asked us to take on some revitalization work in a very poor neighborhood, some of our folks called others in other churches to discuss how to proceed. In the course of those discussions, we began to realize that others had felt crowded out by some of our previous initiatives. We agreed to pull back a little and work more carefully on inclusion of other churches, instead of just jumping in and trying to do it all ourselves, like we had in the past. That has really made a difference in the sense of teamwork. Now that we are true partners, we can do so much more together."

Relating to their larger community is important to Episcopalians, according to our findings. Realizing that the neighborhood in which their church was located had shifted from affluence to indigence and that they had ignored this change in their locale, the members of one Midwestern congregation became energized. "We had a fund drive and raised $150,000 for programs for children in this area. We did a survey and found the number of single parents rising, so now we are preparing to develop programs for them. We feel a sense of responsibility for doing something about the needs of this neighborhood." Another person in this group added, "People are now being drawn to church from the area around here. We are no longer a smug little isolated club. Folks who come here are a little bit of everything, just like the neighborhood. The building is being used; it is open and active. We are changing and growing in ways I never imagined, and it is exciting."

Episcopal congregations in every section of the country report that they are vital and that lay initiative is the source of their vitality. Though there are widespread reports of tensions between lay leaders and clergy, the evidence does not support the supposition that there is a general crisis of lay-clergy role confusion. Among lay leaders, the clergy role is valued and its distinctive responsibilities honored. Consistently, laity cite the need for clergy leadership in worship, education, pastoral care, and administration of the congregation. The clergy and lay leaders to whom we spoke usually sought balanced, shared patterns of leadership. Rarely was there any desire to intrude upon the most basic worship duties ascribed specifically to priests, but neither did lay leaders allow this important precedent in division of labor to cause them to shy away from seeking and ensuring significant lay participation. A strong emphasis on the accustomed features of the clergy role—such as preaching and presiding at the Eucharist—is accompanied by increased emphasis on the role of lay guidance in the congregation's outreach and service ministries.

This understanding of lay-clergy roles reflects a decisive shift in the Episcopal Church over the past half-century. While the place of ordained leaders and such formally designated bodies as vestries remains intact, a broader and more informal view of leadership has emerged. As stated earlier, the "ministry of all baptized persons" has become a widely accepted ideal. The result is that, in almost every setting, a sense of shared responsibility based on mutual spiritual growth and mission is apparent.

The staff of a large, urban congregation expressed their deep sense of responsibility for "helping all our baptized people know how to live in the world." They worried that they had not done enough to create true Christian communities, and they admitted they needed help with nurturing lay persons and redefining lay pastoral ministries. Grateful for a strong clergy and lay staff team, they also fretted that they continued to carry vestiges of an outdated, hierarchical model of the church. The way in which the clergy of this congregation conducted worship—often with little lay involvement—seemed to indicate a leadership style that needed to be revised. "Our Sunday mornings still seem to overemphasize the 'cult of the senior clergy,' which is inconsistent with our emphasis on the ministry of the laity. We have some more changes to make in order to live out our commitment to the ministry of every baptized person."

Another group of respondents declared, "We need to be hosts, receiving and supporting the new people coming to us. More important than the money we raised in our fund drive was the intangible benefit: we saw so many people hard at work on a shared vision. The reality was faith at work—hard work and real deeds of faith. We are a place where you know you are welcome."

The heart of contemporary Episcopal spirituality is revealed in these remarks. The ideal is to build a quality of congregational life that entails shared work to implement practical expressions of ministry. In the process, the congregation attracts and forms new members whose participation enhances its fellowship and its ministries. It is significant that this ideal rests heavily on the role of the laity.

APPRECIATION OF CLERGY

Given the prominence of grassroots lay initiatives in our story, it becomes necessary from time to time to reiterate the good news about clergy-lay relations that our interviewers uncovered in every part of the country. In a number of instances, Episcopalians reported that they respected and appreciated the clergy who served their congregations.

A Southwestern congregation praised their new rector for supplying a fresh sense of initiative:

> He has helped us identify six key areas of need, and one of them was pastoral care. We had hoped he would address this, and he certainly has. His style is to be as inclusive as possible. Before we started on our recent renovations of the building, we did a congregational survey. Their voices were heard, and we got going quickly. It was important in this process to nurture a sense of place and roles for people. We found some new leaders, and in the process, we became more cohesive. The whole experience gave us something tangible, something people could see. And it moved so fast. The changes in the atmosphere were obvious in just a few months.

In the upper Midwest, a small-town congregation applauded its rector after its merger with another congregation. "She did it all so pastorally, and it just worked. We had a few 'bulls in a china shop,' but she led us gently and steadily through it all." Another person added, "There was some grief, with one church having to close for the two to merge. She helped us do that, letting go of the past. Everyone had to say 'good-bye' to so many memories, and we did that. By the time it was done, we felt healed in the process."

In another congregation, a focus group participant emphasized, "Our last rector was a great Bible teacher. I still miss his classes. That's what drew me here. But our new guy is a great 'people person.' That's what we needed, and it's what we found." Another added, "There is such a new sense of spiritual attentiveness here. With so many young families facing problems, our rector has helped us all do a better job of helping. There is a new sense of families becoming stronger."

"Right now we have a right match with our rector, and we are blessed," one woman declared. In a downtown congregation, the lay people we interviewed emphasized the significance of their ministries in the vicinity. "That illustrates the advantage of having a priest who is so deeply involved in downtown," one woman said appreciatively. Clearly, when their clergy are active in community life, Episcopalians notice with gratitude.

Another parish elaborated on the sense of possibility their priest has brought:

> Our biggest challenge is to turn around the decline. We believe our energetic young priest is just the one to help us do that. He has so many good ideas about projects that will draw in people. We want to bring them in 'through the basement door' for activities and then hope some stay on for worship. For example, he got us a small grant from the diocese to start up an arts program for kids after school. That will begin to draw in kids from the neighborhood. One activity just under way is making plaster casts from one of the gargoyles on the roof. We hope to sell them and raise money to expand the arts program even more.

For many members of Episcopal churches, clergy serve as gatekeepers who can either facilitate the dynamism their congregations require or frustrate it. Such dynamism has been evident throughout our discussion, but the leadership styles that help such dynamism—as well as the leadership styles that hinder it— deserve our closer attention.

EMPHASIS ON PROCESS

The dynamism that propels Episcopal congregations forward is evident in their emphasis on shared process, which becomes readily apparent whenever congregations are asked to share their stories. A California parish offered a vivid account of just such an emphasis early in our conversation with them. Having described their Holy Week and Easter worship as "an incredible religious experience," a "stunning performance" that "defined and drew us together as family," they explained that, for their congregation, worship is the center. Worship entails more than weekly ritual; it is the basis of a common spiritual journey. One member observed that, "[We] who have embarked upon a journey of spiritual search, who know, love, and respect each other, [also] break out of the Sunday bonds and meet elsewhere to celebrate who we are."

The theme of journey surfaced repeatedly in their conversation. "I am protected in my journey," one member emphasized. "We want to be a place where you are protected at least temporarily from the slings and arrows of outrageous fortune." Their worship is central to this sense of ministry. "We see ourselves as we struggle through death and resurrection; we're celebrating life and death among us, and here it is encouraged by how word and meal is brought to bear on our own spiritual journeys."

For these California Episcopalians, the emphasis on a shared journey explicitly contrasts with an institutional view of membership. Their parish offers "encouragement toward finding and developing our own sense of identity and...not [trying] to make us something that someone else perceives us to be. We steer away from the institutionalized vision and [do what will] keep us on the path of spiritual growth, attention, nurturance." There was no hint that the members of this parish were hostile to the wider church. In fact, they spoke positively about various ideas they had received at diocesan events. But for them, the Christian life to which they were called stood in clear contrast to the institutional priorities they perceived from the diocese and beyond. They were meant to be different, to embody what the church's institutional structures lacked, namely an authentic expression of Christian community in their locality.

An urban parish in Indiana proudly described the soup kitchen that had been a priority of their mission work. Asked about the relation between this soup kitchen and their link to their diocese, they began with loud praise for their bishop, and they were proud of having hosted a diocesan convention. Several persons in the group warmly recalled a variety of diocesan events. So would their warm feelings about the diocese and its leadership incline them to seek diocesan guidance about their soup kitchen or other parish activities? "Oh no," a woman exclaimed. "We couldn't do that. We have to be self-sufficient." "Self-sufficient?" asked the interviewer. "That's right," another woman replied, "If we're going to be authentic as a church, we have to be self-sufficient."

"Look," a man in the group explained. "We know this area. We know how to get things done. We know who to call to get food for the soup kitchen. If a woman comes with children, we have an arrangement with a motel to provide a few days' shelter. How could the diocese help us do that? We live here, and we know the way to do things here."

"Self-sufficiency" is an intriguing phrase that has appeared directly or by implication in a number of our conversations with members of Episcopal churches. To these lay leaders, "self-sufficiency" links the spiritual aspects of parish life to the practical ones. They mean that the congregation holds primary responsibility for mission in its vicinity. They also suggest that their congregation approaches the level of integrity that is the very ideal of Christian community only when they are defining and enacting their own mission.

Without realizing it, these twenty-first-century Episcopalians have embraced a treasured aspect of the wider Anglican Church's mission history. In the first half of the nineteenth century, as the Church of England began a dramatic period of overseas expansion, a noted English mission leader, Henry Venn, articulated what became the goal of Anglican mission. Taking a position much like the one modern local leaders affirm, Venn declared that the goal of mission is to create autonomous, self-supporting branches of the Church of England around the world.[5] The concept of being self-supporting was also adopted by mission churches launched by the Episcopal Church, such as the fledging church in Japan, which declared that its goal was to seek an appropriate form of self-sufficiency that would allow them to stand independent of external management yet remain open to consultation on general goals and specific strategies. Though Episcopal congregations cannot be equated with entire national branches of the Anglican Communion, there is a true analogy. Anglicans have long believed in the integrity of local initiative and the goal of becoming appropriately self-sufficient.

Hints of what this ideal of self-sufficiency means in the shifting relations between a diocese and its congregations appeared often in our interviews. "We tried the resources of the diocese and were not very happy," said a man on the East Coast. "But the diocese was most often helpful when we went to them and asked for help with what needed to be done." In other words, his parish looked to the diocese for a broad sense of direction and general affirmation of the Christian faith. Specific programs required adaptation to local circumstances; for this task, the diocese could not be helpful. In our interviews, we frequently encountered the sentiment that diocesan programs should grow out of appreciative relationships with local lay persons. Only then could a diocese develop programs that would truly serve and empower its congregations. Only then would the diocese be able to respect the necessity of congregational self-sufficiency and to understand that their role with the congregation must be one of true partnership.

The priority of "self-sufficiency" is evident in the emphasis Episcopalians place on processes which translate a general sense of direction into specific congregational programs. "The reason I see it was a success is because it was not based on the sole striving of one individual person," said a woman as she described a program supported by several churches. "It was a process-oriented program development." Her comments suggest that the quality of group process becomes as important as the eventual results of that process. The process acquires significance that equals the program's outcomes. "It's an open process," commented a lay leader in Texas. It is "not locked into some iron-clad hierarchical structure but open to the flow of the Spirit. We have a structure, but it allows for freedom to move around and deal with issues that come up." It is clear that self-sufficiency is grounded in a sense of being led by God in shaping the church's mission in particular places by a process that is locally led.

The centrality of spirituality and prayer in the striving for self-sufficiency was obvious whenever Episcopalians described their local group processes. In the West, a woman explained why and how she became a member of a committee in her parish: "Well, I was in a program of spiritual direction at a retreat house near here, so this committee provided me with a concrete opportunity to put into practice what I had been studying. The rector asked me to convene and facilitate the committee. That role has drawn upon and deepened my skills in listening and learning to evoke instead of trying to control things."

This woman's statement finds analogues in many conversations among Episcopalians. "Somehow, underneath it all, we are called to follow Jesus," a man in the South said. "Part of what's being Episcopalian," a man in the Northeast commented, "is that there is that room for diversity and for judgment. And for discerning what is important to you either as an individual or as a parish." At a parish in the East that was seeking a new rector, the emphasis on a spiritually grounded process was clear. "We are back to basics: faith and prayer.... Pray the Lord creates a spiritual basis [that produces] ongoing connectedness. [More than] previously in the church, [we need] open dialogue about the search, who will be the new minister."

Rather than turning congregations inward, such intense forms of process usually push them outward. This commitment was evident in the words of one woman in an urban parish. "I really tried to stay in process rather than making it a win-lose situation. Let's all go back and look at our purpose, how the environment has changed, how our church environment has changed, staff environment, school, etc. Look at all of this change, and now that all of that has changed, what does that mean? If we remain static, we are not dancing to our own song, which is about human change, because urban environments go through massive amounts of change continually."

In a parish in the West, a major new form of ministry arose by individual initiative followed by group process. One of their parishioners learned of a church that ran a health clinic. She "got all inspired and...told the rector, and he said, 'why don't we put together a task force and see what can be done.' So we put together a task force. We met, there was a need assessment sub-committee that was going to look into what needed to be done, and we began to target homeless kids." The program succeeded beyond expectations. But the extent of social need and the natural limitations of the congregation's resources meant that the program required broad sponsorship. Soon local community agencies took the lead in running the program, but parish leaders remained involved as volunteers and board members. The parish had been the catalyst for an important program, and the parish maintained a central role in it.

Two essential aspects of group process in Episcopal churches often were highlighted by our respondents. First, the group must be able to mediate among points of view that often are competing; that is, groups are likely to include persons who genuinely differ in their sense of appropriate means and ends of congregational life. Second, the democratic aspects of process are valued, and, thus, the process must include ample opportunities for airing views and seeking to discern a common mind that embodies a Christian sense of shared vocation. Numerous accounts of group processes that exhibited both these aspects—some to greater, some to lesser, degrees—were recorded by our researchers. Many of these group processes eventually resulted in widespread, sub-stantial, and sustained congregational engagement with the needs of their neighborhoods, towns, and cities; perhaps even more impressive is how few of them ended in irreconcilable conflict or self-absorption. The sort of group process emerging among Episcopalians offers encouraging signs about the capacity of locally-initiated, lay-led group process to advance congregational life and to engage in substantive ministries.

OVERCOMING OBSTACLES

Many Episcopal congregations gave compelling accounts of their struggles to find vitality in one aspect or another of their common life, and it is difficult not to be struck by the number of parishes that found it ultimately; few, however, appeared to find it easily. Local reports of successful initiatives frequently were countered by descriptions of the obstacles that congregations had to face before they eventually found new life. In fact, for most of the Episcopalians we interviewed, a large part of their understanding of vitality seemed based on their church's experience of facing obstacles and overcoming them. To reiterate an earlier point: the process acquired a significance equal to the results achieved.

Asked to describe a recent experience of success, the members of a California parish had an immediate response. "In terms of a big, successful something, it would have to be the preschool," one man quickly replied as heads nodded throughout the group. "And I can say that, because I was on the vestry at the time and was completely opposed to it." Laughter cascaded around the circle, and the man who had spoken joined in. Then he continued, "I couldn't see it, because we had so many other problems."

How the preschool emerged despite sincere differences of opinion makes a revealing story. One inducement for proceeding with the project—even amid controversy—was that the clearly perceived need for more preschools in the area augured well for the success of any well-run preschool program. "I think it is now accurate to say that we are flooded with applications from parents who want their children to have a good preschool program and want their children to have religious instruction. And the idea was that the children would bring the parents to church. And there has been some of that. And so, it has been an absolute, astonishing success. All the little pieces have come together."

What "really made it work" was the organization of a committee that "really made it go." But much more than an effective committee was involved. Exploring the idea of launching the school demanded much of the vestry's time to secure a certain level of consensus and a coherent strategy. "In those days," said the man who had spoken originally, "we put half our vestry meeting time into working on the preschool. The rest of us, who at that time were worried about things like stewardship and evangelism, felt all this attention to the preschool was draining us at a time when we had so many other issues to address. But it was absolutely what we were supposed to do, because having the preschool succeed has been an absolute nucleus for this church, and because of it we have been able to address all those other things that worried me then."

Another former vestry member recalled that the "process was a big part of what this was all about. It was a process of growth. And along the way, we had to deal with some problems that were very uncomfortable. By having taken it on, you couldn't retreat." The man who had doubted both the preschool and the process now resumed his account: "Personally for me it was a constant struggle....There was no clear feeling. Every time we turned around, there were new sets of problems. But as we came through this, it was clear what we were supposed to do, and we started to hold hands and love one another. But during the process it was hard."

The greatest obstacle many Episcopalians face is simply profound differences over the priorities of their congregations. In New England, a group of lay leaders cited "a lot of years of frustration, disagreement from every side because of the discussion of differing ideas [without a sense of] community or [being] able to communicate." In a nearby parish, there was "a lot of discussion and disagreement about how we should get the minister to stay and some differing about wanting him to leave."

Reported one member of a church in the East that suffered a devastating fire, "We had to decide whether or not we were going to stay in the city. And all this was happening while the city itself was facing very hard times. We feel like our decision to stay— when it might have been easier to move to the suburbs—was a commitment not only to ourselves but to the city itself. We saw that who we were, and who the city was, were linked." A process of discussing their differences and possibilities allowed this parish to affirm its historic sense of mission in a new way.

A sense of clarity about parish mission does not always come easily, many Episcopalians say. "We're not dealing with the situation," a lay leader on the East Coast revealed. Members of a nearby parish acknowledged fears that, if their congregation grew, it would "lose its identity." In a third parish in the same area, differences of opinion and purpose led its members to pray together often but with no clear sense of resolution.

At times, the open acknowledgment of differences represents a positive step. In the Midwest, a parishioner who left during turmoil in the congregation and then returned described a key change in the local leadership process. "I'd like to speak to how we handled differences: I was really excited two or three years ago when we finally had a disagreement on the vestry. Until then, no one would speak up. No one would ever vote 'nay' on anything. He'd just abstain. When we got to the point that we could positively address differences, I knew this was progress."

Differences may occur in places and under circumstances no one could have foreseen, but plain speaking that is judicious and consistent can produce remarkable resolutions. In one parish, an otherwise successful vacation Bible school suddenly became the subject of concern. A lay leader described what unfolded: "During the week, two members of the adult leadership team approached [the rest of] us with concerns about the discussion time with the children. There were two ladies who, following the curriculum, had asked the children about their fears. One child said he feared death and became upset. Apparently his grandmother had died recently. The two women were concerned about engaging such young children about such profound fears. The women thought that vacation Bible school was not meant for this. They thought that vacation Bible school should only be about teaching Bible lessons to little children."

How did this leader and the other committee members respond to such a profound concern that no doubt came as a surprise to all involved? A thoughtful compromise evolved. "We asked the two ladies what they would be comfortable with; they came up with presenting Scripture. But, after they spoke with me and the mother of the upset child, they agreed that what was needed was a different way to talk about fears other than the original way in the curriculum. They agreed that talking about fears was within the parameters of the original program."

This anecdote sheds clarity on the underlying obstacles Episcopalians face, namely differing perspectives on religious means and ends. It is important to emphasize the uniquely religious dimensions of Episcopal life and not merely to cite psychological, sociological, or organizational aspects of it. For example, a response from a strictly psychological dimension might have warmly welcomed the venting of the child's fears even as it subtly criticized the restrictive behavior of his teachers. This one-dimensional reaction, without regard for the religious dimension, might easily have made all the adults involved become defensive and entrenched in their positions; opportunities for spiritual and educational growth might have been lost; the ties that bound the teachers and committee members might have been loosened; and the children might have returned to an emotionally charged vacation Bible school run by tense and contentious teachers.

It is crucial to encourage fresh perspective on the religious nature of the congregation's struggles and celebrations. And it is necessary to honor the differing religious and theological perspectives that the people of most congregations bring to basic questions of shared purpose and shared ministry. As much as any dimension of Episcopal life, the theological dimension is in dramatic transition as new forms of faith and ministry take hold.

The resolution of the situation described above suggests not only the capacity of local leaders to adapt external resources to congregational realities but the almost constant necessity of doing so. It also highlights the sense of religious vocation among the two teachers and other committee members involved. In part, this sense of vocation is apparent in the urge to adapt congregational life to new contextual realities. Usually, such patterns of adaptation occur as astute laity or clergy, drawing on their personal senses of calling, devise processes of discussion and discernment based upon the shared faith commitment and dedication of their congregation. Through a process of reflection and reconsideration, obstacles usually can be surmounted.

Hints of surmounted obstacles cropped up everywhere in our conversations with Episcopalians across the country: in phrases such as "we talked it through" and in depictions of parish life such as "participatory" or "inclusive" or "honest." However, the preponderance of conciliatory language in the stories of Episcopalians should not be mistaken for a desire for a consensus or close conformity. Consensus in the Episcopal Church appears to be something many strive for, but the object appears to be consensus of overall intent, within which there is considerable room for disagreement, even heated disagreement. With remarkable frequency Episcopalians stress that accepting differences of opinion is one of their highest values.

Left to their own devices, Episcopalians often seem quite capable of clarifying their mission, addressing their differences, and securing their congregation's future. Yet they also understand that their "self-sufficiency" does not imply that they can always be self-contained or completely self-reliant. Often we have heard Episcopalians say that they needed resources that could only be sought outside the congregation. Typically, the term "resources" refers to programs that enhance some aspect of congregational life, such as Christian education curricula or stewardship guidelines. Challenges to do with finances, evangelism, and spiritual formation of children and youth often prompt congregations to look for approaches that other churches have found successful. "We really need some useful resources for training lay leaders, including spiritual growth and practical skills in team building," a Kansas lay leader revealed.

With disturbing regularity, local Episcopal leaders complain that the diocese or the wider church has been the greatest obstacle to finding leader resources and programmatic materials that will enhance their congregational life. "We went to the diocese, but there were no resources," said an Eastern lay leader. She meant that the diocese seemed incapable of appreciating the congregation's situation and responding effectively to its needs. In the Midwest, a small congregation sought financial aid from the diocese for their program needs, but the token assistance offered them caused only frustration. "I wish we could get more support from the diocese for these efforts. That little grant is a miniscule percent of the tax we have to pay the bishop. We are being bled to death by his taxes, and we get so little in return. Whatever he does with all that money and all his time is a mystery."

But in the West, a lay leader revealed an entirely different experience of her diocese. There, "more than any other diocese I've been in, I feel more a spirit of acknowledgment that God might really be in charge of it all." Her religious longing was apparent, and she credited the bishop's style and thoughtful positions on critical issues. Nevertheless, she also noted that the diocese ran "like a bureaucracy." Such a distinction between admiration for individual leaders, especially bishops, and disdain for the church's institutional machinery surfaces often. In a parish that had recently been a mission congregation, a focus group noted that the bishop had "been wonderful." When a new parish building was dedicated, the bishop drove through a snowstorm to be there. His personal commitment was recalled with affection and respect.

It would be too simple to say that all Episcopal congregations are finding vitality or that the vitality they realize comes effortlessly. It would also be much too simple to say that Episcopalians are uniformly disparaging of their diocesan or national leaders and structures. However, the loyalties of Episcopalians, as well as their standards for themselves and their church, are in flux. No longer seeing themselves as members of an institution, they are engaged in building vital communities of faith that reflect their avid spiritual searches. The kinds of initiatives they take and the ties they now form reflect the most dramatic of all the church's changes.

NOTES

[1] David E. Sumner, *The Episcopal Church's History, 1945–1985* (Morehouse, 1987), p. 168.

[2] In response to the insistence of Presiding Bishop John Hines, the General Convention of 1967 allocated $3 million annually for "development of a program" to benefit community organizations in "depressed urban areas." The program proved controversial when it appeared to some Episcopalians that monies were being given to radical groups. This fear was reinforced when Hines encouraged the church's positive response to the "Black Manifesto," a demand for reparations from the white economic establishment for the evil of slavery. Hines acknowledged the "inflammatory" nature of such a demand but urged the church's support at a special session of General Convention in 1967. Hines saw such support less as reparations than as funding further community development programs through the Black Economic Development Conference. But this distinction was lost on many Episcopalians at the time. In retrospect, Hines' leadership and the church's response had both beneficial and harmful effects. While deepening the sensitivities of many Episcopalians, the General Convention Special Program also deepened suspicions of the national church's intentions. See Sumner, pp. 46–59.

[3] Patricia O'Connell Killen, *Christianity in the Western United States Since World War II.* Unpublished manuscript presented at the Spring Theological Conference, Pacific Lutheran Theological Seminary, April 19, 2002. This paper is cited with permission of the author, to whom we express gratitude.

[4] *Ibid.*

[5] Wilbert R. Shenk, *Henry Venn—Missionary Statesman* (Orbis, 1983).

5

IN SEARCH OF LEADERSHIP
The Historic Forms of Religious Leadership

In order to achieve the vigorous congregational life for which they yearn, Episcopalians everywhere are seeking faithful and effective models of leadership. In the past, one assumed that references to "religious leaders" meant clergy, but that assumption is changing. The urgency of the calls for leadership throughout the church compel reconsideration of religious leadership and attention to the forms of Christian life that are emerging from local ferment. How do the people who now constitute the church construe and develop leadership?

The search for leadership engages the most basic aspects of religious life. Beneath all the usual associations with religion, the primal intent of religion is to bind all things together: the deity with human beings, heaven with earth, human beings with their earth, human beings with one another. More than rites, doctrines, or institutions, "religion"—as generally understood from a sociological perspective—refers to the capacity of belief to bind people together in collective pursuit of shared ideals. To make the transition from abstract tenets to concrete expressions of belief, religions require leaders. Human guidance is integral to the realization of religious ideals. To understand how religion binds people together demands attention to the activities of religious leaders. In turn, the forms of leadership rely upon the ways in which religious ideals meet concrete circumstances.

Religious leaders have always performed a variety of tasks. Since ancient times, religious leaders have served as priests and prophets, teachers and administrators, healers and monastics. Ancient religious life centered on ritual practices that emphasized the sacred character of a people and the land they inhabited. The early Hebrews modified this framework to suit their dynamic experience of God. Called into covenant with God by their patriarchal leaders, they inhabited a promised land where they pursued their ideal of nationhood. The Hebrew Bible records the heights and depths of their story and also the ways in which leadership roles arose. As their institutions developed, kingly and priestly leaders emerged to guide them. When moral failure and religious laxity appeared, prophets challenged the people to realign themselves with God and with one another. Only later, after the time of Jesus, did the rabbi become Judaism's central leadership office. The rabbinic role included ritual dimensions similar to those of ancient religious leaders, but this later understanding of leadership focused more on teaching the faith and sustaining its wisdom tradition. This emphasis on ensuring the endurance of the covenant befitted a people whose experience had shifted westward but whose sense of homeland never moved.

Early Christians adapted Hebrew precedent to their new vision of covenant with God. Christianity absorbed the ideal of the kingdom of God but did not align it with one locale. Instead the early Christians rooted their response to God in a new fellowship which they called the church. Within a century after the time of Jesus, a set of offices had arisen to guide the church's development. Bishops directed the church's life in particular places, deacons performed pastoral roles, and priests oversaw ritual life. These offices secured the chuch's mission and distinguished correct belief and practice from heretical challenges. Only a few generations after Jesus, Christian leadership had achieved enduring forms.

But other spontaneous forms of Christian leadership persisted. Martyrs and reformers as well as visionaries and popular preachers have shaped popular Christian experience in alternative ways. Over and over since the time of Jesus, their stories and devotional ideals have transcended the institutional precedents of their period, repeatedly demonstrating the inability of the church's authority structures to embrace the full breadth of Christian piety. Christian history records a series of tensions between leaders who worked to secure institutionalized expressions of faith and leaders intent on reforming or transcending those very expressions.

At times the tension between religious institution and popular piety exploded into lasting division. The Protestant Reformation of the sixteenth century was the most decisive of these. The Reformation was closely identified with such leaders as John Calvin and Martin Luther, whose work began as efforts to purify Christian belief and piety. To that end, they and other reformers explored new forms of church life that often sacrificed Roman Catholic sacramental practice in order to emphasize Scripture and biblical study. The new Protestant emphasis dictated patterns of leadership that created a more clearly defined division of labor between clergy and laity. Clergy were responsible for interpreting, ministering, and teaching the faith as presented in Scripture. Laity shared in the church's governance and ordered their daily work and family life as patterns of faithful witness. The result was a consonance of the everyday workings of politics, religious community, secular community, and family that allowed faith to be integrated in practical new ways with the practicalities of life. As a result, leadership patterns of worship and community began to mesh more easily with political patterns, greatly facilitating the establishment of Protestant churches in much of Western Europe.

Indeed, so successful was the establishment of Protestantism that establishment became worrisome to some strains of the reformed faith. Protesting the seeming compromise of faith's ideals by worldly realities, such English groups as the Puritans of the seventeenth century and the Methodists of the eighteenth century gave rise to enduring Christian denominations. Inspired by charismatic teachers and preachers, these groups advocated a Christian faith that would not be contained within a few, highly organized churches. New patterns of Christian life arose as a result of their reinvigorated search for pure belief and fellowship. Nowhere were these patterns more evident than in the United States; and in the voluntary religious environment that followed after disestablishment, the search for compelling expression of belief only intensified.

For Episcopalians and other mainstream Protestants in the U.S., this intense search for religious expression has meant a continual challenge to readjust their social roles and institutional forms. From the early nineteenth to the late twentieth centuries, America's Protestant establishment seemed to meet this challenge well. These denominations developed deep social roots and built elaborate programs. Among Congregationalists, Methodists, Presbyterians, some Baptists, and Episcopalians, significant differences in worship, ministry, and doctrine remained. But by the second half of the nineteenth century, these denominations—and others such as certain Lutheran groups—found broad consensus on their social role and organizational style. Resolved to function like American corporate entities, they created the organizational framework for mainstream religious life. Through the second half of the nineteenth century, these denominations developed complex structures that linked congregations, developed common mission, and enforced standards of leadership performance.

These complex structures created markedly different roles for clergy and laity. Along with their elaborate organizational frameworks, Protestant denominations developed the corollary that religious leadership was a specialized profession that needed the same steps of qualification, education, and certification required of other specialized professions in America. Consequently, Protestant denominations begin to require more elaborate preparation for ordination and to define more markedly the different

roles of clergy and laity. To be a minister, one received training
and demonstrated competence in a range of fields. Religious
leaders had to be skilled preachers, teachers, worship leaders, and
counselors. They had to be able administrators of the congregation's affairs and loyal representatives of denominational life.

Interestingly during this period, Protestant denominations
were ordering themselves internally in ways almost opposite to
their outward expressions of faith and mission. Internally, they
were compartmentalizing their missions and stratifying their
leadership, but outwardly they sought synthesis of purpose—if
not of identity—among the denominations. Building on what
historian Martin Marty has called the "binding tie of cohesive
sentiment," the Protestant mainstream churches came together
after World War II to create an elaborate institutional network
called the National Council of Churches.[1] The Episcopal Church
played a prominent role in its creation. Presiding Bishop Henry
Knox Sherrill helped to organize it and served as its first president. By then the corporate form of mainstream religion was at
its peak. The organizational structures of most denominations
and most interdenominational agencies were not very different
from corporate America's. Religious America had become a centralized set of organizations that endeavored collectively to be
the primary provider to the mainline Protestant church of somewhat generic resources for most aspects of congregational life;
more denomination-specific programs and resources continued
to be produced separately by the national bodies of the various
churches. By the 1950s, denominational and ecumenical religious
agencies at the national level had proliferated and offered mainstream congregations a wide variety of educational and social service programs. Given the high level of loyalty to denominations,
denominational leaders could assume their materials would be
well received and used by their congregations; leaders of such
ecumenical groups as the National Council of Churches hoped
their materials would be widely known and thoughtfully received
by the congregations of several denominations. Denominational
and interdenominational agency leaders presumed that local

clergy and laity would honor the standards for church life as set by their denominations' national bodies. Religious life centered on institutional processes, and religious leadership was a function of this institutional whirl.

In those years, it was common to experience one's congregation as an extension of a national institution. Centralized authority and local loyalty were not in conflict. Great emphasis was placed on membership in a national church that united its members in a specific religious identity according to clearly defined standards. In such a cultural climate, mainstream denominations presumed a widespread loyalty and a sharp clarity about their identity and vocation, assuring them that their activities would be seen as significant—denominationally, interdenominationally, even secularly. The church's people may have differed on aspects of their denomination's policies and expressions, but they never doubted its religious identity and social place. Well into the 1960s, the church's main concern was how to function better in order to extend the reach of its influence. Toward that clearly defined end, the leadership burden was placed almost entirely on the clergy.

During more than a century of institutional confidence—from the mid-nineteenth to the late twentieth centuries—the Episcopal Church was fortunate to receive the skilled guidance of a number of dedicated leaders. The career of Noble Powell—parish priest in Virginia, Maryland, and the District of Columbia, then Bishop of Maryland from 1941 to 1963—offers vivid illustration. As a young Virginia rector, his biographer records, Powell worked effectively to build St. Paul's Church adjacent to the University of Virginia. His efforts focused on creating parish programs that would extend into the community. Typical of his generation, Powell understood his ministry to be the making of disciples of Jesus Christ within the fellowship of the church. "A heart changed over time was the goal, accomplished with the assistance of divine grace, through the ministrations of the church and not without the human being's own patient striving." The Episcopal Church and the Book of Common Prayer "presented a structure to flawed human beings, a rhythm of contrition and thanksgiving; it offered a pattern of religious practice that was encouraged and supported by a primarily pastoral ministry."[2]

Noble Powell and his generation "did not see a need for the church to array itself against the dominant norms of civilization." Instead, following the prevailing assumption among Episcopalians, he saw the church's role as a "custodian" of American life. Religious functions were not the only appropriate responsibilities of the church; there were social, civic, and educational responsibilities as well. The church's focus was upon socialization within the generally accepted bounds of propriety and morality. The church proudly saw its task as being in step with the culture.[3] To be a religious leader was to act as a custodian of the church and the society it served.

For most of his career, Powell benefited from such justifiable assumptions about the church's identity and vocation. Like other church leaders of the day, his place in society, as established by his office, was widely understood; and with that place came the presumption of authority. Powell used his to good effect, especially during his tenure as bishop. Under his guidance, the Diocese of Maryland expanded its children's programs, its ecumenical activities, and its funding of new congregations. Powell acknowledged the tensions that permeated American life during the Cold War era. But in response, he offered assurances grounded in the church's institutional capabilities. With the first assaults on institutional assumptions that came with the Civil Rights Movement, Powell faced a vocational crisis; the shaking of the presumably unshakeable foundation of the institutional church represented an enormous challenge for which he and others of his generation simply were not prepared.[4]

Powell and much of the mainstream religious leadership had based their confidence and ambitions on the weak presumption that a nearly unanimous American religious consensus underlay their work. Of course, Protestant institutionalism never approached, much less achieved, this level of hegemony. But theirs was a curious understanding of consensus, one that did not deny the cultural and religious diversity in America, but rather tried to appropriate it into the overall view of Protestant mainstream mission. In retrospect, their perspective looks curiously reversed, because this period in America now looks less like the apotheosis of religious consensus and more like the beginning of the heyday of real pluralism in America.

Many Jews and Roman Catholics shared mainstream Protestantism's organizational style and endorsed much of its sense of social responsibility; but their religious sensibilities remained distinct. Still more apparent—as signals of the limits of the mainstream ideal in America—were the ever-growing numbers of Muslims, Buddhists, and others who practiced non-Western forms of religion. Even among Christians, it was clear by the twentieth century that Evangelicals and Pentecostals cultivated ideals of religious life and community that did not take their cues from the mainstream.

As stated above, mainstream religion responded somewhat paradoxically to diversity. These denominations hoped to embrace America's social diversity in ways that ranged from upholding and protecting diversity at all costs to subsuming it. For many years, the very fact of religious diversity has fueled, rather than diminished, the ambitions of mainstream religion. Combining a sense of social prerogative and a professional view of ministry, the mainstream churches tried to devise practical expressions of their ideal of "inclusivity." Had they succeeded, they would have achieved a religiously inspired version of social justice that would have validated and sustained their social role. From a twentieth-first-century perspective, however, we now see that the full implications of the social justice they advocated were actually incompatible with, even antithetical to, the pivotal role in society that they envisioned for themselves. But at the time, the historic mainstream churches were surprised and frustrated to find their hopes unrealized and their social place eroded. From within and without the mainstream, there was a reaction against institutionalized religion. Historic loyalties and habitual efforts to mimic corporate life lost legitimacy. By the late twentieth century, stresses within mainstream religion could no longer be ignored. It appeared that American religion had become more noted for its strains and its diversity than for its coherence. Inevitably, the Episcopal Church vividly illustrated the agonies that mainline religion began to face.

THE TYPES OF EPISCOPAL RELIGIOUS LEADERS

Until the late twentieth century, Episcopalians understood religious leadership largely in institutional terms. The church's clergy were its key figures, because they were understood to be professional persons charged with guiding the church's life. More precisely, the clergy were expected to serve as custodians who attended to the church's institutional well-being and worked to expand the influence of the church's ministries in the world. Episcopalians presumed that their clergy would be men who would be able managers of congregations and dioceses, an emphasis that intensified as the church's program life expanded during the twentieth century. Episcopalians also presumed that, in their preaching and teaching, as well as in their administrative duties, clergy would bring fresh, energetic expression of the church's role in society. There were few Episcopalians who doubted that the church must bring the Gospel to bear on the problems of modern life and that the institution of the church would develop specialized "how to" resources and techniques for handling such problems. Episcopalians simply assumed that the church's heavily managerial style of leadership—both national and local—would be marshaled against these challenges of modern life. They further assumed, until late in the twentieth century, that ordained persons would predominate in such leadership.

By the mid-twentieth century, new styles of leadership were appearing. As we will describe, these styles included reform, activism, guardianship, as well as spiritual guidance, which is the broadest model, including, among other styles, the therapeutic model of spiritual growth. We will explain that these types never fully supplanted the role of the professional serving as an institutional custodian, nor has any one of these types by itself set the tone for the church's life. Each has represented a moment of creative possibility in the Episcopal Church, and each has continuing significance.

REFORMERS

The role of the *reformer* arose along with Episcopalians' awareness of social injustice and an increasingly diverse society. Burning with the desire to create a just society, Episcopal reformers realized that the church would have to become better integrated into secular aspects of society in order to change it; but in order to become truly a part of a diverse society, the church would have to become considerably more diverse itself. The creation of special ministries to African Americans, including the consecrations of a few African-American suffragan bishops to superintend this work in some dioceses, suggested that the church understood its need to adapt.[5] Similar, if somewhat more limited, initiatives also were extended to Native Americans, and a few local ministries addressed the situations of Asian Americans. But these ministries suggested no reframing of the church's ends or means. There was no hint of challenge to the church's institutional structures, religious ethos, or social locus. These ministries represented limited efforts to incorporate additional people into the church without changing it.

But increasingly, the emphasis on custodianship—and even on limited patterns of adaptation—was challenged by an impulse to reform the church. The new impulse was apparent first in liturgical revision, which was sparked by late-nineteenth-century English and European academic movements which sought to recover early Christian emphasis on the Eucharist as the center of worship, and which then gained pastoral impetus from the social and theological challenges of the two World Wars. By the 1950s, when the liturgical revision movement gained momentum, some church leaders felt that the ancient liturgies could be adapted to modern circumstances in a manner that would serve the church's identity and vocation in times of social crisis. As a result, the Episcopal Church's Standing Liturgical Commission began publication of a series of booklets exploring liturgical reform. Behind this series was the influence of several reformers, notably Massey Shepherd of the Church Divinity School of the Pacific. A liturgical scholar who was conversant with innovative studies of ancient worship in Britain and the Continent, Shepherd—along with Canon Edward West of New York's Cathedral of St. John the Divine—helped to launch a reform-minded group, the Associated Parishes, in 1946. Under its auspices, conferences were held to explore worship and parish life. The result was increasing momentum for revision of the Book of Common Prayer.[6]

The ideals of worship that emerged in the 1950s have proven strikingly definitive of Episcopal life. Shepherd, West, and other liturgical reformers imagined redesigning worship to incorporate ancient forms and apply them to modern realities. Specifically, they recovered the ideal of worship as an expression of the life of God's people in particular places. They also advocated elaborate vesture, music, processions, and imagery to enhance the sacramental character of the moment. In their eyes, worship should be viewed as celebration, the gathering of God's people in thanksgiving for God's blessings and in assurance of God's guidance. Worship became the core of a new ideal of a church composed of people drawn together on a divinely inspired journey. The achievement of this ideal required leaders willing to reform worship.

A key aspect of the reformist view of worship was its emphasis on the laity. Of course, the lay role has always been prominent in the Episcopal Church, but that role had been restricted when it came to ministry and worship, aspects of church life which always had been reserved for clergy. With the dawning of the idea that worship was the work of the entire church, however, a new emphasis on lay involvement arose. At first, the notion of having lay people read the lessons or prayers in worship seemed a monumental step, but it was a step that allowed lay people to see their roles in the church as ministries in ways that overlapped with clergy but remained distinct from them. Reform of worship inspired review of the role of lay persons, not only in the church but in all aspects of their Christian lives.

Nor did this reformist view of the church as a worshiping community end with revising the role of lay people. During the 1960s, the General Convention gradually removed obstacles to the full participation of women in the church. Previously women had been restricted to running their own "auxiliary" organizations or entering religious orders and had been prohibited from the sorts of roles occupied by male lay leaders. Apart from deaconesses in some dioceses, there were no ordained women.

In 1964 came a significant indication of change in the role of women in the church: women deputies gained seats in the General Convention's House of Deputies. Then, in 1966, a Convention committee endorsed the ordination of women to the priesthood, an action which lead to the Convention's approval of the ordination of women as deacons in 1970. In 1974, a few sympathetic bishops ordained small groups of women as priests without the Convention's approval. The Convention finally approved the ordination of woman to the priesthood in 1976. Meanwhile, other significant reforms had been underway. In 1967, the Convention permitted lay people to assist with the chalice at Communion. During the same Convention, the revised Book of Common Prayer received the first of two approvals required by the church's canons. The second approval came in 1979.[7]

Behind these historic reforms lay a new sensibility. An interesting insight into the tenor of the times surfaces in the autobiography of Pauli Murray, an African-American woman and lifelong Episcopalian who had a distinguished career as a lawyer. Murray never lost the faith her church inculcated, but for years she felt relegated to the margins. Eventually her "growing feminist consciousness led me to do battle with the Episcopal Church over the submerged position of women in our denomination. Challenging inequalities in religious life was more difficult than challenging similar inequalities in the secular world," she continued, "because church practices were often bound up with questions of fundamental faith, insulating them from attack."

"As a child growing up in the church," she recalled, "I knew that I could never be privileged to carry the cross or serve at the

altar as an acolyte. Only boys were permitted to do so. I grudg-
ingly accepted these limitations...and serving in the capacities
open to me—as choir member, Sunday school teacher, member
of the Altar Guild, and occasional organist." Although she experienced the appeal of the Christian faith and the lure of its
expression in the church's worship and ministry, she also felt—as
a woman and as an African American—the sting of the church's
exclusion. Thus, "I could neither stay away entirely nor enter
wholeheartedly into Christian community."[8] In 1966 she protest-
ed to the rector of her church that she, and all women, should
have a role in the liturgy, and he proved receptive. No decisive
change happened immediately, but she perceived that a door had
begun to open.

Ultimately, Murray would not attain her appropriate role in
liturgy on the basis of protest. Though she had experienced the
sting of discrimination, the crystallizing moment that led to
proper place of ministry occurred as she ministered to a dying
friend. Afterwards, she began to recover a sense of her family's
heritage in the church, and as a result, she discovered a sense of
her own life as a spiritual journey that eventually led her to ordination as a priest early in 1977. In a dramatic way, Pauli Murray's
experience matches those of many women and men who have
sought to expand the church's structures that they might affirm a
broader range of spiritual experience. In the process of pursuing
their calls, many gifted Episcopalians like Pauli Murray have
reformed the church. A similar spirit remains today among people
who believe that the first task of leadership is to ensure that the
church's actual functions match its Christian intentions.

ACTIVISTS

It is tempting to think of the first women ordained to the
priesthood as *activists*. Not only did they mobilize to compel a
basic change in the church's life, but a few of them stepped outside the church's normal procedures to be priested in an ordination
service that preceded the church's official recognition of women as
priests. But for the majority of women clergy and their supporters,

their efforts were not focused on radical change of the church's structures but on an energetic search for equal participation in those structures.

A critical stance toward the church and American society developed among some Episcopalians, as well as among leaders in the other mainstream churches. A new style of leadership that featured activism for radical change surfaced in the 1950s. It had its roots in a movement that originated in the seminaries: the "theology of crisis" that began in Europe between the World Wars and then secured roots in American public discussion. The sense of crisis arose from the shock of theologians and church leaders at the devastation caused by war. Also known as Neo-Orthodoxy, crisis theology absorbed some of the concerns and activism of the Social Gospel movement that arose in the United States in the late nineteenth century and also the Christian Socialist movement that entered a new phase in Britain at the end of the nineteenth century. But unlike the optimism about society that fueled these earlier movements, crisis theology sought to distance the churches from naïve responses to complex social problems or from the appearance of complicity with the societal structures that create such problems. Crisis theologians believed that the task of the churches was to recover their distinctive identity and vocation by adopting a critical view of society. Among Episcopalians, Virginia Theological Seminary became a center of crisis theology in America. Professors Albert T. Mollegen and Clifford T. Stanley proved so adept at conveying the message of crisis theology—and public hunger was so great for a return to basic Christian beliefs and their biblical sources—that they began a lecture series. "Christianity and Modern Man" became so popular that, for nearly twenty years (well into the 1960s), they offered this series annually in the Washington, D.C. area.[9] These and other theologians conveyed the idea that the role of the church was to critique society.

The idea of a critical theological stance encouraged a few church leaders to advocate an aggressive, uninhibited questioning of the Christian faith and the church. As Dean of the Cathedral of St. John the Divine in New York and later as Bishop of California, James A. Pike became noted—and, to some, notorious—for his challenges to traditional Christian belief and church life. For example, his book, *Time for Christian Candor*, published in 1958, referred to the Trinity as "excess luggage."[10] Articulate and insightful at times, eccentric and outrageous at others, he became a champion of breaking old molds for some; for others he was an embarrassment or even a heretic. Few could follow in his erratic footsteps, but his example as a voice of challenge was not lost. Activism as a way of confronting the church became a priority for some Episcopalians.

But the voices criticizing church and society gathered force in the 1960s with a series of books that moved from challenge and assertiveness to confrontation. In *The Suburban Captivity of the Church*, sociologist Gibson Winter, an Episcopalian, issued an indictment of the church's role in suburban culture and neglect of America's declining inner cities. In *The Comfortable Pew*, Canadian Anglican Pierre Berton challenged the tendency of congregations to avoid difficult social issues. Episcopal theologian Joseph Fletcher's book, *Situation Ethics*, argued that inherited assumptions about ethical norms needed to be replaced by standards that acknowledged contextual realities. Paul Van Buren's *The Secular Meaning of the Gospel* issued a call for new ways to think of God. Thus, a variety of critical voices, with Episcopalians prominent among them, revealed that activism for change in church and society was gaining momentum.[11]

The activist leadership style spread far beyond books and the quixotic personalities who wrote them. In the post-World War II era, there had already been notable Episcopal efforts at inner-city ministry. Thus, pastoral experience combined with the social critique that was gathering force to lead some Episcopalians to become active in the Civil Rights movement. It is difficult to estimate the extent of involvement by Episcopalians in the movement's diverse aspects. It is even more difficult to define the extent of Episcopal participation in protest against the Vietnam War, the other great social cause of the 1960s and early 1970s.

But the formation of the Episcopal Society for Cultural and Racial Unity (ESCRU) in 1959 and the revival of the Episcopal Peace Fellowship (EPF) during the same era helped to focus the social activism of Episcopalians.[12] When Episcopal seminarian Jonathan Myrick Daniels was shot in Alabama in 1965 because of his work for civil rights, many Episcopalians saw the struggle for equality in personal and immediate terms. Activism for justice gained urgency as a form of leadership. Presiding Bishop John Hines adopted an activist approach in urging the General Convention to respond with funds and programs to address major social issues.

By the late 1960s, the time had passed when custodianship or reform represented the dominant assumptions about leadership style in the church. Instead, activism characterized the prevailing leadership approach. Motivated by the urge to make the church authentic in its practice and faithful in its belief, the activist emphasis widened the division between liberal and conservative Episcopalians. Ironically, across a yawning ideological divide, only an energetic activist style can be embraced by both liberals and conservatives. To the extent that such a culture-war divide persists in the Episcopal Church, the activist leadership style remains influential. But activism can also be glimpsed locally when congregational leaders speak of their intention to transform congregations or aspects of the wider church. While the style of confrontation that characterized the Civil Rights and war protest movements has diminished, a long-term commitment to institutional and social change retains great appeal.

GUARDIANS

The extensive changes in the Episcopal Church's worship and ministry have not been welcomed universally. For some Episcopalians, one change or another has not been palatable; instead, change has been viewed as surrender of church tradition or even as abandonment of the Christian faith. The Episcopal Church is not unique in generating this response to change. Within all the mainstream denominations, the seeming ascendancy of liberal views of the faith and church has unsettled many clergy and laity. Liberals have appeared too centered on human experience rather than divine revelation and too aggressive in advancing their concerns within the church. While liberals have envisioned their ideals as the church's next form of consensus, their assertiveness has sparked a broad response that embodies a new style of leadership in the church. A variety of individuals and groups have begun to see themselves as *guardians* of faith and order, and *guardianship* has become a notable leadership theme.

Some guardians have formed highly publicized dissident groups. Some have broken with the Episcopal Church while others have remained within as active critics.[13] The American Anglican Council is a group that espouses the theme of guardianship of tradition and faith while proclaiming fealty to the church. Ironically, their commitment is similar at its core to that of liberal groups in that both seek to achieve a pure expression of the Christian faith as they interpret it. Their principal motivator is fear that the church's foundational beliefs and practices are in danger. Threats to the church come from several sources: there are, of course, the avowed opponents of the faith who publicly align themselves with one or another of the modernist heresies; more difficult to locate but almost as insidious are those Episcopalians, clergy and laity alike, who appear to be going about the proper business of the faith but who have in fact grown careless and lax in holding the line against apostasy; then there are those faithful Episcopalians who are too "nice," who try too hard to accommodate their fellow Episcopalians who have fallen into error. At root, guardians believe the world is riddled with evil, and they are determined to guard unchanging doctrinal and moral standards as the church's safeguard. But guardianship should not be equated only with fear or extremism. Among Episcopalians, the spirit of guardianship runs broad and deep. More than simply reactive, guardianship enlists a wide range of thoughtful leaders who work to clarify and adapt belief and practice or to preserve Episcopal identity and vocation as past generations have received and expressed them.

An example of guardianship as a leadership style comes from Philip Turner, a noted scholar and teacher. In a recent article, Turner urged that theology in the church "has to do with passing on, exploring, explaining, and defending the language and forms of life that lead to common knowledge and love of God." He identifies this process with the tendencies inherent in healthy parish life, and so he strikes an optimistic note about the church's life at the grassroots.

Turner believes that it always has been the responsibility of bishops to serve as guardians of the faith, but he believes their guardianship is especially required today, when the faith seems under unprecedented attack. But Turner criticizes the church's bishops for failing to lead as guardians of the church's basic beliefs and practices. "The job of a bishop is complex, but its primary aspect is to see that [the] language and forms of life of the local church are in accord with those of the apostles. It is, however, just this aspect of the office of bishop that has moved steadily out of sight within the life of the Episcopal Church." As evidence, Turner cites the bishops' increasing "inability and unwillingness to address the various theological crises that have come before the Episcopal Church in the last fifty years, and by their insistence that respecting differences is more fundamental to the life of the church than finding a common mind." As a result, there has been an "abdication" that creates "a sort of theological congregationalism at the level of both parish and diocese."[14] Turner may be unusually pointed, but his sentiments are typical of those guardian style leaders who call upon the church's offices and structures to guard the Christian faith as the Episcopal Church has received it.

The primary duty of guardianship is less about grumbling over liberal innovations and more about affirmation of the church's beliefs and practices. It would be easy to ascribe the Episcopal Church's tensions to a rivalry between traditionalists and progressives, conservatives and liberals. We have heard some Episcopalians protest an alleged surrender of faith and mission to liberal ideology and institutional processes. For liberals, on the other hand, the church's greatest threat comes from a well-organized conservative phalanx equally bent on imposing its will by seizing power.[15] But neither liberalism nor conservatism can be blamed for conflict and the loss of momentum at the Episcopal Church's national level. As we will describe in subsequent chapters (and have alluded to previously) the loss of organizational momentum has been profound but cannot be ascribed to ideological causes.

In response to these challenges, the new and largely grass-roots ideals of leadership that have sprung up in the church function in various degrees as custodians, reformers, activists, or guardians. But more than any of these, Episcopal leaders now serve as spiritual guides.

SPIRITUAL GUIDES

Since the last third of the twentieth century the most profound religious current in America has been the spiritual search. There has been a turn toward unconventional religious sources and forms of expression so diverse and numerous that their overall influence is difficult to trace. The new spiritual energies represent personal and shared efforts to realize a dynamic way of life that blends explorations of historic religious traditions with practical experiences of community and expressions of benevolence. Consistently, the emphasis is upon finding a way of life in one's setting that is "authentic," that is, which succeeds in integrating religious ideals with daily life. This public spirituality stresses personal and shared forms of integration; this means that it is more pragmatic than esoteric. To be genuine, spirituality must inspire practical results that improve not merely one's own life but the lives of those in one's vicinity.

Though spirituality is often presumed to be inherently and even strictly individual, our findings point to signs of a public, collective dimension that we believe is becoming central for many Episcopalians. Popular understandings of spirituality do *not* appear to be solely individualistic. The spiritual hunger that has been described to us inspires a collective effort to construct religious community. The realization among many Americans that they have little or no religious background, or are consciously shedding their pasts in order to grasp a more authentic sense of possibility, often fuels this search. To reach their goals, these seekers devise new forms of religious community. They experience occasions of discovery and celebration that ground them in tradition, awaken vivid belief, and structure habits of prayer and discipleship. For them, the religious leader must blend worship, inquiry, and formation by creating times of encouragement and exploration, pastoral care and empowerment of initiatives that advance collective searches.

For these tasks, the religious leader must primarily be a *spiritual guide*. The leader must speak not merely about the sources of belief and practice but about the affinities and contrasts between Christianity and other religions. Such a leader strikes the delicate balance of embodying a very specific tradition in a very specific locality, yet remaining broadly appreciative of pluralism in the community and in society. Appreciating the unparalleled pluralism of American society, the religious leader must embody a tradition in a locality. The leader must give evidence of personal authenticity and must suggest strategies for finding personal spiritual vitality. Meanwhile, historic religious leadership responsibilities continue. The leader must continue to teach and to preach and to administer local religious life. More importantly, the religious leader must weave these tasks together in ways that form religious community in local contexts. In short, the religious leader must be a spiritual guide who draws individual journeys together into life-giving patterns of shared discovery and social responsibility. This turn toward spiritual guidance is the outcome of at least two considerable shifts in American religious life over the last century: a shift in the meaning of the term "pastoral care"; and a shift toward an increasing focus upon laity.

Historically, pastoral care has meant the "cure of souls"—that is, the guidance religious leaders offered in order to secure personal salvation for their flocks. Catholics, Anglicans, the Orthodox churches, Lutherans, and other mainstream Protestants traditionally have envisioned a gradual form of salvation based upon various forms of growth in the Christian faith, whereas Evangelicals have focused upon a dramatic, decisive moment in which the pastoral goal was to shepherd the person toward the offer of salvation. In either case, the salvation of souls was the historic emphasis of pastoral care.

For most mainstream Christians, "pastoral care" began to be put to different use approximately one hundred years ago, when the focus turned from salvation of souls to personal well-being. In the early twentieth century, Episcopalians were in the forefront of creative efforts to integrate psychology into pastoral care. At Emmanuel Church, Boston, a movement to integrate insights from psychology with traditional emphasis on pastoral care encouraged the spread of a new therapeutic approach to the clergy role. The integration of pastoral care and psychotherapy deepened as clinical pastoral education became an important practical aspect of clergy training. The Episcopal Church readily incorporated this clinical pastoral approach to clergy formation.

Episcopalians also were among the key figures active in another scholarly enterprise that eventually had a profound effect at the grassroots level: the search to retrieve ancient Christian liturgical and spiritual practices. A variety of leadership trends have been influenced by this development; they range from Anglo-Catholic borrowings from the past that would appear to reinforce clericalism to indications that women once played a larger role in the church, thereby encouraging the push for senior leadership roles (including ordination) for women. But the most conspicuous use of precedents retrieved from the ancient Christian past has been to ratify the increasing responsibility and authority of the laity. So convincing are these lessons from the Early Church and later Christian periods as well that, especially during the final decades of the twentieth century, the professional emphasis on the clergy diminished steadily while the role of laity increased steadily. Locally, regionally, and nationally, lay persons act in ways that until recently were reserved for the clergy and religious. It would be wrong to suggest that this trend signals an anticlerical shift, just as it would be wrong to suggest that spiritual energies in the culture will sweep away religious institutions. But the priority of the spiritual search means that religious life has taken a decisive turn, and that turn requires adjustment of the forms of religious leadership.

Of course, religious leaders will continue to have social roles, and religious leadership often will be the prerogative of persons who fill professional roles. Certain tasks, such as preaching, teaching, presiding at worship, and guiding people through key transitions in life will remain largely or exclusively the role of ordained ministry. But there will also be a growing need to clarify the respective roles of laity and clergy. Whether ordained or lay, religious leaders increasingly must craft styles of leadership that match their personal gifts to the demands of their contexts. As situations differ, leaders must alternately become custodians, reformers, activists, and guardians. They also must exhibit attributes of pastoral care-giver—but of the more personalized and less professionalized variety. Finally—whether they are clergy or laity—they must be attuned and committed to full lay participation. Today, the role that best unites all these styles and attributes is that of the spiritual guide.

THE CHALLENGE OF GOOD LEADERSHIP

LEADERSHIP FORMATION

The ideal of the spiritual guide has emerged from grassroots ferment about the religious life and the form of the church, and it has spread to the point of becoming a broad consensus. But how do Episcopalians express this ideal? How can they translate their new vision of the church and of its leadership into practical forms of church life? A variety of challenges confront them and make this a daunting task. Yet, as a whole, these challenges confirm that leadership has become the central issue for Episcopalians. In our interviews, numerous respondents expressed ambivalence regarding their own leadership capabilities as well as those of persons in the church hierarchy. Many respondents told of having sought help with difficult issues only to be disappointed with the responses of diocesan offices. We explored their stories and noted their emphasis upon the leader as spiritual guide. Then we asked them what characteristics distinguished effective leadership from ineffective. Respondents were eager to discuss how well Episcopal leaders and holders of church offices perform. They identified challenges and reflected on the steps good leaders take. They reported approaches and practices they considered ineffective. Many demonstrated awareness of expectations of leaders and impatience with styles and structures that remained stuck in the past. These observations reveal the outline of good leadership.

Effective leadership is understood to be complex and challenging. In the words of one respondent, "I wish somebody would finally put the basics of faith in order for everyone but do that without sacrificing the rich and creative differences we bring. We want to be engaged with and own our programs, but we find our time and energy just stretched beyond their limits. We really do want to be welcoming to others, but we find some of those who come through the door beyond our tolerance and threatening our core commitments."

To repeat a very useful quote on leadership already used in chapter three, another leader said:

> Developing lay leadership is a major need here. We want to be more effective leaders in the church and the world, but where is the preparation? I don't think we're just supposed to be junior priests. We have different roles and responsibilities. But how do I practice my faith in my job, where power and authority are such issues? How do I practice my faith in my neighborhood and right here in church? What should I do when a volunteer drops the ball? I wish there were resources to help us become better leaders.

Learning how to be effective leaders in voluntary religious organizations is a challenge, especially to people with strong work experience and demanding careers. Those who have come through difficult experiences in congregations agree that they should place inclusiveness and community above efficiency, even when important decisions have to be postponed to find mutual solutions. However, respondents often wondered by what authority and guidelines they should proceed. Some sensed that their approach to situations in their congregations should be different from work situations. Some grasped the differences between informal influence and formal authority. But many were unclear about how and when to use each approach or in what ways their Episcopal tradition might instruct them and others in the church.

"We are so busy here that we're just exhausted, and then we aren't sure how to work together effectively on our ministries," explained one woman. "Every one of us works full-time in a demanding job, and only the retired people have much time and energy to work on church projects. I try to think of my job as a form of ministry, but often it's really just busy work. By the end of the day, I don't have anything left to give to anybody. There are so many needs, but you just can't do everything. How should I set priorities in my efforts? How do we become effective leaders and develop useful ministries? We need help with such issues."

Confusion over priorities, authority, and responsibilities were not limited to lay leaders in congregations. Among seminarians and clergy, similar sentiments were heard. At one Episcopal seminary, a group of students quickly identified leadership as a major challenge. "Our church needs to have a clear vision for forming leaders. Many of us are on different terrains, and we need to decide where we are going together and how to get there. We should be about forming true leaders."

How they would distinguish between the leadership roles of clergy and laity was not clear. "Stronger lay leadership is important," offered one student. "It can't be just the priest's responsibility." "But what does that really mean," asked another; "Who should do what?" A third added, "It is easy for some people just to dismiss the clergy and others discount the laity. We need to find good ways to get experienced CEOs involved and together learn about truly *religious* leadership."

This discussion began with a strong endorsement of better lay leadership but then grew ambiguous when participants tried to differentiate the roles of clergy and lay persons or to specify the distinctions of religious leadership. "Simply saying 'leadership must be the catalyst' is appealing but still incomplete," summed up one participant. "We've spent a lot of time and energy on aspects of leadership but have few clear conclusions to show from the effort, beyond the observation that we aren't happy with what we've seen going on."

Yet on one broad aspect of leadership, Episcopalians readily agree: the leader must be one who embodies certain personal traits and must be someone of unquestioned character. One lay person emphasized that a priest must be "able to communicate and [be] sensitive to people's need to know what is going on." Another lay person in the Midwest contrasted a cold, dogmatic, former rector with a recent one who appealed to lapsed members. He "really tried to draw them back. He had meetings with them and with the parish. There were lots of tears. Then there was lots of healing. We realized we ought to persevere on this. We sought reconciliation. Now the anger has passed." In one parish after another, tributes were offered to admirable clergy whose character proved trustworthy and compelling. Consistently, such praise centered on the ability to encourage growth and reconciliation. For Episcopalians, personal character is the greatest clue to the sort of leadership that is desired.

ALIENATION

Respondents in many congregations expressed uncertainty about the reliability of church structures and confusion over differences between the roles of ordained and lay leaders. Many people sense that changes are going on that involve shifts from clerical authority to lay initiative and shared responsibilities, but often there is confusion over how to conceptualize such issues and how to practice effective leadership.

In many congregations, parishioners described conflicts with clergy that had actually strengthened lay leadership. The lay leaders of one historic congregation recounted their conclusion that the rector who had been there for more than two decades had lost the parish's confidence and was not performing productive ministry. "We felt powerless to do anything, and frustration was building up without any outlet. We brought in a mediator and called a large meeting, but it turned into a bloodbath. It was really wrenching. Then things seemed to improve, but just when we thought we had turned the corner, the rector abruptly announced he was leaving. So looking back, as hard as we tried, we just failed to handle it well. I still feel a sense of failure. We're not over it yet; there are still divisions. I wonder what we should have learned from the experience."

A more positive report came from a congregation in the Southeast. "We spent a lot of time and money to find a new rector. We just knew this one was going to be good for us. But he immediately started creating problems. We got nowhere trying to talk with him. Then suddenly, he announced he was leaving. On his last day, he told everyone this congregation was going to die, so we should just sell the property and leave. We were really down, but I'm glad most of us didn't listen to him. We just hung on and slowly turned things around. We built a lot of strength by coming through all that."

Someone from a congregation that had experienced clergy misconduct shared this experience: "We were a broken family, and the bishop didn't do anything to help. We spent a lot of time together in prayer, group discussions, and then searching for a new priest. That eventually led us to a sense of hope for a new beginning."

Many of our respondents were notably negative in describing their relationships with their dioceses and their views of national church officers. It was clear that some people had awaited an opportunity to express pent-up feelings. In the eyes of many participants, we were viewed as representatives of the church hierarchy and therefore appropriate targets of their anger. Those responding to our mailed survey were even more critical than those in the discussion groups, suggesting that we may be underestimating the degree of dissatisfaction among Episcopalians with their denominational leaders and structures.

In part, the disconnect between local and denominational leaders is fed by the expectations of many newcomers to Episcopal churches, who have no experience of a denomination with diocesan structures or bishops and who think only in congregational terms. The feeling of disconnection also is fed by experiences of disappointment with the efforts of dioceses to address congregational needs effectively. Many respondents expressed (and illustrated with highly emotional stories) their distrust of diocesan and national leaders and their disappointment with seminaries and Commissions on Ministry. Clearly, most people in the pews have little faith in the capacities of these organizations to grasp and help with local needs. National and diocesan conventions and convocations were criticized for preferring controversy to cooperation and having little relevance to congregational concerns.

At the same time, there is a longing for effective connections with the wider church. To be linked with the rest of the church is to have one's perspective and needs appreciated and addressed. Yet many people are frustrated after years of seeking effective linkages with their own denomination and feeling rebuffed. "The national church is devoted to causes, while the local church is devoted to Christ," is how one lay person viewed the matter.

"Our congregation had two priests in a row that got involved with personal misconduct," related another church leader. "We tried to get help from the bishop, but he just avoided us. In one of those situations, he eventually showed up and announced he was replacing our priest with another one, without asking our opinion about anything. He implied that somehow the problems were our fault. Then he put the priest from here over into another congregation, where he did the same thing." Another member of this group added, "I sometimes think the diocese is really just a priests' protection society, rather than any real resource for our ministries. What in the world do those people do if they aren't even looking out for the quality of priests? I'm sorry, but I just don't trust them anymore. I hope it isn't too late for them to change and become a useful resource for us in some way."

In another diocese, a senior respondent who was also a corporate executive said:

I hope we will see some major changes among the bishops. Those guys see themselves at the top of some pyramid of power, telling us what to do, when really they ought to be at the bottom, asking us what we need, supporting us and helping us do our jobs here better. The local congregation is the church. The church isn't some set of abstract ideas, reports, or announcements coming from Manhattan. Do they understand what it means to model your faith? Businesses are recognizing the importance of servant leadership and teamwork, but the church hierarchy seems stuck in the past and incapable of change. Their behavior speaks louder than their words and sends a clear message they don't have a clue about what we are facing or learning or needing. That chasm is just going to get wider and wider unless somebody wakes up and makes some serious changes. I hope it's not too late.

Another respondent expressed a widespread opinion:

I have no idea what anyone in New York or in the bishop's office does at all, and I don't really believe they want to know about us or serve us. I'll be surprised if your report makes any difference at all. Are you sure they asked you to do this, or is this just one more empty gesture of pretending to listen?

LINKAGES

Our data indicate that most congregations develop informal linkages with other churches and para-church organizations to find ideas and resources to meet their needs. A few dioceses make intentional use of such linkages and arrange opportunities for congregational leaders to come together to exchange resources, practical ideas, and support for local applications. Some networks include explicit attention to leadership development in these efforts.

Some of these networks have been sought out by congregational leaders—or indeed have been created by congregational leaders—along traditionalist lines. This traditionalist perspective expresses concern over untenably liberal positions on basic questions of belief and morality and over what is viewed as a loss of the church's commitment to the Bible and to mission; traditionalists have inspired the formation of such networks as First Promise, the Episcopal Synod, and the American Anglican Council. Participants in these networks express a sense of having been excluded by the rest of the church and a fear that the church is failing not only its people but also its divine mandate. Traditionalists are not the only Episcopalians to organize along ideological lines. A variety of "progressive" groups are committed to the inclusion of gay and lesbian persons and to other issues that they perceive as matters of social justice.

In between the traditionalists and the progressives are numerous networks that include many priests, musicians, educators, and outreach and service programs. Such relationships offer valuable opportunities for the support and expression of shared interests. However, most who participate in them also see their informal linkages as replacing functions they hoped would have been served by the church's formal structures. There is a widespread sense that the church needs to reconsider its expectations and to reformulate its ways of being the church. In one way or another, almost every respondent shared a deep sense of longing for ways to draw the many parts together into a more effective whole.

While local and special interest networks will likely continue to provide important kinds of resources, many respondents expressed the wish that formal offices and leaders at all levels would become more responsive to their concerns and serve their needs. Their disappointment with formal offices can turn to disaffection and diminishing interest in providing financial support or participation from congregations. Such occasions as diocesan and national conventions draw especially sharp criticism for their reliance upon legislative models that invite conflict and polarize issues, rather than draw people together to work on shared concerns and affirmations. A broad range of Episcopalians believe they have no influence with official leaders and see bridging the chasm between the local and institutional church as hopeless; others no longer even hope for any reconnection, considering it pointless, even undesirable. Without such changes, local financial support for wider church offices and structures can be expected to decline.

"The diocesan and national conventions are taking us away from the important issues of faith and discipleship and into more political conflicts and self-righteous judgments," observed a senior leader in one congregation who had participated in a number of these conventions. He continued:

> Who plans those agendas, and what in the world are they thinking? I wish we could find a way to just stop all the resolutions and debates and voting. Can't we spend the time on what we really care about in congregations? We are searching for good ideas about developing missions and carrying out ministries, about engaging newcomers and teaching our children, about leading and serving and growing. I hope we can find ways to learn practical things from each other and grow together in faith, instead of debating right versus left political issues and voting things up or down. That certainly has nothing to do with us, and I just don't see any reason for going to them anymore.

On the other hand, many Episcopalians find that their linkages to official church structures have been beneficial. Even in congregations where lay initiative is emphasized, there is often a strong sense of personal relationship between the lay leaders and their bishop. Asked to name their most important resources, they cited the bishop and the canon missioner of their diocese. "We're the bishop's pet," one person joked. But as they chuckled, their respect for their bishop and diocese was clear.

In summary, Episcopal congregations are vital in their faith and actively engaged in ministries in their communities. Clergy and lay roles are changing, with greater emphasis on lay leadership. Many of these lay leaders are impatient with wider church structures and offices, and in their place they are developing extensive networks for sharing ideas and practical resources. Popular stories of the decline of the church do not fit local Episcopal congregations, but they do convey the substance of some local sentiment toward the church's diocesan and national offices.

EFFECTIVE LEADERSHIP

While there are a variety of challenges to finding good leadership, Episcopalians are devising creative ways to do so. Episcopalians have become convinced that leadership must be rooted in a lively spirituality, the sources of which should be diverse, and the outcome of which should be innovative forms of local initiative. As a result, Episcopalians at the local level seek effective leadership in a wide variety of ways, picking and choosing among resources as practicality permits. As they do, several themes surface consistently: mission, organizing for action, networks, and coping with problems. We begin our descriptions of these with the one that our respondents consistently emphasized when they discussed leadership: *mission.*

MISSION

Along with local dissatisfactions expressed over the actions and offices of the wider denomination, our respondents had much to say positively about leadership and teamwork in the Episcopal Church, but their stories usually drew upon encounters with local leaders. Only occasionally did they include regional leaders whose approaches and practices were considered helpful and inspiring. Their descriptions of effective leadership experiences suggest patterns of new life in the church.

The element of leadership they emphasized most often was the importance of a clear sense of mission or vocation. Many local groups told of having spent time examining local circumstances, identifying issues or problems needing attention, coming to agreement about one or more challenges they felt called to address together, and initiating programs or activities to work on them. They reported having discerned a clear and shared sense of being called by God to carry out their work. Issues addressed by these groups varied widely, ranging from homeless shelters, supportive services for immigrants, after-school activities for children, spiritual formation programs, and various forms of support for clinics and schools in their communities and in other countries. Some programs occurred within the congregation; others

occurred without. Some were cooperative efforts with other congregations or organizations. The intent or format varied widely;
what mattered to these congregations was that their program life
arise from a clear sense of mission. In turn, the congregation's
mission dictated the shape of its leadership style. Often, both the
mission and the style of leadership that accompanied it took a
strikingly innovative direction.

Explained one respondent who chaired the board of a new
Episcopal school:

> Our congregation had gone through a strategic-planning
> process. We concluded that there were several important
> things we were being called to do. Among them was the
> matter of education for our children. The public schools in
> this city just aren't doing a very good job, and there is
> absolutely no attention to the religious dimensions of life.
> We were delighted to learn that some people in the other
> large Episcopal church across town were coming to the same
> conclusion. So we began getting together to discuss what we
> might do together to address the gap. But immediately we
> ran into some big barriers. There were people in both con-
> gregations opposed to the idea of developing a private
> school under church auspices, saying that would detract
> energy from improving the public schools. Others said we
> would eventually "sell out" to the interests of wealthy cor-
> porations. They contacted the bishop, who joined in opposing
> our effort. He sent the suffragan, who said we would not be
> committed to diversity but just set up a little-needed white
> 'finishing school.' When it comes down to having to choose
> between money and diversity, you will choose money,' he
> charged. But those of us who saw the importance of some-
> thing wholly new pressed ahead and developed a planning
> team.

She continued, "There were lots of challenges and differences among us about how to proceed. But we spent a lot of time
talking and praying about how to move forward. We felt a growing
sense of interest, energy, and commitment to a mission of serving
children, not just our own but also those who couldn't escape the
worst schools in the inner city. That became a powerful energizer.
The process seemed to take on a life of its own. We felt called to

do this and make sure the school really served the community and stayed linked to our churches. We have clearly demonstrated that the critics were wrong."

When asked what was the most important thing they had learned about leadership, members of this group were unanimous and clear in their response: "Be clear about mission and vision. Know who you are before you get started, and then make sure your mission is the frame for every decision you make."

At the outset of such efforts, leaders such as these took the initiative and expressed a sense of calling or vocation to work on some problem or concern in the world. They invited others to join them in addressing the matter. They had the credibility or even the charisma to draw together people who shared the concern. Taking initiative, articulating the issues, and inviting open discussion among participants were essential early steps. In a few cases, diocesan leaders invited such discussions, urging local congregations to attend to needs in their communities, but most often such initiatives began among members of local congregations.

Sometimes, a congregation's leaders find that it is difficult to shape a new initiative. The ends and means may not be apparent. The challenges facing a congregation may be ambiguous or not clearly defined in the minds of parishioners. In such instances our respondents told us that a phase of group discernment and clarification was necessary. Many participants told of examining the current realities of their external environment or community as well as the internal environment—the gifts, talents, capacities and track record of the people involved. In the words of one respondent, "Get to know your market, the need for and interest in what you think should be done. Make sure there is a demand for what you want to offer and not some other good resource already filling what you think is a gap. At the same time, you have to see if you have the people and resources necessary to do what you think needs to be done so the project can be carried out."

Another explained, "We reflected together on questions of what were the most important challenges facing us, what gifts we had to use, who we are, and what was God calling us to do and be." In these deliberations, participants identified and examined opportunities, barriers, problems, threats, and possibilities for their action, considering all of them in light of their core beliefs and values.

In the words of another respondent, "Our group talked a lot and prayed together about questions like: What are the specific circumstances we want to address? How do our values, beliefs, and sense of shared vocation shape how we want to direct such change? In what ways does our faith transform our assumptions about the situation and possible actions? What gifts, skills, and resources do we have that can be applied to the situation? Who else is working on this matter and how might we link with them?" Drawing upon such considerations, the respondent and his fellow committee members formulated a statement of shared vocation, purpose, and mission that set forth their intentions for the future.

The data demonstrate that any common stated purpose tends to exhibit differences of value and intention in the beginning, but effective leaders will take an adaptive approach and work to make sure that all views are heard and respected and that the concluding statement of mission is not only acceptable to all but motivated by all.[16]

The respondent continued his narrative:

> When the social service agency first asked us to provide shelter in our common room for the homeless in this town one night each month, several of the parents of young children objected, due to the possible danger to kids. We went slowly and engaged everyone in extensive discussions. Eventually, we agreed to try it for one night and see what happened. Of course, nothing bad happened, so we extended it a little longer. Soon, those same parents and their kids were here to help set up the cots, make the beds, prepare the meals, and do the cleaning up afterward. Now we wonder why it took us so long to get going. Those with the vision had to have lots of patience with the rest of us.

ORGANIZING FOR ACTION

Once the foundation of a shared mission was in place, teams were able to identify the particular tasks needing to be done to carry it out. Formulating work plans for achieving intentions began with specifying goals for each dimension, answering the question of "What specific results do we want to see?"

One respondent explained, "We identified what we wanted to accomplish and what evidence of success would look like. Then we set clear work assignments and timetables, based on the various particular talents and gifts of participants. Unexpected things came up, so deadlines had to be adjusted as we went along. There were some gaps in our skills and resources, and we soon recognized we would have to recruit others to join us for the vision to become reality."

Specifying tasks, allocating them to people for implementation, and devising ways to coordinate efforts and communicate progress are essential components for effective action. Whether they are volunteers in a congregation or paid staff in a community service program or school, the group must make sure that the required people and skills are recruited, linked with the mission, and then deployed efficiently.

One respondent explained, "We soon outgrew the office space the church had given us and had to look for bigger accommodations. Some members of our project team from another church found some unused rooms there and persuaded the vestry to let us move there. That led to greater visibility for the project and to more volunteers from that congregation. We came out of the experience far stronger than we went in."

Effective leaders sought to make sure that everyone understood what was expected, how that made use of their gifts, and how they linked to the group's overall vocation, goals, and commitments. The leader reminded participants of their responsibility for solving problems as a team and maintaining accountability for use of resources. They invited members to identify how they would communicate progress and barriers as well as what the group would do when problems arose. They also looked for ways to recognize successes.

"We couldn't afford a new building for our program so decided to move ahead temporarily with some prefabricated structures. Of course, we would have liked better facilities, but this step allowed us to move ahead in a big way and do so more quickly. We proudly invited everyone to an open house, so they could see what we were doing. We were as proud of those little buildings as kings in a castle."

Roles and responsibilities for carrying out their projects were developed with careful attention to ensure that energy and resources were used efficiently and effectively. In addition to assigning very specific duties, they also identified those people who would coordinate people and tasks in order to sustain communication among participants and congregations, guide new participants, obtain and distribute materials, and lead periodic meetings to plan future activities. Care also was taken to differentiate lay and clergy roles to ensure that responsibilities and expectations were understood by all.

"Make sure everybody knows what is expected of him, or you'll have unnecessary conflicts," advised one program leader. Another added, "Don't wait around for the rector to do things or for people to guess what needs to be done. Draw upon lots of people's skills, interests, and expertise by describing what is needed and asking them to take on specific tasks."

The work and organizational structure of these groups tended to be horizontal or collegial, rather than vertical. That is, groups shared decision-making responsibilities and worked out goals and plans together, rather than waiting for some central authority to tell them what to do. Challenges or barriers to implementation were brought back to the group for mutual solutions. These teams saw clergy and diocesan leaders as resources rather than controllers.

"It is important that you get the resources needed to sustain the program," explained another project leader. "But you can't always know everything in advance. We aimed high, and found some surprising moments of God's grace and provision along the way. Some doors opened that we didn't expect, and some closed that we thought would be open."

"Don't limit your growth by settling for small visions and small resources," advised another. "Know your dream and plan for it. Then find creative ways of locating and making use of resources. You don't have to do or create everything yourself. We found space at the Y and more at a nearby church. Collaborative efforts not only enable you to accomplish more; they enrich the quality of your program, and they benefit the other partners, too."

NETWORKS

As discussed above, groups with a vision and a mission often need to look beyond themselves to realize their goals. Although groups sometimes reach out for support of their ideologies, most groups reach out for help of a hands-on, practical nature; they are looking for very specific skills and resources that they have not been able to identify within their own congregations. Such groups develop relationships with a wide variety of national para-church organizations and networks as well as with diocesan staff, other congregations, and local community organizations and networks. National and regional networks tend to supply learning materials, program ideas, and speakers to local congregations; local networks provide facilities, volunteers, and financial support. Mutual support and encouragement are exchanged at all levels of network relationships.

One interesting conclusion we have drawn from the data is that congregations and congregational groups who reach outward for those resources not available within are demonstrating proficiency rather than deficiency. For one church, which had been contentious and divided, the movement outward was an indication of new healing. According to one member, "some in the know decided to do concerts. We have done one—a professor put it together." This savvy leader was able to create an effective program that combined a variety of talents in the congregation, energizing them and drawing them into the larger community. In another Northeastern congregation (a parish which previously had had no outreach programs), the rector's focus had been to develop an outreach program for very young children. "With children, our parish is a much more welcoming place. The focus on children is a big focus for the growth of our church." Effective leadership inspired an effort that not only brought people together but, for the first time, pushed them outward in ways that addressed needs and joined the congregation to its vicinity more effectively.

As already stated, effective leaders link people to one another, but effective Episcopal leaders do something more: they link people in distinctively Christian ways. As one respondent explained, "We were led to who we are and called through prayer. The rector has led us in spiritual growth endeavors, programs for Advent and Lent. We have been persistent in prayer and see concrete success in developing a training program for health care. We are linked into the network of social service agencies that care for the homeless. They asked churches in this community to take turns providing shelter for people they couldn't care for." Consistently Episcopalians describe the pride they feel at having launched new ministries in their communities, even when such initiatives are accompanied by significant challenges. The effort to build a new ministry typically encourages a new feeling of the congregation as a Christian community in mission and creates strong bonds among those parishioners who have invested themselves in doing such work.

COPING WITH PROBLEMS

"You can expect some healthy disagreement along the way," one seasoned leader of group efforts offered as advice to others. "Don't be put off by it. Rigorous probing of ideas enriches the final decision. This isn't just conflict and disagreement for its own sake, but multiple perspectives are important. Let complex problems 'cook' for a while. Take time to explore alternatives together, and wait for a sense of the group's wisdom to emerge. That will strengthen everybody's ownership of the conclusion."

Rather than trying to *fix* the inevitable problems along the way, the good leaders we kept hearing about took those problems back to the group for prayerful consideration and for exploration of mutually acceptable solutions. In times of difficulty, several respondents stressed, it was important to avoid slipping into blaming or scapegoating individuals. Problems belong to the whole group, as does responsibility for finding solutions. Questioning familiar assumptions and staying open to the possibilities of better ways of proceeding or understanding issues were vital for the success of efforts to deal with problems as they emerged.

"Problems inevitably come up. When they do, it's important to take them back to the group for solutions. Get everyone involved in finding solutions. Unilateral announcements and conclusions are destructive of teamwork and commitment," stressed another respondent. "Stick together in the tough times," advised another. "Insist that you are going to find ways to move ahead together, and then hang in there with the hard work of finding those ways that will enable you to move forward with your mission."

"There were tensions we never anticipated," said a leader of a preschool program in one church. "For example, some folks wanted to charge higher fees so we could have smaller classes, while others opposed that on the grounds that it would discourage those with less resources from participating. It is a delicate balancing act. We finally decided on a sliding scale, so those with more money could pay and enable us to offset the losses from serving those who couldn't pay anything." Another school that struggled with establishing an equitable fee structure decided to set one fee for every paying student but to set it high enough to fund full scholarships for children from families with lower incomes. Both groups took a great deal of time to come to shared conclusions on such an important issue.

Astute leaders understand that communication is the key to coping with difficult situations in religious life. "The issue of communication...is an important one," acknowledged one member of a congregation whose rector had been applying small-group process techniques to vestry members, rather than the usual protocol for a board of directors, "and these people are really getting to know one another." A member of another parish also had high praise for the quality of communication in her congregation, but she went further, discerning a denominational element—the Anglican principle of *via media*—in the way members had resolved a difficult dispute: "What was distinctively Episcopal about how we handled it was that we talked it through. We were inclusive of everyone, and we found a middle way." Unwittingly perhaps, the leaders of this parish recovered a core feature of the church's tradition. Remarkably, the very process of addressing their tensions became an opportunity to affirm the congregation's identity and vocation.

Truly effective leaders understand the crucial need for forms of reconciliation in the congregation. Tensions and even open conflict occur in many forms, but the two most common are differences over the congregation's programs or worship and conflicts having to do with leadership styles. Ultimately the function of leadership is to convey a clear, healthy, faithful sense of direction about a chosen course of action, but an action-oriented definition of leadership risks acknowledging only the end results and edits out the process and even the essence of leadership. An effective church leader who truly is interested in seeing results also probably will be attuned to reconciliation. In group dynamics, as in classical physics, bodies tend to stay at rest; if movement occurs there necessarily is friction. An effective leader simply presumes that results will create some social friction and therefore is ever ready to be the reconciler.

ASSESSMENT AND ACCOUNTABILITY

The stories we have gathered indicate that members of effective teams monitored the impact of their efforts upon the intended beneficiaries as well as upon the team itself. They sought out and made intentional use of candid, honest feedback to reflect on their efforts, make changes in their approaches, and strengthen the effectiveness of their work. "Cultivating leadership skills requires that we listen to feedback, especially when it is critical," said one respondent. "It is too easy to avoid bad news. Becoming effective involves learning how to consider others' views and use them to assess the impacts of our attitudes, words, and actions on them."

Assessment was essential to learning in these groups. It enabled participants to identify successes and barriers, gaps needing attention, and possible steps for improving their efforts. As they discovered ways to assess the effectiveness of their congregation's programs, lay leaders and clergy usually found that their capacities to address challenging situations were enhanced. By returning to their underlying sense of calling or vocation, they were able to overcome most obstacles, because they knew how to consider ways to solve problems while remaining focused. In the course of solving difficult situations, many congregation leaders told us they discovered renewed commitment to the congregation and to their role in it. They discovered that, even in the midst of adversity, they were living out the Christian faith through ministry, becoming connected to their religious community, deepening their spiritual lives, and evoking the ministries of others.

"Keeping focused on our mission enabled us to survive the many obstacles along the way," said one. "We couldn't satisfy everybody, but we finally concluded that it wasn't our mission to do that. Of course, we wanted to avoid polarizations and sustain an atmosphere of collaboration. But that's not always possible. When it came down to one person's demand and the whole program's long-term well being, it became clear what we had to do. Our mission was the guidepost in times like that."

In the words of another respondent, "It was hard for us to hear what some people were saying about us, because we wanted to think everything we were doing was just great. After all, didn't we have great intentions? But once we started taking the feedback seriously, we realized it could be an opportunity to grow. We found a way to include them in our process of deciding on how to rethink our approach to the matter, and they became involved, instead of just sitting back and criticizing. Now they're some of our biggest advocates."

Another group described how they worked together. "We took some time every so often to step back from all the work and ask ourselves how well we were doing, what was working, and what wasn't. That included looking at ourselves as the leadership team, as well as the program. We identified some things we had been doing that put people off, like rushing through their concerns without much serious respect for their viewpoints. Some things you can't anticipate, like having to say 'no' to somebody's demand. But there are ways to listen and come to conclusions that reduce the hurt feelings. It just takes time for a team to develop such skills, especially including how to listen."

Throughout these steps, their leaders continued to articulate the connections among the group's calling, their faith commitments, their actions already underway, their results already achieved, and their ultimate goals. They drew attention to movement and conspicuously celebrated their successes, both inside and outside the group. They also noticed and nurtured the emergence of new leaders, preparing them for expanding responsibilities in the future. Most importantly, stressed several respondents, their leaders modeled the behaviors expected in others, demonstrating accountability, commitment, faithfulness, and openness to feedback for learning and growth. "You've got to walk the talk if you expect people to take you seriously," said another leader. "A good example says more than all the declarations and directions in the world. If you want people to listen to others respectfully, you've got to do so yourself first. Then talking about the principle has some value for them."

Effective leadership based on the ideal of the spiritual guide is taking hold. But can such ideals be formed as practical steps in the life of the congregation? What are the key features of forming persons first as Christians, then as leaders who will serve as spiritual guides? Our research has clarified the stages of leadership formation that many Episcopalians now follow in their local churches.

FORMATION OF RELIGIOUS LEADERS

Developing good leaders is crucial for the future of the church, stressed many of our respondents. Some of them went on to identify important steps in this development. "Becoming a leader is an ongoing learning process, not a weekend workshop," said one experienced leader. "It involves nurturing one's inner and outer journeys. Often leadership isn't something people recognize in themselves until someone else begins responding to it and commenting on it, naming and affirming the gift."

Mentoring is a key ingredient for many. For one respondent, "finding an experienced mentor or wise elder to guide one's efforts was an invaluable resource for me in learning how to lead." More experienced people often described the qualities found in effective, faithful mentors. "Being able to see events and ourselves from multiple perspectives is a capacity that comes with guidance and practice," another added. In her experience, an effective mentor had encouraged these qualities in her and thus shaped her ability to lead. But she added that her continuing development as a leader was largely self-directed and not associated with the church's programs. "I've searched out people and resources on my own. Wouldn't it be great if our diocese offered opportunities to support these efforts?"

Clergy respondents were virtually unanimous in their reflections that seminary education had done little to prepare them for the complexities and challenges of leading volunteer organizations. Some had benefited from continuing education courses relating to aspects of the topic (such as "conflict resolution"), while others told of mentors who had been vital in their on-the-job education. A few had participated in Cornerstone Project sessions that provided reflective opportunities to examine their own growth as leaders.

Some dioceses have begun projects that address lay leadership development. However, these are usually framed in terms of preparing new vestry members and wardens to carry out the prescribed duties of these positions effectively. Innovative leadership styles rarely are covered; traditional forms and approaches tend to be taught in trainings such as these. Only a few dioceses are stepping outside these familiar assumptions and sponsoring programs that truly encourage lay leadership. Respondents surveyed or interviewed who had attended such a diocesan training expressed gratitude to their bishop and diocesan staff for demonstrating their commitment to lay leadership. Participants in lay leadership development programs (diocesan or otherwise) also reported to us that the major insights they had gained as a consequence were more about building a collective, congregational spirituality than about acquiring any particular skills a lay leader might need. "Growth is a shared process as much as a personal one. It involves realizing a shared vocation in a particular time and place, with particular needs and specific individuals. It involves mobilizing resources and solving problems *together*, not just alone," explained one leader. Shared problem-solving is vital, especially in an age when spirituality is thought of as private and personal.

"Becoming agile and capable of changing perspective and direction involves sustained practice in thinking creatively, adapting to unexpected developments, and learning from mistakes—rather than hiding them or avoiding them," said a respondent. "At its core, learning to lead is a shared process, including attending to the development of others' skills and spirituality as well as our own, understanding their motivations and concerns, empowering them, encouraging them to stretch, take risks, stay faithful to the mission, and learn from attending to the results of our and their efforts," reflected another senior respondent.

Some lay leadership issues may not apply to clergy, given the particular skills and specialized professional education expected of ordained persons. The fact that parochial clergy usually have paid, rather than volunteer, status also creates differences between lay and ordained leadership styles. But the same ideals, and many of the same dynamics in the congregation, pertain to both lay and ordained leaders. Above all, both are equally affected and challenged by the ideal of the spiritual guide. For this role, both clergy and laity require new sorts of skills that arise out of a new perspective on religious life and the church—a perspective that views the church not as an institution with a fixed form but as a spiritual community that must be built and rebuilt in dynamic fashion in each locality. To secure this necessary perspective, leaders and would-be leaders require formation and re-formation of a new sort.

Today, growing as a leader has become a life-long learning experience. To sustain one's development as a leader requires acknowledging that, inevitably, situations will arise for which one is ill equipped. The leader who is committed to further development will ask for input and feedback from others and then will consider alternative game plans, shifts in expectations, and new approaches as the work progresses. Effective, spiritual leadership involves caring deeply about others as well as oneself and staying committed to mutual growth and well-being. Encouragement, faithfulness, loyalty, spirituality, teamwork, commitment, respect for the dignity and worth of others are all matters of the heart more than the head. As one respondent concluded, "When we encourage others, we give them heart. And when we give heart to others, we give love."

In conclusion, we found wide recognition among Episcopal congregations of the importance of effective leadership. This is not surprising, given that effective leadership has been a long-established ideal for Episcopalians. But the sources and intentions of effective leadership have acquired new dimensions. Effective leadership today is born within the personal spiritual journey. As personal stories interweave in Episcopal congregations, the locus of leadership becomes clear. As people become involved in conducting programs or assisting with worship, they often discover innate gifts and possibilities of expressing them. They begin to see how the Christian faith, as it is proclaimed and lived in this congregation, makes sense of the rest of their lives. If they are fortunate, these nascent leaders in local congregations also find mentors and guides among veteran members of the congregation. They grasp the long-standing devotion of older members and learn to love the congregation with equal affection. These emerging leaders also look to the clergy for guidance and usually find encouragement and hope. Together, older and emerging lay leaders, along with their clergy, find common cause in building the congregation anew. They are united in commitment to Christian mission in their locality.

Such lay leaders may draw on diocesan resources for leadership and mission that seem apt. Lay leaders increasingly sense that bishops and their staffs intend to be catalysts for renewed mission. But often lay leaders turn to informal, even interfaith coalitions of nearby congregations. They also tap the unofficial networks and para-church resources that are proliferating. As our respondents see it, few dioceses, seminaries, and other regional and national structures are addressing this extensive grassroots phenomenon in the Episcopal Church. Faced with the growing divergence between their institutional agenda and the needs and interests of people in the pews, the church hierarchy is carrying on with "business as usual." "But we already have more responsibilities than we can manage," was what we heard from many official church leaders when this issue was broached. Few of them realized how little credence people in local congregations gave such efforts. Those who were aware of local dissatisfactions tended to blame others for their dilemmas. Such institutional avoidance of adaptation to the realities in the field can only fuel increasing investment in alternative resources.

Meanwhile many local congregations continue on their innovative journeys.

NOTES

[1] Martin E. Marty, *Modern American Religion, Volume 3: Under God, Indivisible: 1941–1960* (Chicago, 1996).

[2] David Hein, *Noble Powell and the Episcopal Establishment in the Twentieth Century* (Illinois, 2001), p. 55.

[3] *Ibid.*, p. 67f.

[4] *Ibid.*, pp. 78–95.

[5] Harold T. Lewis, *Yet With A Steady Beat: The African American Struggle for Recognition in the Episcopal Church* (Trinity, 1996). Gardiner H. Shattuck, *Episcopalians and Race: Civil War to Civil Rights* (Kentucky, 2000).

[6] Prichard, p. 240f. William L. Sachs, *The Transformation of Anglicanism: From State Church to Global Communion* (Cambridge, 1993), p. 312f.

[7] Prichard, pp. 255f.

[8] Pauli Murray, *Song In A Weary Throat* (Harper & Row, 1987), p. 369.

[9] Prichard, p. 223, 230.

[10] Prichard, p. 258.

[11] Gibson Winter, *The Suburban Captivity of the Churches: An Analysis of Protestant Responsibility in the Expanding Metropolis* (Doubleday, 1961). Pierre Berton, *The Comfortable Pew* (McClelland and Stewart, 1965). Joseph Fletcher, *Situation Ethics: The New Morality* (Westminster, 1966). Paul Matthews Van Buren, *The Secular Meaning of the Gospel, Based on an Analysis of its Language* (Macmillan, 1963).

[12] Prichard, p. 261. Shattuck, p. 101.

[13] Amanda Porterfield, *The Transformation of American Religion: The Story of a Late Twentieth-Century Awakening* (Oxford, 2001), p. 3. Prichard, p. 265f.

[14] Philip Turner, "When Worlds Collide: A Comment on the Precarious State of Theology in the Episcopal Church," in Robert Boak Slocum, ed., *A New Conversation: Essays on the Future of Theology and the Episcopal Church* (Church Publishing, 1999), p. 128f.

[15] A notable example of this theory can be found in Lewis C. Daly, "A Church At Risk: The Episcopal 'Renewal Movement'" in *IDS Insights* Vol. 2, Issue 2 (Institute for Democracy Studies, 2001).

[16] Thomas P. Holland and David C. Hester, eds., *Building Effective Boards for Religious Organizations: A Handbook for Trustees, Presidents, and Church Leaders* (Jossey-Bass, 1999).

6

MAKING CONNECTIONS
Team Approach

The physical appearance of a church can mask its true situation. A beautiful façade may cover a reality of conflict, or a building in obvious need of repair may misrepresent the sterling quality of common life within. But for one congregation on the West Coast, the church's physical appearance matches its spiritual reality. Adjacent to the well-maintained, neo-Gothic sanctuary, there is a new parish building with classrooms, a kitchen, and a large meeting hall. With well over 30,000 square feet, the building is a welcome addition and a major accomplishment for a growing congregation. Impressive as this physical structure is, the parishioners point to a deeper accomplishment than the physical completion of the building: "I don't think our success is in material achievement," one member injected after the new building had been cited as a major success by this parish. "Our life together is what makes us, as a people, successful."

"As a community, we came up with the idea, sat with it, prayed about it, worked out details, planned for it, and raised the three-fourths of the needed money before we started and built it," another member explained. A powerful, collective sense of process had carried them forward, through the building program as well as the development of several other successful parish programs. They spoke of several of these other accomplishments, then returned to the newly completed building to reemphasize the point they had been trying to make. "The building is sort of a symbol of our success," said one person. And another member of the group concluded: "Our success is not just program but...our feeling of being a community."

As the members of this congregation described their common life, an unexpected sense of belonging was evident. It was unexpected, even startling, because the sense of commitment among these people defies several common and closely related assumptions made by the media and other commentators. One of these assumptions—from which, perhaps, the others are derived—is that Americans are becoming increasingly private and individualistic in their patterns of believing and living their beliefs. Instead, we found consistent evidence of powerful new forms of shared faith and practice. Against the popular view that religious life is having less social impact, we have recorded numerous instances of Episcopalians carrying out effective ministries in their localities. Against the prevailing wisdom that the conflict in congregations and denominations—particularly in the Episcopal Church—is irreversible and therefore fractious, we have uncovered many instances of ferocious congregational conflicts that not only were resolved but brought the community closer than they ever had been before.

All these assumptions are corollaries to another mistaken theory: that the ties once binding Episcopalians have disintegrated. The truth is that Episcopalians are forging new and surprisingly resilient connections with one another, not only within their own churches, but also beyond. Perhaps it is the phenomenon of the formation of ties beyond the congregation that is the most surprising. Sometimes regional, sometimes national, sometimes exclusively Episcopal, sometimes ecumenical, these new ties—or networks—also sometimes have ideological agendas, bringing together people who align on one side or another of a charged argument. But more often, such connections have been made for specific, ministry-related reasons. Consistently the ties that bind Episcopalians to one another and to others now arise out of opportunities for shared mission in the name of Jesus Christ.

The ties that bind Episcopalians today do not take the familiar forms of yesterday, such as unquestioned institutional loyalty or primary reliance on institutional programs, staff, and resources. There is significant erosion of historic institutional allegiance today, but there are as many positive and proactive reasons for this complicated and sometimes paradoxical phenomenon as there are negative and reactive ones (such as the cynicism, conflict, and decline that receive much more media play). In this chapter, we will build upon themes previously covered and add such disciplines as business management theory and group dynamics to the mix in order to discern more about the new connectedness that is reshaping the church. What we have discovered by analysis of our data is that the new forms of connectedness have produced a grassroots horizontality of leadership that does not intersect easily or naturally with the older, institutional verticality of leadership. We also discovered that this disconnectedness of local and institutional leadership styles ultimately has surprisingly little to do with ideological polarities or "us-versus-them" grudge matches and everything to do with the completely different origins of these understandings of leadership, each of which arose as the church's necessary adaptation to the cultural and religious trends of the day. In some precise sense, the old vertical and new horizontal styles of leadership never were connected, and to characterize them as disconnected due to conflict and culture war is to miss a profounder truth.

THE SINEWS OF COMMUNITY

In one local situation after another, Episcopalians described the strength of the bonds that now unite them. Their stories have brought the new shape of faith community into focus. For example, in a parish in the Southeast, there was impressive awareness of the parishioners' strong connections with one another. "Disagreements are put in place, rather than overshadowing what we're really all about."

The way in which members of this group endorsed each other's comments offers an important insight. Explained one of them, "We are learning about the strengths underneath our differences."

The ties that bind Episcopalians have unlikely origins, beginning in the most disparate of ways: with individuals who are searching on their own for spiritual clarity. One cannot speak with groups of Episcopalians for long before references to individual spiritual journeys appear. The personal longing for clear belief, for assurance, and for the means of addressing life's basic questions seems central.

In this respect, Episcopalians illustrate the insights of sociologist Robert Wuthnow, who has traced the changing understanding of spirituality over the last half-century. As described in chapter three, Wuthnow observed that, in the mid-twentieth century, Americans thought of spirituality in terms of fixed places and institutions. In the twenty-first century, by contrast, the prevailing American view of spirituality features the theme of the journey.[1] Since journey is the literal way of life in fluid America (where people change careers and locations frequently), the word does perfect double duty as a spiritual theme for a people who change avocations and interests monthly if not weekly as they pursue their relentless personal quest for happiness, coherence, and meaning.

Evidence of this personal quest for happiness, coherence, and meaning is unmistakable in almost any gathering of people in Episcopal churches. And if that gathering happens to be one of the thousands created in the "small group" tradition—which may collect people who would not normally come together but for some shared interest or need—there also may be unmistakable evidence of the longing Episcopalians have to connect beyond their congregations. A story told by a priest in the Northeast who had just become dean of his diocesan deanery gives evidence of both personal quest and the desire to reach outward. "At some point last spring I got in touch with the clergy of the deanery and asked, 'would you be interested in meeting on some kind of a regular basis, informally?' Almost everybody said they thought they would like to do that. This fall, we started doing it. I can only speak for myself, but I've really enjoyed the meetings. It means a lot to me.... I think that has been a success. It is hard to quantify. This kind of fellowship in the deanery, I would count that—for myself—as something we've done as a deanery that has been a good thing." Heads nodded emphatically from all around the circle of clergy who had been listening.

These priests carried the small-group pattern into their congregations. Increasingly, the priorities of leadership for Episcopalians feature appreciation of each individual's spiritual journey and response to the personal search for grounding in shared possibilities.

Among a group of Episcopal seminary students, there was energetic discussion of how leaders must respond to the spiritual searches they encounter in congregations. "Last year in the parish where I was doing field work, I organized a men's spirituality group," one student related. He spoke carefully but with barely restrained enthusiasm, as if wanting to be certain his account was complete and conveyed the depth of his experience. "It was hard work, but over the course of the nine months, a men's spirituality group became a reality, and I'm confident that group will continue." Other students nodded energetically. They were eager to speak, and one did, immediately echoing the previous speaker's emphasis on spirituality. "The parish I was in did a survey and found that people were looking for some changes in worship and education. So we devised and revised our programs, and in the course of those efforts, we discovered a new sense of this parish as a place of worship."

All across the Episcopal Church, such conversations and the sense of enthusiasm that accompany them reveal how new ties have emerged, reshaping the common life of Episcopalians. The primary source of this ferment is obvious: the individual spiritual journey does not remain isolated. We have found that the heart of the spiritual journey for the people in Episcopal pews is that their search required some sort of shared expression.

In turn, as people find their story taking collective form in small groups, they usually begin to discover its practical implications. At the heart of congregational small-group process is the longing to connect the spiritual journey with daily life in ways that will bring practical benefit to the congregation, the neighborhood, and beyond. It is this ability to connect the individual to the group and the group to meaningful, practical forms of shared expression grounded in Christian tradition that constitutes the heart of life in Episcopal congregations today.

The small-group phenomenon is not limited to Episcopal churches. The proliferation of small groups for study and worship is characteristic of our times. Unlike task forces, which have a habit of turning into standing committees, small groups offer immediate and intense forms of community; and they can convene, address specific issues or shared tasks, and then dissolve without giving in to the temptation to "institutionalize." According to Wuthnow, it is this basic shift from a fixed sense of religious loyalty to a dynamic sense of spiritual journey and local community that is the most important change of the past half-century.[2]

Those who journey together in small groups often see themselves as independent of old hierarchical church structures and formal roles. Leadership is no longer the exclusive domain of professionally trained experts or ordained clergy. Instead, emphasis has moved to lay persons carrying responsibilities for leading ministries and programs within and outside traditional religious organizations. The old distinctions between clergy and laity are giving way to more widely shared functions, and formal denominational structures are less credible than informal networks of people sharing similar concerns and ministries.

Throughout the nation, thousands of local groups meet for worship, study, and service, and only some are using church buildings and ordained clergy to carry out their activities. Interest in lay leadership is growing rapidly and prompting changes in the roles and expectations of lay persons as well as clergy. Historical developments in approaches to leadership in corporations, in the popular culture, as well as in religious institutions have shaped the emergence of these new patterns and practices.

ORGANIZATIONS AND LEADERSHIP

Earlier chapters have outlined the shaping influences that the wider American culture has had on the Episcopal Church throughout its history. Let us now consider some patterns in the wider culture—including the corporate and public sectors—that have contributed to the most recent changes in Episcopal approaches to religious leadership.

BUSINESS ORGANIZATIONS

Members of Episcopal churches often hold positions of responsibility in the corporate and public sectors, and they bring ideas, experiences, and perspectives into their church roles. But they also often bring expectations of leadership from their professional context into the religious context, expectations which often facilitate—and occasionally hinder—group efforts in the congregation. In order to examine how business leaders apply what they have learned from the corporate sector to the church's work, we first must examine business leadership styles more closely.

In the business sector, the clear-cut dictate of profitability as a single, overall purpose makes for an easier beginning in the study of leadership styles than do the multiple purposes of the religious environment. Any corporate leader who intends to be successful knows that his or her main task is to find ways to adapt to and cope with new circumstances and expectations in order to sustain the organization and grow in profitability. Additionally, the business leader has the advantage of legions of scholars and writers who study leadership issues and produce a steadily growing stream of literature on how to address such matters as a rapidly diversifying and increasingly mobile population and how such factors affect marketing and sales.

The diminished loyalty to employers and to name brands that necessarily comes with a fluid population puts tremendous pressure on companies to attract and retain employees and customers and yet to remain flexible enough in operations to be ready for sudden change. According to experts, the business organization of today must not only be strong but also nimble. Survival in the market-place requires business leaders to change strategies and tactics readily in order to maximize profitability of their corporations. Under pressures such as these, the professional fates of individuals are not of primary importance. In other words, the fluid business environment means that, at any moment, employers may return the diminished loyalty of their employees (mentioned above) in the form of cutbacks or layoffs.

The corporate literature makes a distinction between leadership and management. Both require many of the same skills, such as good interpersonal relationships, self-direction, good communication, and a willingness to demonstrate accountability; but there also are profound differences. Management is the more quantifiable; management involves creating and implementing the processes of work, monitoring results, and ensuring accomplishment of goals. Leadership emphasizes creating environments that encourage employees to achieve group goals. It involves goal-setting, communicating in ways that motivate people to pursue them, recognizing human potential and building cooperation, and overcoming conflict and change.

The distinction between the roles may be summed up this way: management involves doing things correctly and completely, producing the intended results, while leadership involves backing up to reevaluate how things are being done, whether the right people are doing them, what the priorities are, and even whether the goals are the right goals. Managers seek order and consistency in current situations of complexity and change, while leaders anticipate complexity and change and bring people together to understand and prepare for them.[3]

Exactly what it means to be an effective corporate leader has changed extensively over the past generation, shifting from an earlier emphasis on managing to the current emphasis on leading. In the period after World War II, the focus was on logical and rational ordering of tasks to ensure efficient productivity. But the emphasis on process rather than product eventually became all too apparent. As customers began complaining about shortcuts in products that limited their durability and reliability, businesses began to place more attention upon quality. In the 1970s and '80s, business managers emphasized excellence in all aspects of their organizations. The old emphasis on efficiency began to acquire new meaning. The organization and its means of production had to be adaptable, drawing on new technology and compelling personnel to be fluid in their responsibilities. The new meaning of efficiency required that the organization be dynamic.

This trend led to extensive dislocation; some people were "down-sized" and others were replaced by workers who were more eager to demonstrate excellence and productivity. In order to retain the best employees, however, managers had to relinquish some of their hierarchical controls and traditional authoritarianism, relying instead upon teamwork and collegial decision making by those closest to the production line. The "flat organization" came to be seen as more effective than the hierarchical one, as it was more nimble and adaptable to changes in market conditions.

By the turn of the millennium, those studying corporations had begun to recognize limits to the unqualified push toward excellence in everything. Trying to "manage" every aspect of the corporation toward a flexible, team-based production process began to be seen as contradictory and self-defeating. What business organizations really needed was more visionary leadership and less operational managing. Tapping the creative potential of an increasingly diverse work force meant finding ways to identify mission and goals that could be shared and operational procedures that could be mutually designed. Being a good leader involved working with staff to define a mission that everyone could believe in and then to identify tasks and allocate them according to individual skills and interests. The good leader no longer was just the person who assigned tasks and demanded results but, rather, a facilitator, coach, team-builder, communicator, and resource for everyone. As the dimensions of good leadership changed, a new philosophical basis appeared. The essence and tenor of organizational leadership became nothing less than spiritual.[4]

Contemporary experts on corporate leadership maintain that there is no one way to accomplish such a variety of leadership functions; no single style of leadership fits all circumstances. Rather, there are multiple approaches or sets of skills to be used, depending on the situation. Leadership skills are like the variety of tools in a toolbox, and the skillful carpenter selects the right tool for the present task and another for the next. Some people prefer one tool or approach to others, but the best leaders draw selectively upon a range of approaches in order to maximize overall effectiveness. One respected corporate expert, Daniel Goleman, has summarized these styles of corporate leadership and their applications as follows:

- *Coaching*: The leader seeks to develop people for the future, drawing upon empathy and self-awareness. This style works best when trying to improve performance and build long-term strengths of employees.

- *Pacesetting*: The leader sets high standards for performance, drawing upon conscientiousness, initiative, and drive for achievement. This style works best for getting quick results from a highly motivated and competent team.

- *Democratic*: The leader forges consensus through participation, drawing upon collaboration, teamwork, and communication. This style works best for building consensus or getting input from valuable employees.

- *Affiliative*: The leader seeks to create harmony and emotional bonds, drawing upon empathy, relationship-building, and communication. This style works best for healing rifts in a team or motivating people during stressful circumstances.

- *Authority*: The leader seeks to mobilize people toward a vision, drawing upon self-confidence and an ability to instill changes in organizational life. This style works best when changes require a new vision or when clear direction is needed.

- *Coercive*: The leader demands immediate compliance in a manner that activates the drive, initiative, and discipline of employees. This style works best in a crisis, to kick-start a turnaround, or to deal with problem employees; however, it has a negative overall impact on organizational climate.[5]

According to major writers on leadership, the best leaders need to be able to draw upon all styles, depending upon the situation. They should expand their repertoires, building skills in the areas less familiar to them in order to get the best results in the various circumstances they will face. Such learning involves developing greater self-awareness, self-management, social awareness, and social skills. Leaders must be able to learn from situations as they unfold and be willing to use structured forms of process and reflection to review recent situations in search of refinements to their leadership practices.[6]

Beyond developing their own skills, effective leaders understand that they must nurture the skills of others. One of the most important skills that leaders can nurture in their work teams is "emotional intelligence."[7] Emotional intelligence is developed by encouraging group members to express their feelings about work. As they do, their ability to handle challenges constructively increases, because they begin to invite "reality checks" from customers or suppliers. Just as individuals can grow in emotional intelligence, so can groups. A group's emotional intelligence is an entity unto itself; it is more than the sum of its individual members. The emotional intelligence of a group represents the way in which a group develops a collective understanding of its purpose and expresses that understanding in group culture. Inevitably groups develop norms that regulate their internal life and structure their contacts with the world outside their circle. These norms build trust, group identity, and a sense of group efficiency. These attributes, in turn, build the foundation for true collaboration and cooperation—helping already skilled teams to reach even higher potentials.

PUBLIC SECTOR LEADERSHIP

Experts on leadership in public organizations have taken an approach similar to that of experts in the corporate sector. However, their area of study is complicated by the nature of public sector challenges, which can be less clear-cut than corporate ones, and by prevailing attitudes to public leaders, which can be changeable, even contradictory. Experts point out that, although we tend to look to those in positions of political authority for direction and answers during times of social stress or crisis, we usually are ambivalent toward—even distrustful of—them. Some have disappointed us in the past, and so we discount all of them, or else we shift our support from one to the other in hopes that our problems will be solved, if only we can find the right one. Some of us believe that public sector problems are so complex that no one has the answers.

Ronald Heifetz—author of *Leadership Without Easy Answers*, instructor at the School of Government at Harvard, and popular lecturer to church groups, including the Episcopal Church's House of Bishops—suggests that it is useful, when examining public sector issues, to distinguish problems that are "technical," from problems that are "adaptive" in nature.[8] Technical problems can be solved with technical solutions; technical problems have a fix—often a complicated fix but a fix nonetheless—and it is our task to find it or to find someone who can provide it. Examples would be a broken water main or an unsafe bridge. The problems are definable, and solutions are known to experts and available from them. Solving technical problems calls for skills that the corporate field categorizes as "managing."

Adaptive challenges are more complex. The problem is not clearly definable; neither is a quantifiable solution available. Examples would be how to deal with urban sprawl or racial and class discrimination. Such situations are frustrating because there are no ready remedies, only questions when we want answers. Learning and adaptation are needed to define the issue and to develop a solution. Dealing with such challenges involves drawing upon a wide range of information and views, struggling to find new perspectives that may help us move forward, identifying and experimenting with novel solutions, and learning from watching the results. Such efforts need leadership, not management.

Addressing adaptive problems constructively requires an environment conducive to honest, protracted interaction among a group of people whose shared efforts will find mutually acceptable solutions. Leadership is crucial to such processes, maintains Heifetz, yet leadership is difficult to sustain when there are no apparent solutions at hand. Because of the complexities of the challenge, participants may become frustrated, disappointed, and polarized, causing tensions and assignments of blame to surface. The key role of the leader is to build trust, maintain the focus, and hold the attention of participants upon the shared but difficult challenge of finding new answers. Key to the success of such efforts is staying focused on the shared goal and on continuing to search for and consider all possible solutions.

Adaptive solutions require every participant to examine the decision-making process on several simultaneous levels. It is not enough to assess the data, the latest project proposals, the performance of colleagues, and other "external" aspects of the process; each participant also must make internal assessments in order to determine whether his or her attitudes, values, habits, assumptions, or working relationships may be hindering the search for mutually acceptable solutions. However, the leader who guides participants toward examining their underlying assumptions and expectations about problem-solving may encounter resistance from some group members. The notion that certain cultural norms and beliefs are but options among many others may provoke anxiety, even denial. Such a leader will be testing, not the assumptions of certain participants, but their very realities, and the exercise may be rejected angrily as useless nonsense.[9]

The idea that the individual is the standard unit of productivity and that individual skills and interests (or defects) are the most important determinants of action is an example of a popular assumption that many people hold as intractable truth, thereby handicapping their group processes. Groups often are understood to be merely aggregates of skilled, self-interested individuals. Groups are means by which solutions are found, never ends in themselves. The way to solve problems is to find the least stressful of familiar solutions and search for answers within the accepted framework of assumptions and practices of the participants.

From this perspective, problems tend to be defined in terms of conflicting individual interests rather than the group's reassessment of how assumptions and patterns of response may have contributed to their circumstances. A typical "solution" is to blame an individual for some failure and to expect that finding an acceptable replacement for him or her will solve the problem. Such cultural assumptions are held tenaciously, and it is difficult to direct attention toward other explanations of what may have disabled the group.[10]

The role of the effective leader is to help group participants to identify the adaptive challenge they face and to explore how their assumptions, definitions, norms, and practices might threaten their collective goals or create conflict within the group. The effective leader resists the pressure from others to scapegoat individuals or to adopt assumptions or solutions too quickly. Work is continually returned to the group itself, and attention is kept focused on issues instead of stress-reducing distractions. Along the way, the leader draws attention to what the group is learning and supports recognition of its movement and change.

MISSION AND LEADERSHIP

The complexities and challenges of leadership in religious organizations are at least as great as those in other types of organizations; indeed, the challenges probably are greater, given the complex and multiple purposes of most religious organizations. However, many ideas about leadership from the corporate and public sectors are surprisingly applicable to religious organizations. Even more surprising is how applicable to secular sectors some spiritual principles have proven to be.

The core organizing principle of religious organizations is their concept of mission—and of coming up with a formal, written statement of that mission. This principle, first emphasized by religious organizations, has been widely borrowed by a variety of other organizations. Without a clear and compelling sense of mission or purpose, no organization will thrive. One basic task of leaders is to push for a persuasive statement of mission that all participants in the organization can share in pursuing with dedication and commitment. Peter Drucker, an Episcopalian and an expert on corporate organizations who turned his attention to nonprofit organizations, emphasized that, if a mission statement is to be effective, it must be intelligible, meaningful, and motivating to organizational members as well as to outsiders. A clear statement of mission defines the organization's identity in a way that offers substantive purpose to participants in the organization's work. A sufficiently dynamic purpose statement will encourage others who are not yet enlisted in the organization to offer their support.[11]

In addition to inspiring people to fulfill a mission, religious leaders must also do most of the things secular leaders do. They must be managers in the sense of running things efficiently. No less than a business, a religious organization must be concerned about the bottom-line, fundraising, and marketing, however different their vocabulary may be to describe such endeavors.

Religious leaders must also be leaders in much the same style as corporate and public sector leaders. They must take risks, think creatively, act proactively, plan strategically, and convey a sense of commitment to a vision of the future, basing their tasks and resources on that desired future.[12] Unlike the corporate leader, the religious leader may work predominantly with volunteers—indeed may *be* a volunteer—but overall, effective leadership in any field of endeavor draws upon a similar range of competencies that enable the leader to attend equally to the people and operations of the organization and to the foundations and strategies that support its purpose and mission.[13]

While effective leadership in all sorts of organizations calls for many similar skills, there are distinctive requirements for religious leaders, who must go well beyond the reactive basics of managing and even beyond the proactive creative functions of leadership. Religious leaders must offer those involved in the mission of their organization a level of meaning and fulfillment that are not strictly necessary in other sectors.[14] Studies of outstanding leaders of religious organizations invariably found them to be focused on the deeper meanings of life events and experiences. They spoke of grounding their lives in an awareness of the presence of God and of seeking to demonstrate the importance of faith and values to those within their organizations as well as those without. Awareness of the presence of God was spontaneously mentioned by these leaders, both as a source of spiritual support for what they were doing and as a source of energy and dynamism for their work. They were in ready touch with the spiritual aspects of their roles, talked often about the religious significance of what was happening in their organizations, and drew often on their mission and their faith in supporting and energizing others.[15]

In a preliminary report on a study of Episcopal clergy leadership conducted by Seabury-Western Theological Seminary, the study's co-directors, John Dreibelbis and David Gortner, found that the characteristics of the most effective clergy include:

- Strong emphasis on mission and vision in their work, that is, on the importance of religious development in the personal lives of parishioners;
- Active cultivation of networks, partnerships, alliances, and mutual relationships;
- Frequent use of inspiring symbols to sustain participants' focus on goals;
- Extensive use of active listening in dealing with others;
- Intentional cultivation of contexts that will support the ongoing enthusiasm of groups of people and foster their creativity;
- Engagement in multiple innovative projects linked to long-term goals for congregational development;
- Proactive engagement in potential conflicts, seeking to build mutual understanding and collaborative relationships;
- Strong emphasis on a sense of bearing God's presence to others, and on the importance of religious development in the personal lives of parishioners;
- Sustained interest in ongoing development of their own and others' leadership skills;
- Concern over disconnections between their seminary education and the actual practice of congregational leadership and ministry;
- Appreciation for the leadership mentoring they received after seminary.[16]

NEW APPROACHES TO MINISTRY

Changing expectations of religious leaders have shifted many roles and functions from clergy to lay people. In earlier generations, the functions of ministry became professionalized, and ordained clergy were seen as having the specialized skills and expertise to hold formal offices of religious leadership. Members of congregations and other religious organizations expected clergy to fill the major roles in ministries and religious education. Laity assisted in subordinate and supportive functions. Most seminaries trained their students to become the professional experts in spiritual, religious, and theological matters for congregations. Clergy expected themselves to be the ones who carried out these specialized functions in the churches they led.

By the turn of the millennium, there had been a strong shift toward lay leadership. Many members of local congregations came to see themselves as called to carry out various ministries and services in a variety of situations within and beyond the old, formal structures. Instead of identifying leadership with clerical positions, leaders are seen as embodying the gifts, charisma, and vocation of the community in general. Growing emphasis on the ministry of *all* believers, not just a few official experts, is seen as a return to the experiences and models of the earliest churches.

The rise in lay initiatives prompted changes in the roles of clergy, as they no longer directed all religious activities. Supporting others' ministries and broadening the notion of ministry to extend well beyond the church itself are new and unsettling ideas to those comfortable with familiar old approaches. Loren Mead—an Episcopal priest and founder of the Alban Institute, which has become the country's premier congregational consulting organization—wrote of this emerging emphasis in congregations:

> Ministry in the past age was the task of professionals in the pulpit...and the people generously supported that ministry. The new ministry is the task of the people where they are involved with life—at work, at play, at home, whatever. Clergy who used to BE the ministry and were trained to be the ministry do not know how to train the new ministry, are

unsure how to support it, and often cannot even get out of the way. Similarly the people are not universally enthusiastic about the new responsibility that is theirs, are not clear what they are to be and do, and are often afraid to get started.[17]

Moving from solo clerical ministry to shared and mutual lay ministries involves transformational changes in the approaches of both groups. Evoking the ministries of every member involves increasing their awareness of their gifts, talents, skills, values, and interests. Author and church consultant R. D. Phillips describes this new emphasis:

> People are energized and fulfilled when they interact with their world from within that core of themselves.... They are most likely to live effective lives when they are helped to live from that inner center. Rather than helping members discover how the congregation can serve their needs, we sought to energize them by encouraging them to learn who they are in their God-given uniqueness, what they can become, and how they may be able and ready to be of creative use in the world.[18]

Underlying this approach is the belief that "we are all called to use our gifts to share in God's ongoing creative and redemptive activity on earth and to grow toward wholeness in the process. The mission of the church is to facilitate this process.... Sharing the ministry is what it means to be the 'church.'"[19]

This new understanding of ministry is in sharp contrast with the assumptions expressed to us by older Episcopal laity and clergy. Their (often implied) assumptions about congregations usually could be summarized as follows:

- To provide a friendly place where the emphasis is on being friendly at the expense of not addressing underlying tensions or destructive behavior by influential individuals in the congregation;

- To assume that the most appropriate pastoral response to people who have been victimized in some way is to devise institutional programs that analyze victimization without considering how to address it;

- To provide an organizational outlet for people who need to feel they are making a difference in the world;
- To attract ever-increasing numbers of people into membership in the congregation and to retain a large percentage of these by granting them ceaseless committee and program duties that will impress upon them the importance of the congregation's administrative minutia.

Such "pseudo-missions" divert attention from the true issue: What is God calling us to do? New writers on leadership such as Phillips advocate that congregations draw people together to reflect on what they believe their church is here for, what it stands for, what it hopes to bring about, and what conditions it wants its presence to help establish in its community and the world. Once shared concerns are established, discernment of vocations and calls to service follow, after which the group works together to carry out its ministry, drawing upon the strengths, values, assets, aspirations, and talents of particular people in the specific locale, but also drawing upon a wide and often informal network of resources. As these ministries go forward, continuing formation of members helps them grow spiritually.

Thus, contemporary congregations are different from those of previous generations. We have described the expanded place assumed by lay people and the adaptation of the clergy role toward an emphasis on the practical dimensions of shared ministry with laity. These shifts are signs of a change in how Episcopalians construe and express the Christian faith. For increasing numbers of people in the pews, Christianity has lost its institutional guise. No longer presumed to be grounded in static, impersonal structures and programs, the Christian faith must be discovered anew and lived afresh among a local community of fellow spiritual pilgrims. The journey upon which these pilgrims have embarked becomes substantive as they engage in local ministries that give practical expression to their faith development. While their initiative as laity has become the marrow of congregational life, they look to their clergy as spiritual guides who teach, encourage, and counsel them on their collective journey. The discovery of shared Christian purpose has become the goal of the congregation's life. Both this intention and the various changes it encourages in role, authority, and organization mark the lives of today's congregations as significantly different.

This difference includes more than the internal functioning of the congregation; it also includes the outward functioning of the congregation, as exemplified by the new congregational emphasis on mission. As we have already observed, Episcopalians generally do not seek refuge from the world in church; rather, they use the congregation and its leaders to make sense of their lives in light of the Christian faith. Grateful for what they have been given by engagement with their Christian community, they are anxious for similar engagement with the other parts of their lives. Accordingly, Episcopalians often are anxious to "give something back"—to the church beyond their own congregation, to their neighborhoods, and to the wider world. In some sense, mission would appear to be the final "destination" of the Christian journey: the individual inward journey that brings one to church in the first place becomes collective journey as part of a Christian community; then one journeys outward as the natural result of this gift of Christian belonging. While this characterization of linear journey to an eventual destination may be partially true, a circular metaphor may be more telling. Mission may be said to bring Episcopalians full circle: they move outward, wanting to "give back"; they return to the congregation for sustenance; in the process, others follow them—others who then begin *their* individual inward journeys. But here is what many Episcopalians actually told us about mission, and it is a perspective that plays strange tricks on both our linear and our circular perceptions of journey; Episcopalians say that mission is the basis of their sense of being an authentic Christian community. This is remarkable news about the transforming influence of the community of faith, because, surely, any objective, outside perspective would view the phenomenon of mission as the result of the phenomenon of Christian community—not the other way around! And yet many Episcopalians we spoke to saw mission from a perspective altogether different from the understanding of mission as a destination or even as a return. Their view is strangely transformed, even telescoped; for them, mission is not the end—it is the means. Christian community does not create mission so much as mission creates Christian community—and that is a perspective every bit as drastically altered and spiritually exalted as Zacchaeus'!

Mission exhibits other surprising characteristics as well. Mission tends to have a diffuse quality. Because mission today is grounded in the spiritual searches of a congregation's members—not in the programs generated by the church's diocesan and national structures—mission is an open-ended pursuit. The goals of a congregation's mission may be vague, the criteria for success unclear, and the roles and responsibilities required to attain it ill defined. Typically, the path to mission entails careful attention to a process of discernment. That is, mission requires clergy and laity in a congregation to engage in forms of group process to clarify what they mean, what they might seek, who might benefit, and what is entailed. While the overall mission impulse may seem diffuse at first, the discernment process is not nearly as abstract. Indeed, Episcopalians today strongly emphasize that integration of Christian spirituality with the practical and sometimes very specific demands of congregational life is the hallmark of mission discernment. But, because broadly spiritual criteria dictate how mission is pursued, the organizational dimensions of mission have become difficult to define and can vary widely from one congregation to the next.

This reconfiguring of spirituality and mission is appearing today not only in congregations but at the diocesan level. We have found encouraging signs that increasing numbers of bishops and their staffs are incorporating creative approaches to mission into diocesan life. The theme of revitalization is prominent in a number of dioceses. These dioceses are now emphasizing mission rather than "maintenance," a sign of conscious efforts not only to increase church activity and membership but to do so by means of discernment processes that link mission to personal and congregational spiritual growth. One example comes from the Diocese of Texas, where a well-publicized emphasis on mission has attracted interest from across the Episcopal Church. The Texas initiative has created something of a model for mission that various dioceses are adapting to their own work.[20]

In an effort to renew the church's mission, a number of bishops are creating retreats and conferences for congregational leaders to consider the state of their congregations and the common life of the diocese. Such occasions focus on the continuing formation of congregational leaders and on the practical resources required for congregational life. These times apart with the bishop and diocesan staff also give congregational leaders a sense of working with the diocese to shape a collective mission together. Lay leaders and clergy report that, because the diocese has dared to listen to their needs and to join in shaping their visions of their congregations' futures, they are more likely afterward to turn to the diocese for the support their congregations require. Most leave such gatherings with an unprecedented sense of stake in the life of the diocese.

Bishops who take this tack are addressing two of contemporary religious leadership's foremost themes. Not only are they taking a collegial approach to reframing congregational and diocesan life, but they are stepping into the role of spiritual guide. We believe that effective leadership requires these two dimensions: first, the bishop as leader must pose a new view of the church as an organization and must reframe that organization's life around the theme of mission; second, the bishop as a religious leader cannot simply be an organizational engineer but rather a spiritual guide who has adapted to a horizontal style of leadership. That is, the bishop's character must befit one who speaks and acts in the name of Christ. More specifically, the bishop must model a life of continuing discovery, of ceaseless learning, and of humility and humanity. Rather than act as a remote authority figure, the bishop must inspire congregational and diocesan processes that will discern what God would have the church be and do in order to proclaim the love of God revealed in Jesus Christ. While affirming the essential tenets of Christian faith, the bishop today must ask more than answer, must encourage and inspire more than order or direct, and must embody more than administer. We are encouraged to find a number of bishops who understand the contemporary shape of organizational life and leadership and who can adapt its precepts to the changing life of the church. Increasingly, there are bishops who grasp that the church is becoming more a spiritual community than a religious institution.

Across the congregations and dioceses of the Episcopal Church there are lay and ordained leaders who are taking new approaches to leadership. There are common features to these approaches though hardly complete congruity. Often lay and ordained leaders emphasize mission; in pursuit of it, today's Episcopal Church leaders attempt to integrate broadly spiritual themes such as "place" and "journey" with the practical dimensions of congregational and diocesan life, such as the administration of property, fundraising, and staff oversight. There is a shared, horizontal sense of being a religious community rather than a hierarchical, vertical sense of being a religious institution. Authority is presumed to flow from the egalitarian functioning of the congregation and the diocese. Accordingly, lay and ordained leaders emphasize the ministries of all baptized persons and seek to nurture leadership skills and participatory forms of activity so that ministries, outreach programs, and community service projects will effectively address the needs of the congregation and beyond.

New wine is splitting old wineskins; religious organizations are being transformed by new views and practices. We now turn to see how these trends help to create the new ties that now bind Episcopalians.

BRIDGING GAPS

New patterns of connection among Episcopalians require leaders who are alert to opportunities. But opportunities do not necessarily arise as we expect them to. Curiously, carefully defined goals and clearly managed programs do not always create the best context for opportunities, which have a way of popping up spontaneously. A much better context is to gather people and resources around some acute need or compelling possibility; the people and resources may come from one congregation or several, or there may be a network of organizations involved. Details or even broad outlines are not necessary yet and, in fact, may only dampen the newly convened group's enthusiasm. The only thing that should be clear to all is that they have found some need that is acute, some possibility that is compelling. Once there is clarity on this level, the group or congregation will begin to respond— not as a denominational outpost, but as people on a journey who must consider how their search for spiritual authenticity might shape new congregational priorities and new forms of ministry. Stories abound in the Episcopal Church about congregations that have gone through just such a moment of intense if undefined calling, resulting in a group which begins to coalesce, wanting to do something...*anything*...to help the homeless or to do something for the children in the neighborhood; and very quickly, opportunities begin to present themselves. Our interviewers often discovered several Episcopal congregations in close proximity sharing the running of a soup kitchen or a homeless shelter, building a Habitat for Humanity house, or collaborating on a vacation Bible school. Regardless of their internal resources, Episcopal congregations told us that they were enriched by devising forms of cooperation that responded to practical needs.

Sometimes the acute need that galvanizes a congregation can be a very painful one to have to face. In a small Southern city, on either side of the road and only one hundred yards from each other, stand two Episcopal churches—one historically black and the other white. The white congregation, which we will call Christ Church, is over one hundred years old and has a membership of more than four hundred families. The predominantly black congregation, which we will call Trinity Church, is about seventy-five years old and has a membership of nearly one hundred families.

Trinity is adjacent to a university that historically has been black. The university's first president was an Episcopalian who encouraged the development of Trinity Church as a resource for students. Soon, Trinity drew the elite of the African-American community. Yet through the middle of the twentieth century, the same white priest served both congregations (although members of one rarely ever attended the worship services of the other). Trinity's current rector has served for nearly five years while his counterpart at Christ Church has served for almost eight years.

The late 1960s began a period of unrest in this community, as elsewhere in the country. Tensions over segregation policies on campus erupted into protests and eventually violence. Years later, when the worst of these episodes—a protest that ended in several deaths—was commemorated, the rector of Christ Church was one of only two white clergy present.

In an interview with us, the rectors of Trinity Church and Christ Church explained their commitment to take a conscious course toward long-overdue reconciliation. Said one of them, "We are called to be examples of reconciliation to others through our own behavior and relationships with one another. We are God's children first, and only then members of other groups. The Bible tells us to love one another. There is just no way that the sin of racial prejudice and separation is acceptable in God's sight."

Members of both congregations joined the rectors' initially amorphous efforts at reconciliation with increasing enthusiasm and hopefulness. Their vestries began to have periodic joint meetings, and Lenten services were held together, alternating each week from one sanctuary to the other. They began to collaborate in providing a free community soup kitchen and later began to develop a shared youth ministry program. At the time of our interview, Christ Church was recruiting physicians and nurses for a free health clinic that operates out of Trinity. The two priests fill in for each other whenever needed, and they are planning regular pulpit rotations. Joint newspaper ads include information about both churches, and they even share "Episcopal Church Welcomes You" signs that greet visitors on roads coming into town. These churches demonstrate Christ's love through loving one another.

They also are committed to responding appreciatively to the increasing diversity of their vicinity. "The recent immigration of numerous Latin Americans and Asians has added to the racial, ethnic, and class tensions around here, all highlighting how far short of God's will for us we continue to fall," a member of one church observed in the focus group that included lay leaders from both congregations. Another person reflected: "People fear anyone who is different from themselves. There are some people of every race who are elitists and will never trust or accept anyone from another, whatever our efforts. There are forms of discrimination that go on *within* racial groups as well as between them. Nevertheless, we must follow God's call to us to love one another and live together in peace. Rather than criticizing anyone else, our task is to deal with the fears and shortcomings within ourselves, find forgiveness, and then demonstrate how to live as God wants. Each of us fears losing our identity and security, being overcome by those different from us. Only in Christ's love can we find the foundation of security that will enable us to overcome such limitations."

Members of the two churches are taking steps to establish an Episcopal school in the near future. Together, they are undertaking to purchase the property that will allow them to proceed with their plans. As a next step—one of many before they reach their ultimate goal—they are creating an after-school program. Meanwhile, these congregations are developing other joint projects as well: collaborating with other churches to establish a homeless shelter, working on Habitat for Humanity houses, and developing a recovery treatment center for persons with addictions.

The diocese has been supportive of these collaborative efforts, everyone in the focus group agreed. Their bishop has emphasized that the Body of Christ should not be torn by the "divorce mentality" of the popular culture. "Each of us was invited into the house by God's grace," explained Trinity's rector, "so none of us has any right to tell another he shouldn't be there, too." The two congregations jointly nominated the new suffragan bishop because of his work on behalf of racial reconciliation, and they noted his strong support for their efforts in this community.

Asked what lessons they had learned, they emphasized the connections between the two congregations: regularly scheduled meetings between their rectors, frequent joint meetings of their vestries and other committees, and the role of joint prayer and Bible study. Their deliberate processes of discernment have encouraged very frank, sometimes difficult, but always respectful discussion. Consensus has not always been easy to find (and there have been misunderstandings and frustrations along the way), but their sense of unity is palpable. Their contributions to each other and to their community stand as tangible proof to that unity. In this Southern town, there is a new sense of ties binding Episcopal churches that were never closely linked in the past.

In a small parish in an older, urban neighborhood on the West Coast, a remarkable new pattern of cooperation sprang from an unprecedented challenge that appeared in their neighborhood. Over several decades, the area had declined steadily and the congregation, which we will call St. Mark's, declined with it. By the late 1990s, only a handful of older people remained as members. By several estimates, the congregation's average age was well over sixty. The Sunday school had few children, and there were no signs of any sort of evangelism that would attract young families. The building had deteriorated, and the small congregation could not afford repairs. Few in the congregation or the diocese believed that anything could be done to enliven and sustain the church. When a new vicar came, most parishioners assumed—probably correctly—that he had been sent by the bishop to close them down.

Then, by chance, a church member heard of an African woman in the neighborhood who needed help with the paperwork necessary for residency in the United States. In offering assistance, she discovered that many refugees from the Sudan were moving into the neighborhood. Several more members of St. Mark's became interested in the plight of their Sudanese neighbors and also began to advise and assist them. They became interested in inviting the Sudanese to worship with them, especially when they realized that many had been Anglicans before immigrating to the U.S. Indeed, some had been lay leaders in their homeland. Welcomed to St. Mark's, the Sudanese began to attend worship tentatively at first and soon regularly. Meanwhile, the vicar who initially had seen only a failing parish quickly responded with encouragement to the congregation's new vision of evangelism.

As more and more Sudanese began to attend, the real challenges began. The Sudanese had few resources—material or cultural—to help them in their new country. Apart from advice and friendship, the older members of this poor, blue-collar parish were ill prepared to help with such enormous need. And yet the "Anglos"—as the new Sudanese members called them—were galvanized into action. They began to scour the metropolitan area for Episcopal congregations that would donate money, food, housing, and clothes and who would provide leads on jobs and counseling for dealing with the legalities of becoming residents and eventually citizens of the U.S.

Ten members—four Sudanese and six Anglos—gathered in their parish hall to tell their story. Though they had told it often to people outside their congregation, in an attempt to connect to networks of support, they seemed to have lost no zest for it—or for their common life together. What had happened to them was nothing less than a miracle.

"It began seven years ago," a woman explained. "We started by providing transportation to worship services. And it grew from there. We got to know people and got to know that they needed a lot of help to get settled. We saw the depth of the needs and looked for ways to respond together." "Our people go out and speak, to tell the story of this ministry," an older Anglo man described. "We go all over the state. And we've built a web of churches to support this work." "Shucks," another older man emphasized, "There must be ten to fifteen parishes that have helped us. Every Saturday, I get in my truck, and we go wherever we can to find clothes or food. We help 'em find jobs and we help 'em with their green cards and with the citizenship exam. Isn't that right?" He nodded toward a young Sudanese woman across the circle of chairs. She chuckled, then added, "Yes, and I have an announcement: I passed my citizenship examination. I am going to be a citizen of the United States!" She began to weep with joy.

The conversation halted, the focus group format abandoned. Instinctively people stood and moved toward her. Across the room, old and young, white and Sudanese hugged in joy. "You should see when we pass the peace," a young Sudanese man said, and everyone chuckled as they filtered back to their seats. Then the conversation took a serious turn, because their deep sense of unity had not come easily; there have been profound cultural hurdles. "Well, let's say it," an older man said, "there is racism everywhere, including in our church. And I can say it because I am Anglo."

"And there have been practical obstacles," a woman added. "Many of the Sudanese don't understand English. But they are willing." A man smiled with good humor as he pointed out a real cultural barrier, "Then there is the Sudanese concept of time, like when you're trying to give someone a ride and get them to church on time."

A young Sudanese man responded, also smiling. "Yes, and for us it is natural to have our children in church with us. But the Anglos don't like children in church." There was gentle laughter as the group recognized the truth of his comment. Then an Anglo woman added, "And boy do we have babies now! I'd guess our average age at worship went from somewhere in the sixties to somewhere below twenty. And our Sunday school is filling up, and it is mostly Sudanese."

"Look," added a Sudanese man who had not spoken previously, "Many of my friends say to me, why do you go there with those Anglos? But I say, this is an unusual church." There was an outburst of laughter around the circle. Then the man continued, "I say, look, being in church with the Anglos works."

"God made it work," a Sudanese woman affirmed. More comments came quickly as each person tried to express some feature of this congregation's new life. Said one of them, "Because we're a diverse congregation, we're starting to pull in different Anglo people as well."

"It is gratifying to see that the Sudanese are taking over a lot of the duties around here," an older member affirmed. "But the cultural differences are still hard," another person cautioned. "We just resolved to come together and find common ground. We want to understand one another, and we have to be flexible," added a man. His comment elicited nods around the circle.

St. Mark's gave a ringing affirmation to their diocese and to its other churches. They also endorsed the church-related agencies that provided money and guidance. The resources St. Mark's needed came through both official and unofficial channels of the church. And the result is clear: St. Mark's has been reborn. St. Mark's people have found a way not merely to survive, but to enter a new era. And they are clear about what the experience has taught them. "The important lesson is that you have to ask, 'what mission is the Lord calling this church to do?'" a man declared. And the lesson of their vicar's leadership is also abundantly clear. "He taught us that we are all God's children," one person after another affirmed. "This gave us the vision for what we could do and had to do."

St. Mark's success began in crisis. Faced with the question of survival, the congregation's aging members realized that their future lay within reach, if they could adapt and embrace the unexpected opportunity. They gained new life as a congregation by adopting a new sense of themselves as a dynamic community of faith joined together in a new way.

As older, existing congregations discover new means of adaptation, entirely new congregations are being born under surprising circumstances. In a small town on what is now the fringe of a rapidly spreading metropolitan area, there is an Episcopal mission congregation, St. Alban's Church. Less than ten years old, the church has office space in a small shopping center, and the congregation worships in a local gymnasium. Each Sunday, a truck the congregation owns pulls into the parking lot and the members unload folding chairs and a portable lectern, prayer books and hymnals, and all the items needed for a makeshift altar. With these things, they make their worship space. After worship, they efficiently clear the worship area and repack the truck. This congregation (as mentioned in chapter four) occasionally arrives to find that the gymnasium has not been unlocked and that no key or maintenance person can be found; so they set up for worship in the parking lot. But this is a congregation that sees such occurrences as opportunities, not crises. If worship must be held in the parking lot, then they rejoice in their parking lot. In fact, they now sometimes prefer to set up in the parking lot when weather permits.

True to form, this resourceful congregation manages to be both eager to build their own building and capable of celebrating their process of growth, which includes thankfulness for and appreciation of their unorthodox worship spaces. They are in complete agreement about the necessity of building their own sanctuary and have even purchased land. Their continued growth (at nearly three hundred members at the time of their interview with us) suggests that they will have a bright future, including relatively few problems financing the new construction. But they also agree that their initial investment—in mission and community rather than bricks and mortar—was the correct one. As one of them said (and others echoed): "The church is the people of God, the community of disciples, not a building."

When we spoke with them, the theme of community pervaded the conversation. Most were eager to affirm what St. Alban's has meant to them. "Being a part of this community draws and sustains me. I am nurtured, taught, stimulated to grow in faith, shown how to care for myself and others," said one. Another added, "Being part of this community has become the way I live out my Christian commitment. We are engaged in mutual support and nurturing. It's just healthy personal spiritual growth to be involved in caring for others." "We value deeply the spiritual journey of each individual," another person added, "and we recognize that we're all in this together, regardless of how we express it. The principle of community has really come to be central to our identity."

Asked about the challenges they faced, they were equally forthcoming. "We are facing very rapid growth in numbers. How should we cope with that? Should we all try to stay together and make use of small groups for community and support, or should we divide up and become several communities?" Clearly the congregation's growth, which its members celebrate, is changing its dynamic. They realize that they face a crucial period of adaptation if they are to move from the close intimate cohesion that their smaller numbers once allowed to the formalities of organization and common life needed to hold much larger groups together in community. Adding to this challenge is a reality that most fast-growing communities must face: as they grow larger, they also become increasingly diverse. If growth patterns continue, the entire congregation may not be able to fit into the single worship service, which has been the most conspicuous tie binding them together as a community; but if the influx of diversity continues, a single service with a single style of worship may not be appropriate anyway. One member explained that their new members often come "from other denominations and have absolutely no background in Episcopal traditions and practices. How do we teach them about the meaning of those traditions yet remain open to change and innovation?"

A vestry member offered a focused sense of their challenge. "I think the biggest challenge will be to differentiate management from pastoral care. Our vicar is a priest, not a manager. Yet we really need to take care of management issues. I think our vestry should face this issue squarely and come to some conclusions that will sustain both functions. If we don't, we'll undermine the priest and mishandle the organization." In other words, their strength as a community requires dividing among themselves the various tasks involved in their common life, with attention to whose role and gifts are most appropriate for facing different circumstances.

When asked more questions about sharing the work of mission, the group demonstrated enthusiasm and clarity. "Our most important resource is the pool of talents and skills and faith of our people," said one member, and others promptly agreed by making similar statements. As they talked about the people and skills available to them and how people and tasks were matched up in their community, it became obvious to our interviewers that the practice of discernment is a constant in their lives together.

As the meeting concluded, one member spoke fervently: "Could we pray together before we conclude? I think the issues we've discussed here are so very important, and our church really needs God's guidance in dealing with them."

In Southern California, there is a new Episcopal church that faces many of the same challenges as St. Alban's, but in very different circumstances. Cristo Rey began when a young Episcopal priest sensed a need and began offering Eucharist and Bible study for Mexican and Central American people. Initially, they gathered in a downtown park. Eventually the group grew, and they rented a nearby building in a blue-collar neighborhood. As a storefront church, the congregation continued to grow and later found a larger and more suitable building.

Unlike St. Alban's, Cristo Rey began and has remained a ministry to very poor Latino people. About one hundred people belong, but only several dozen can make financial pledges. They have received strong support from their diocese and from some of the large churches in it. But Cristo Rey has learned to be "self-sufficient," a word their vicar chose carefully. The congregation runs a janitorial service, a thrift shop, and a community development corporation, all of which have become successful. Most of the employees are members of the church. "We went looking for the disenfranchised. We hire people in recovery and kids from street gangs for companies," the vicar described. They have also built a ministry to poor Latino people who are gay. "Most of them live in the poorest parts of the city. They have experienced much hostility from their families," he explained. Cristo Rey offers a striking emphasis on Christian community.

When we later met with church members, the theme of community was prominent. They pointed out that, when economic and pastoral needs were acute, it was easy for people both within their congregation and without to fall into trouble. For some, it was a matter of falling into street gangs. For others, there were gnawing questions of self-worth and the experience of being rejected. But the parishioners at Cristo Rey are determined to address these issues together. "We can change people's conception of what the church is," one member explained. "We accept people to the church. You come to the church, and you will not be rejected." Another added, "We encourage people to leave addiction, to be responsible to their jobs and to their families." Yet another declared, "We are an inclusive community of transformation, and we try to give people spiritual support and help them to survive in this society."

Some of their personal stories proved riveting. One person revealed: "In my case I considered myself an atheist before I came to Cristo Rey. God showed me this place and that my work out there was to reach for other people. Now I consider myself an evangelist.... I touch people's lives, and I just never thought of myself doing that before." After listening patiently, another man in the group added: "What God wants is economic development here." He paused, then continued: "Economic development for poor people. Our company is not about the material. It is the spiritual basis to develop. Everyone is equal and respected." Another said, "God wants us to work for dignity, for justice, and for this society." And yet another said, "We have worked in both sides—spirituality and real life, real stuff. Work, social issues, and justice."

Cristo Rey has a powerful and innovative sense of being a faith community. But their success has created issues similar to those of St. Alban's. They are growing in members and programs, and their businesses are succeeding. As a result, what will become of their sense of community that began in the park? Are there any Episcopal models that they might follow as a rapidly growing Latino congregation? Or, should they follow the precedent of large Roman Catholic parishes? In what ways might they draw on historically Catholic spirituality from Latin America yet retain their Episcopal identity? Can they blend people who are gay and straight and who come from various countries from Mexico and further south? The mission of Cristo Rey is entering an exciting but challenging phase.

EXTENDED CONNECTIONS

What do these vignettes reveal? Surely one important revelation is that the dynamics that define and guide congregational life are less simplistic than some have suggested. Many of those who write and consult on religious life view the congregation as the basic unit of American religious life. While we agree generally, we differ on the assumptions about congregational insularity that usually follow.

According to the theorists, congregations are naturally aloof from their social and religious environments and are often in conflict with them. Heroic efforts are required by local leaders to pull their congregations out of their natural inertia and isolation in order to get them to look beyond themselves for resources or connections with others, official or unofficial. The likeliest way to motivate congregations to reach outside themselves—according to this line of argument—is to tap into their desire to form like-minded coalitions of an ideological (and often emotionally charged) nature. But motivations such as these prove ephemeral.

Against this popular and influential view of congregational life, we pose a different assessment. We disagree that the cohesive force that qualifies the congregation as the basic unit of religious life in America necessarily leads to insularity, and we offer as evidence the many Episcopal congregations that are creating and sustaining a wide variety of extended networks. These vary from clusters of congregations committed to sustaining shared ministries, to coalitions of interested people from various congregations who combine their resources to launch innovative ministries, to more formally organized networks. Far from being narrowly and inwardly focused, Episcopalians are extending the reach of their concerns in multiple ways, and they do so readily, widely, and effectively.

CLUSTERS OF CONGREGATIONS

In a middle-class suburb of a major metropolitan center, there are three Episcopal churches in close proximity, with closely linked histories. The Church of the Holy Comforter is the oldest of the three; St. Clement's was begun as a mission parish of Holy Comforter; Church of Our Savior also was begun as a mission of Holy Comforter, although St. Clement's played a role.

From the 1960s to the 1980s, the suburb experienced considerable growth. In the early stages of this growth spurt when there was only one Episcopal Church in the area, it seemed only natural to prosperous Holy Comforter that the Episcopal Church should grow along with the community. Encouraged by their bishop, Holy Comforter began a mission parish called St. Clement's in a nearby section of the suburb. In truth, there was more to the story of St. Clement's founding than mere mission zeal on the part of Holy Comforter. Partly because of growing pains and partly because of new church party tensions within the mother church, a disgruntled group of Evangelical-minded members were only too happy to leave Holy Comforter and homestead the new mission parish.

Church party divisions deepened between the two parishes as the years passed. What can only be described as an air of competition intensified when St. Clement's began to grow dramatically in the 1980s and Holy Comforter began to decline. St. Clement's leaders went from Evangelical to stridently conservative as they grew larger. One of its rectors contributed to the growing ill will by bitterly criticizing the diocese for various reasons and the national church for Prayer Book revision and the ordination of women.

The founding of the Church of Our Savior makes for an even more complicated story than does the founding of St. Clement's. Technically, the founding parish was Holy Comforter, though the establishment of St. Clement's had mostly to do with factions in their membership and little to do with missionary zeal. For one thing, the parish at that time was not in the financial shape one would expect of a founding parish. In fact, Holy Comforter had been in decline for over a decade. At its low point, the parish had been financially dependent on the diocese. The congregation had had to tear down the venerable old sanctuary because of structural problems; and they rebuilt it—and their programmatic life together—on a greatly reduced scale. Not surprisingly, there was tension in the parish. Some members may have pushed the mission initiative because they were weary and simply wanted out. Other St. Alban's members who had come under the reviv-ifying influence of the Renewal Movement had a brighter, more energetic motive: they wanted to begin afresh with a new style of worship and community and a clean slate—free of hard feelings and entrenched politics.

St. Clement's also played a role in the establishment of Our Savior. The increasingly polemical tone of St. Clement's clergy had begun to wear upon the more moderate Clementines. Disil-lusioned with their parish's stridency, many moved to the new mission church. Some Renewal Movement parishioners from St. Clement's also moved to Our Savior. Meanwhile, the continued growth of the area made the mission a going concern, bringing in many members without prior history with the other two parishes.

By the early 1990s, relations among these three Episcopal churches in the same suburb were characterized by suspicion, dis-trust, and competition. If one showed strength in any area of congregational life or mission, the other two felt jealous and threatened, fearing their members would be drawn to the more vibrant congregation. But in the mid-1990s, the context in which the three parishes functioned began to change. All three churches gained new rectors at approximately the same time. A new bishop urged the diocese to begin a new era of mission and cooperation.

Fortunately, the bishop's message was well received at each site, perhaps because he was willing to try anything that might work. He even suggested to the three embittered, embattled parishes that they consider merging! Perhaps it was the absurdity of the suggestion—given the legacy of ill will among the parishes—

that got their attention. Whatever the reason, the clergy and lay leaders of the parishes began to dedicate themselves to building up their congregations—but in the interest of mission rather than competition. And once they rediscovered the true nature of mission, competition easily gave way to collaboration.

The leaders of these three churches got together to tell us the story of how they reversed many years of destructive patterns. As they spoke, it was obvious that they considered this reversal to be a momentous one; the sense of tentative beginning and increasing momentum in the room was palpable. Here is how one lay leader described the initial period of détente:

> The three priests and senior wardens came together first around a common Lenten series, including dinners, worship, and speakers. The bishop's new mission statement was the focus of some of the discussions. It worked out so very well, so we continued it in the subsequent years. Then we added shared annual picnics and Thanksgiving services and dinners together. These were all very well attended, too. They were rotated among the three churches. In fact, there developed some competition to see which group could put on the best dinner! We tried to notice what worked well and what didn't. We tried some things and kept those that were well attended.

Today, there are numerous shared projects among these churches. The people with whom we spoke listed women's groups, EFM (Education for Ministry) groups, a joint youth program, and shared outreach projects. The variety is impressive in itself; but when the prior period of hostility and resentment is taken fully into account, the change is arresting. Clearly, the leaders of these churches are aware of how far they have come. As one person put it, "There has been lots of healing and a restoration of hopefulness. At the same time, each church has enjoyed many newcomers who know nothing of the past history. They just see the good will and think that's the way things have always been. I'm delighted that is becoming true."

We went on to ask what sustained their healing process. Once again, their answers were clear, candid, arresting. "I think we have just grown up, gotten more mature, and let go of our fears," explained one lay leader. "Our priests have set a great example. They fill in for each other and each tells those at the other places: 'I'm not here to get you to move over to my site. We are all God's church and serve in our respective neighborhoods. We are all stronger when each of us is stronger. We're all in this together.'"

The group affirmed the roles of the bishop and the diocese in their healing process. According to one,

> Our bishop has been a great support. He is clear that supporting local churches is what the diocese is about. His vision encourages us and expands our thinking. He welcomes our ideas and input. His conferences for congregational leaders have brought us together with other parishes of similar size and provided many ideas as well as a sense of partnership in something bigger. There is a sense that we're all part of one big, extended family. Our priests are very encouraging of our participation in diocesan activities and support our service in ministries beyond the parish.

The assembled leaders were proud to note that several of their number had taken roles in diocesan committees and programs. In perfect agreement, they envisioned an expansion of their cooperation and of their roles in the community and the diocese. They named opportunities for more youth programs and also for men's groups. They noted some previously overlooked opportunities for evangelism, such as the increasing number of single parents and retired persons living in the area. As their ideas continued to flow, so did the obvious joy of their newfound collaboration.

One observation seems paramount: with the healing of these three communities came a natural discernment of mission and a natural movement outward. "The local church remains the basic unit of identification," one person in the group affirmed. But "when that is strong, then outreach will grow." Looking back at the pivotal moment when these churches decided to turn from negativism and end polarization, one leader remembered that what "really helped us was the conscious decision to withdraw our attention from all the political controversies that dominated the national church. We decided we wouldn't fritter away our time and energy with those impossible conflicts. That's not what the church is about. We focused on being Christ's church right here in our neighborhoods." As their priority became mission, they saw hopeful signs in the wider church. "Now it's good to see that the Presiding Bishop and our diocesan bishop have taken a similar stance. It is very encouraging."

COALITIONS OF PARISHIONERS

While impressive, the story of shared ministry among these three churches is not unique, especially in urban areas where congregations are likely to cluster around common circumstances and needs, developing coalitions that link congregations in unprecedented ways. In one urban area that straddles two dioceses, a dozen Episcopal congregations have run mission programs together in Haiti for more than fifteen years. When we spoke with participants in this effort, they described how it arose and evolved:

> The Haiti program has been going for quite a while," one person recalled. "It began when a group of physicians in this city who were also Episcopalians got interested in providing medical care in Haiti. At first, one or two groups a year would go from two churches; now we have twelve parishes involved from both of the dioceses in this region. Five or six groups go every year. One of our goals is to have a group going every month. And each of the parishes is linked to a specific village there. There is a steering committee for the program, and we have built up a small endowment fund for the work.

Notable was the fact that a high school student had recently become prominent in guiding one of the projects. The young man spoke proudly of his involvement, which had grown since his first visit at the age of nine: "I helped to organize the first youth trip to Haiti. We were never able to organize a youth trip before. I guess there were a lot of fears about political conditions. I finally thought it was time and got several of my friends together. It was a small trip; we had seven youth and two adult advisors."

Also notable was the sensitivity and restraint shown by the Haiti coalition leaders as the young people organized their budding youth program. Although the amassed experience and organizational resources of the coalition were formidable, the leaders did not dictate the goals of what a youth trip might accomplish. "We set out with an unclear idea," continued the young man. "All we knew was that we wanted a youth trip to Haiti. By the end, we had furnished a church with pews. And we had furnished the school room with benches. We also repaired old benches." He paused, his eyes darting back and forth while he considered how to assess what the trip had meant. Then he drew a deep breath and continued. "The other point to make is that, when we got back, everybody felt they'd accomplished something. We got more than we imagined we would. Like at the medical clinics. I ran a vitamin A screening program. One hundred sixty-two children came to see us. We also gave eye exams and deworming medicine. I guess you can see that my dad is a doctor, and I want to be one!" By this point in his story, he was beaming.

His father had been listening quietly and proudly. As his son caught his breath, the father spoke. "A Haitian nurse wrote me after this group left to tell how impressed the Haitians were with the maturity of our youth group. She was very complimentary. People thought they were actually physicians! She told me how well people were cared for and, in her own words, she said this is true evangelism. It's more than words from a priest in a pulpit. This is true evangelism. The presence of these kids did it."

Asked what helped the trip, the young man was eager to respond. "Well, the facilities there were Episcopal Church facilities, and the priest there was very helpful. In everything we did, he was so helpful." He also took care to emphasize that "all I know is the Episcopal Church. I'm a cradle Episcopalian."

But when asked about his involvement in his home parish, the young man struck a decidedly different note. "For me, the youth group at our church—I've never been able to relate to that." He frowned, paused, then added: "For me it's the way it's arranged. It's hard for me to relate. I don't like all those games or skits." His younger sister—who had accompanied him on his first trip to Haiti several years earlier—had been sitting quietly during her brother's remarks about the youth trip but responding to most of his remarks with facial expressions. Roused by his negative remarks about the parish youth program, she smiled broadly, playfully undercutting her brother's remarks by muttering, "I like games and skits."

"That's my sister," the young man said, somewhat defensively. "It's not just me; there are others who feel like I do—why just play games? But we are not the majority. You cater to the majority, I guess. But when you do, you miss out on others." Nevertheless, he took care to endorse the work of his parish's rector and youth minister, who had supported the Haiti program and encouraged his initiative as a youth leader in it.

The young man seemed to realize that the program and his parish's role in it were not of the usual institutional variety; in fact, it took the institutional church some time to embrace and encourage their program. For a while, the diocese had encouraged overseas connections with a different part of the Anglican world, even as the Haiti coalition in its very midst was flourishing. He was gratified that the diocese eventually became supportive of the program. Above all, for him, for his family, and for other youth and adult leaders in their mission coalition, regular trips to Haiti represented the doorway to mission and to life-changing spiritual depth. "I think we're really fulfilling the Scriptures by doing this," he declared.

NETWORKS

Heretofore, the term "networks" has been used generally for almost any connection made by Episcopalians outside the usual unit of their congregation. But apart from the local clusters and coalitions, there is a distinct category of networks that recognize and respond to core needs of grassroots Episcopalians by focusing on particular issues of Christian and Anglican life. They sometimes are well organized, with offices and paid staff, but more often are decentralized and fluid in their structure, able to assess emerging aspects of congregational life, to sense and respond rapidly to broad trends, and to deliver guidance and resources that consistently prove effective. Typically, the themes they address include basic Christian education for children and for adults, faith development and spiritual growth, and lay leadership development. Although there are theological differences among some of these networks, most take no ideological stance, Some are premised in opposition to some aspect of church leadership or structure, but virtually all of the most prominent among them energetically voice their loyalty to their church and their commitment to strengthening every aspect of its life.

Nevertheless, these networks stand as implicit criticisms of the church as an organization. Their very existence attests to the readiness of grassroots Episcopalians to reach out, make common cause, and share vital resources; by implication, their presence also points to the apparent unreadiness of the church's "official" channels to do so. Virtually every Episcopal congregation demonstrates this grassroots readiness for connection, most of them doing so by connecting with one or more of these networks. The remarkable success of networks can be explained by their accurate perceptions of the needs of Episcopal congregations and by their effectiveness in offering responses to those needs. In the process, all these interactions show how profoundly the Episcopal Church has changed and how it functions after that profound change. It is a church whose members function less as parts of a highly structured religious institution and more as participants in fluid and constantly evolving spiritual communities.

The course of American social history can be seen to a great degree as a history of the development of civic and interest groups; and the sorts of networks now proliferating among Episcopalians represent an updated version of historic American patterns of social organization. In the wake of independence from England, Americans entrusted key aspects of their nation's development to various voluntary associations. Some voluntary groups arose among immigrant groups to secure the education, housing, and social services that would facilitate their adaptation to American life. Some brought together hobbyists of various sorts, or persons with various illnesses and their families, or the parents of school-age children, or people committed to the betterment of their neighborhoods, or people simply seeking social outlets. In historical perspective, the proliferation of these specialized groups and the diversity in the population that they represented are impressive. From a modern perspective, the highly organized nature of today's groups and their advanced communications technologies—which promote their messages and keep their constituents in touch—are equally impressive.

For the purpose of the current discussion, it is important to emphasize that such voluntary groups arise largely from local patterns of experience but can acquire sophisticated forms of national expertise. Typically, such groups gain a social role by filling social niches that institutions overlook or are reluctant to acknowledge. Frequently, new voluntary associations emerge as a way to mobilize public opinion and to give voice to people who have been ignored by official channels.

A flurry of new voluntary groups embodying grassroots perspectives have often foreshadowed major institutional reforms in American life. Voluntary associations are laboratories for new ideas, new forms of expression, and new forms of organization. Their innovations may find common cause with those proposed by other nascent groups in other local or regional settings, each one voicing concerns, floating proposed solutions, and testing coalitions with other new groups.

The next stage in the reform process occurs when a few such voluntary groups develop widespread audiences and promote programs designed to address specific needs that are poorly addressed or addressed not at all by existing institutions. In the recent history of the Episcopal Church, a good example is Cursillo. A retreat-based, small-group movement of personal and congregational renewal in the Christian faith, Cursillo became widely popular among Episcopalians in the 1970s and has retained a core following ever since. It acquired national organization, though—as is typically the case with such groups—it retained a decentralized form of governance which allowed for some regional variations in style. In some places, Cursillo became more

Evangelical, in others more Catholic. In some places, its following was small but intensely devoted; in other places it attracted wide but less fervent participation.

The members of one West Coast parish with a history of Cursillo participation sat down with our interviewers and gave us a valuable twenty-first-century perspective on the program's impact in their lives. St. Matthew's Church is located in an affluent suburb of a major city where homes seem to be either large estates or well-appointed condominiums. Founded in the 1950s, the parish was led by its first rector for more than thirty years. It grew fitfully, but at the time of the interview seemed to have entered a new phase of dramatic growth, and as a result, the parishioners who spoke with us described the welcome but acute problems of an overcrowded sanctuary and insufficient Sunday school space. Besides rapid growth and overcrowding, there were other compelling aspects of their lives together, such as their outreach projects, of which they were proud. But neither growth nor outreach was foremost in their minds; they wanted to describe the impact of Cursillo upon their church.

One man blurted, "[Cursillo] has mobilized people. We've gotten to know hundreds of people in the diocese. And Cursillo has motivated a lot of people. We discovered that the Creed is for real!" In his enthusiasm, he kept thinking up points and adding them in staccato fashion: "And it involves networking and leadership development. And Cursillo is very intentional in this church. And there is over thirty years involvement by this church." When he paused, several others in the group picked up his pace. "A lot of people here are heavily involved," a woman said, "Our youth are leaders in the diocese for Cursillo." Another man said, "My life has never been the same. It has encouraged me to be involved. My wife and I have had leadership roles. It has been very exciting."

Another man acknowledged that Cursillo had had tremendous impact on St. Matthew's but had not always produced consensus. "In the past, there sometimes was some misunderstanding. Maybe people think Cursillo made them superior.... It was easy to have a perception that there were only outsiders and insiders. But not now. We have to be open and not be secret about Cursillo." Another person, who responded by saying that the very purpose of Cursillo was to make connections, not break them, explained it this way, "It was an emotional experience when I went to Cursillo. It was awfully hard to come down the mountain. It was a new realm for me. It involved allowing a few others to be a mirror so I could see and hear God. It took me out of a vacuum. I learned to look and to listen." This thought elicited similar powerful testimonies, such as this one: "Cursillo helped me to realize that I could become who God wanted me to be. I wondered for a while what that was. Then I discovered—my role is to be an encourager of others."

How extensively had Cursillo made its mark upon this parish? According to one respondent, "The essence of this church is defined by Cursillo. People feel encouraged. We've spread something that permeates. Our kids have picked it up. And they spread that same sense of God's strength." Others were not as full of praise, but neither did they want to diminish Cursillo's influence. "Well," one man said slowly and thoughtfully, "Cursillo supplements our driving force. And that is the rector. We hear God's Word coming through. Cursillo is in a supporting role." The woman sitting beside him agreed: "This is not a Cursillo parish; but Cursillo is very supportive of this parish, just under the surface."

The experience of St. Matthew's Church with Cursillo is illustrative of how a network program can be adapted to enhance parish life. It is also important as an example of one network's influence on a generation in the life of the parish, one which may suggest something about how a network's influence is manifested over time in a community. The number of networks—each with a distinct point of emphasis—has grown enormously in recent years. It is not possible to give a comprehensive list or assessment of them. But brief reviews of three such organizations will enhance our picture of how the ties that now bind Episcopalians have reached beyond the congregation in elaborate ways. The three that we will summarize, compare, and contrast are Alpha, Stephen Ministry, and Total Ministry.[21]

Alpha began at Holy Trinity Church, Brompton, in London, England. The current format was developed by Nicky Gumbel, a Church of England priest, in the early 1990s. His works, *Questions of Life* and *Searching Issues*, provide foundational content for the ten-week course in the basics of Christianity. Alpha is now in use by about fifteen percent of the more than 7,000 Episcopal churches and enrolls upwards of three million people worldwide. Its appeal grows out of its attention to unchurched persons, but its proponents also emphasize that it can deepen faith as well as awaken it. Alpha's format employs lectures on such topics as the Bible, Jesus, and prayer, followed by discussion in small groups. People who have participated in Alpha describe its ability to create an atmosphere of open inquiry and unconditional acceptance. Like Cursillo, it speaks to a widespread longing for grounding in the Christian faith's basic affirmations.

Like Cursillo, Stephen Ministry began outside the Episcopal Church (Cursillo has Roman Catholic origins, and Stephen Ministry grew out of the work of Lutheran minister and psychologist Kenneth Haugk in the 1970s in St. Louis, Missouri), yet both of them have acquired significant Episcopal followings. Of the 8,000 congregations enrolled in Stephen Ministry, nearly one in ten is Episcopal. The program can be found in all fifty states, nine Canadian provinces, and twenty countries. Based on Ephesians 4, "equipping the equippers," and named for Stephen, the first deacon and first assistant to the Apostles, Stephen Ministry is a program to train lay people in Christian caregiving in their congregations. After fifty hours of training, Stephen ministers are assigned a church member, whom they visit and provide with caregiving under clergy and group supervision.

Unlike the other two programs, Total Ministry *did* originate within the Episcopal Church as a set of guidelines or ideals that take many different programmatic forms. Total Ministry, as one ardent supporter described it, is more of a "principle of Christian living" than a program. The idea for Total Ministry grows out of

the baptismal covenant in which all Christians are commissioned by Christ to serve in ministry, applying the gifts God has
given them. Although Alpha and Stephen Ministry rely on distinctive formats and curricula, Total Ministry has no such blueprint for personal or congregational life. Among Episcopalians, it
grew out of the needs of small and rural congregations for leadership when clergy were not available or affordable. But it has
become less a means of addressing scant resources and more a
basis of affirming a new principle of congregational life, as we
shall describe. Since the term, "total ministry," was first used in
the Episcopal Church at the General Convention of 1976, the
Total Ministry ideals have inspired an elaborate network of
groups and informal relationships These include the Living
Stones Partnership, Sindicators, Harvesters, Leaveners, and the
Ministry Developers' Collaborative. Arguably, Living Stones is
the best known. A loosely organized cooperative network that
includes twenty-two dioceses, many (mostly rural) parishes, and
organizations, as well as interested individuals, the network has an
annual meeting sponsored by the member dioceses, at which
elaborate patterns of cooperation are featured. Some of those
who affirm the Total Ministry principles and participate in Living
Stones describe their network as a laboratory in which new ideals
of church life and leadership are tested and assessed.

Though the differences among these three networks are
notable, their common features are more striking. As described
below, these include emphases upon spiritual growth, leadership
development, community, implementing change in the local
church, and envisioning a new kind of "wider church."

Spiritual growth: Using small groups extensively, these networks promise a deepened spirituality for participants. A Living
Stones member noted that "spirituality is at the heart of Total
Ministry. I find the commitment to deepening our spiritual life in
the context of local ministry development to be a strong, emerging theme and concern, and there are many in the partnership
who are working creatively and energetically on this."

Leadership development: Groups such as these help people to
understand group dynamics, set goals, develop appropriate

strategies for meeting those goals, and manage conflict. Even the most basic small group must be run with a purpose, an element of structure, an agenda, and a timetable. One author noted that "this is grassroots organizing and, taking into account the ceaseless proliferation of new groups, leadership is astonishingly widespread," by which is meant that the preferred and the increasingly prevalent style of leadership in religious America is "flat" or "horizontal."[22] Or, as one Episcopal participant in Alpha said: "Alpha is a leadership development track. It incubates small groups and allows the groups to move into the home environment. Small group ministry grows out of Alpha. It throws people directly into the midst of action and makes them 'start swimming.'"

Community: The small-group movement has set important standards for these networks. Community in small groups is fluid, diverse, and attuned to the emotional needs of their members. Community is informal and spontaneous but embodies sufficient structure and purpose to give adequate direction. In small groups, participants acknowledge the limits of "me" individualism, but in small groups containing people from more than one church, parishioners find that they can belong to a diocesan or regional or even national "we"—"to something bigger than we are." The idea of the kingdom of God becomes real, even in the midst of the church. One small-group participant remarked that "the kingdom of God is being expressed more fully in the diocese." The marks of community that our respondents noted included: healthy patterns of interaction with each other, a common language that reinforced their common sense of purpose, and a deepened commitment to the identity of the Episcopal Church. The last point may be particularly significant. The networks we examined functioned outside the church's structures in a manner that offered explicit and implicit critiques of them. But at heart, these networks seek ways to enhance the church.

Implementing change in the local church: It is clear that these networks aid individuals and congregations through crucial times of transition. As they do, they promote new ideals and propose adoption of new patterns of common life. The flexibility of their strategies and the clarity of their ideals allow them to be mid-wives for change in diverse circumstances. Indeed, these groups often build their constituencies among people who have already resolved upon change and seek direction for it. One woman, from a largely rural area of the country which often calls local parishioners to be "Canon 9" priests due to clergy shortages, noted the shifts in thinking and behavior that the Total Ministry guidelines—with their emphasis on rural and small-town leader-ship issues—has had on the Commission on Ministry in her diocese. "The way they conduct their business has changed—living first into the conversion process; it is of the utmost importance. Conversion is stressed. Conversion must be a corporate, organic process."

Envisioning a new "wider church": Networks gain much of their energy from the longing of Episcopal congregations for an experience of a "wider church"—albeit wider in ways other than diocesan or national. Utilizing the small-group format and emphasizing biblical principles, these networks encourage lay people and clergy to work toward a new ideal for the church. The church is to be seen not as set institutional structures and programs but as a vocation to be accepted, a fellowship to be built. These networks convey a sense of mission and equip people to pursue it. "At work, since [becoming] a Stephen minister, I just listen. Stephen Ministry has given me the knowledge and empowered me to know that listening and reflecting is Christian caregiving." Or, as a woman offered: "Stephen Ministry makes one step outside the boundaries, outside of the church, and outside of old behavior." There is a "blending of life with the church" and "a sense of being the church outside the walls."

These networks work because they take local concerns and connect them creatively to basic Christian affirmations and wider connections among Christians. Their widespread popularity may say something important about the Episcopal Church in par-ticular and American religious life in general: a deep longing lies beneath the disillusionment with historic religious institutions, and this longing is being acted out in congregations all across America as a search for new and life-giving patterns of connection.

NOTES

[1] Robert Wuthnow, *After Heaven: Spirituality in America Since the 1950s* (University of California, 1998).

[2] Robert Wuthnow, *Sharing The Journey: Support Groups and America's New Quest for Community* (Free Press, 1994).

[3] John Kotter, "What Leaders Really Do," *Harvard Business Review* (December 2001).

[4] Alan Briskin, *The Stirring of Soul in the Workplace* (Jossey-Bass, 1996). Lee G. Bolman and Terrence E. Deal, *Reframing Organizations: Artistry, Choice, and Leadership* (Jossey-Bass, 1991). See also Bolman and Deal, *Leading With Soul: An Uncommon Journey of Spirit* (Jossey-Bass, 1995).

[5] Daniel Goleman, "Leadership That Gets Results," *Harvard Business Review* (March 2000).

[6] Daniel Goleman, "What Makes A Leader?" *Harvard Business Review* (November 1998). See also his *Emotional Intelligence* (Bantam, 1995).

[7] Vanessa Urch Druskat and Steven B. Wolff, "Building the Emotional Intelligence of Groups," *Harvard Business Review* (March 2001).

[8] Ronald A. Heifetz, *Leadership Without Easy Answers* (Belknap, 1994). Ronald A. Heifetz and Donald L. Laurie, "The Work of Leadership," *Harvard Business Review* (February 2000).

[9] Edgar H. Schein, *Organizational Culture and Leadership* (Jossey-Bass, 1992).

[10] Thomas P. Holland et al., "Culture and Change in Nonprofit Boards," *Nonprofit Management and Leadership*, Vol. 4, No. 2, (Winter 1993), pp. 141–155.

[11] Peter F. Drucker, "The New Society of Organizations," *Harvard Business Review* (September 1992).

[12] Robert D. Herman and Richard D. Heimovics, "Critical Events in the Management of Nonprofit Organizations," *Nonprofit and Voluntary Sector Quarterly*, Vol. 18, No. 2 (1989), pp. 119–132. E. Burt Knauft et al., *Profiles of Excellence: Achieving Success in the Nonprofit Sector*, Jossey-Bass Nonprofit Sector Series. (Jossey-Bass, 1991).

[13] David J. Nygren, CM, and Miriam D. Ukeritis, CSJ, *The Future of Religious Orders in the United States: Transformation and Commitment* (Praeger, 1993).

[14] Max De Pree, *Leading Without Power: Finding Hope in Serving Community* (Jossey-Bass, 1997).

[15] D. J. Nygren et al., "Outstanding Leadership in Nonprofit Organizations: Leadership Competencies in Roman Catholic Religious Orders," *Nonprofit Management and Leadership*, Vol. 4, No. 4 (1994), pp. 375–388.

[16] These preliminary findings of the Lilly-funded project, "Markers of Strong and Effective Clergy," were announced at a gathering of church leaders and scholars in Evanston, Illinois, in 2000.

[17] Loren Mead, "Reinventing the Congregation," *Action Information*, Alban Institute (1990). *The Once and Future Church: Reinventing the Congregation for a New Mission Frontier* (Alban, 1991).

[18] Roy D. Phillips, *Letting Go: Transforming Congregations for Ministry* (Alban, 2000).

[19] Jean Morris Trumbauer, *Sharing The Ministry: A Practical Guide for Transforming Volunteers into Ministry* (Augsburg, 1995).

[20] Claude E. Payne and Hamilton Beazley, *Reclaiming The Great Commission: A Practical Model for Transforming Denominations and Congregations* (Jossey-Bass, 2000).

[21] We are grateful to Susan Johnson of the Episcopal Church Foundation for her groundbreaking research on these and other networks that attract scores of Episcopalians.

[22] Nancy L. Rosenblum, *Membership and Morals: The Personal Uses of Pluralism in America* (Princeton, 1998).

7

THE WAY, THE TRUTH, THE LIFE
A New Consensus

A SEEMING PARADOX

Ask a group of Episcopalians to define the church's belief and their responses probably will be vague. "What is distinctively Episcopalian?" a lay person asked, parroting the question that had been posed to her focus group. Then, struck by something about the question, she looked puzzled and rephrased it as a larger question, "What is Episcopalian?"

Her perplexity with the word was not an isolated reaction. "We are all from different backgrounds, so we don't know what 'Episcopalian' means," observed one respondent, acknowledging the uncertainty even as she tried to explain it. With wry humor, one Midwesterner went even further, saying that "no one can say what Episcopalians are...not even how to spell it." In another Midwestern church, one member was uncertain even about the uncertainty: "We hear painted upon us not having doctrinal cohesion within the denomination. I don't know whether that is accurate or not."

For many Episcopalians, the inability to give a quick, definitive answer to the question of Episcopal identity is a strength, not a weakness. Where some see vagueness, they see breadth. "The Episcopal Church is structured but loose. It is not judgmental. It is not out there trying to find who they put down next," according to one Midwest lay person. A Texas church member declared, "I am almost an Episcopalian as a defense against what I see as a Fundamentalist outcry that has swept this country, and it frightens me. The Fundamentalism frightens me." "I like the tradition, the intelligence of Episcopalians, the focus on Scripture, and the sense of worship," stated an East Coast church member clearly and confidently, without further comment.

But for many people in the pews, uncertainty about Episcopal identity is disturbing. Of the several reasons cited for this uncertainty, the diversity of religious backgrounds among Episcopalians is one of the more common. Referring to newer members of the parish, a church member in the South said simply, "Most of the newcomers have no background in the Episcopal Church." Other Episcopalians we interviewed felt that the explanation lay in the lack of programmatic resources to address basic issues adequately. "We needed dialogue about sexuality and faith. There were no resources in the Episcopal Church to help the dialogue," said one lay leader.

Some leaders, however, locate the problem at a deeper, even core level of the faith. To them, the Episcopal Church has surrendered to a theological pluralism that, at best, obscures basic Christian beliefs and the church's mission and, at worst, undercuts its Christian identity entirely. Related to the concern about pluralism is the fear of some leaders that the most disruptive aspects of America's individualistic culture have been incorporated into the church, with dire consequences for its identity and vocation.[1]

According to one local leader, "We don't have a doctrinal center in what we are doing. I miss the doctrinal center." For another, the lack of understanding of Episcopal identity and of its foundation in Christian belief has hindered appreciation of the church's strengths. "We have to know who we are, identify our strengths, and get the word out about the quality of our priests. We have to explain who we are. No one knows what Episcopalians are."

At least one noted Episcopal theologian is concerned about the core of Episcopal identity, citing what he calls the "precarious state of theology in the Episcopal Church." To revisit a quotation we used in chapter five, Philip Turner believes that the attention of the church's national leaders "has moved steadily away from instruction that draws baptized members of the church more deeply into a *common* knowledge and love of God (which is the proper subject matter of theology in all its forms) and toward various forms of social action or pastoral practice designed to address either the perceived ills of society or the experience and perceived needs of individuals." Although theology should be the basis of the church's identity, in actuality it "tends to follow along behind commitment and experience and is trotted out, if the occasion demands, to provide a blessing for what our commitments and experience have already told us is right and good." Instead, Turner maintains, theology should serve as the "grammar" of faith. That is, theology is the articulation of both the church's tradition and its lived experience. In this way, theology offers "the basis on which one can learn to understand and live out a form of belief and life."[2]

On the evidence, theologians probably are correct to be concerned about the lack of appreciation for the "grammar" of faith—that is, for the basics of Christian faith and Episcopal identity—among people in Episcopal pews. But when one probes local belief and practice, a more intricate reality emerges. In most Episcopal churches, uncertainty about specific aspects of Episcopal belief does not necessarily reflect theological confusion or lack of substantial Christian faith. But the problem with trying to assess the extent and nature of disconnection between theology and local practice and belief is similar to the conundrum we encountered with the inability of the vertical and institutional leadership styles of the church to intersect with the horizontal leadership styles being employed at the grassroots. What we determined about the disconnection between the two leadership styles was that they were not disconnected at all—at least not in the strictest sense of that word; they were not disconnected because they never had been connected in the first place but rather had evolved quite separately in response to very different cultural circumstances. Similarly, the "grammar" of denominationally based theology may not be working well at the grassroots level today, but that does not necessarily mean Episcopalians in the pew are not attuned to the issues at hand. Perhaps the theologian and the lay person are talking about the same core issues but using two entirely different languages to do so, in which case our anxiety and surprise that the grammar of one language does not function well in the other may be misplaced.

Episcopalians at the grassroots level appear to be motivated by the same basically integrative impulse that motivates theologians. People in the pews long to understand and to embody Christian belief in their personal lives and in the lives of their congregations. This effort springs from a deep desire for clarity about the basic tenets of Christianity and the essentials of Episcopal tradition. Episcopalians are energetically seeking to identify and to embrace the truths of the Christian faith. They long for a center, that is, for certainty about the core of Christian faith and for understanding of Christian tradition, especially in its Episcopal expressions. They also seek effective means of appropriating and expressing Christian belief and Episcopal tradition. They long for effective bridges to the past, that they might comprehend the church's history and draw upon it for guidance in facing the challenges of Christian life and witness. This longing is neither casual nor secondary to the lives of their congregations.

In many places in the Episcopal Church, the longing to find the core of Christian faith and tradition has a decidedly Episcopal expression. "We are part of the Anglican Church," one lay person affirmed. "We all consider ourselves to be part of that tradition and that is something that holds us together." But in other places, this Episcopal component is less obvious. Unlike similar longings in past generations of Episcopalians, many members of

Episcopal churches today do not presume that Christianity's essential truths and institutional formulations of them are necessarily the same. Institutional matters no longer carry the urgency they once bore; nor are controversies about institutional forms and dynamics likely to have the weight that a focus on broadly Christian belief and life must bear. To be faithful today, many members of Episcopal churches say, one must adopt a new approach to being an Episcopalian. Most do not presume Episcopal identity to be a fixed expression of Christian belief but a dynamic one that must be continually reclaimed from its institutional guises. The traditions of the church are viewed as a living deposit of faith that must be appropriated and expressed anew in today's novel circumstances.

One respondent who was asked to say what was uniquely Episcopalian about his parish's life said something that may help our discussion: "I think the fact that we are unable to answer this question is distinctively Episcopalian." There had been an awkward silence in the focus group until he spoke; then the group became more animated. "We are focused more on Christianity, not on the denomination," one of them said. One man in the Northeast emphasized that his parish's life dwelt "more on being Christian than on being Episcopalian." When asked to characterize the vitality of his parish, he answered, "I don't see it as Episcopal but as Christian." Then he conceded, "But Episcopal resources helped."

In this chapter, we explore the nature, rise, and pitfalls of the consensus on belief to which most Episcopalians now subscribe. We will emphasize that this consensus is a seeming paradox, for it entails both an affirmation of the doctrines of Christianity and an innovative, dynamic view of Episcopal tradition. We will show that the core idea for the majority of the church's members now focuses on Episcopal identity as a way of life that is secured by basic beliefs and practices. Episcopalians today believe that this way of life is most compelling when it is shared. Above all, Episcopalians presume that belief can no longer be handed down through institutional channels as unchanging forms nor be defined by institutional process. Rather, the Episcopal Church's beliefs and their expressions find validity as they are lived in the particularity of local circumstances. More to the point, Christian belief, as Episcopalians now affirm it, finds its primary expression in building spiritual community. The truth of Christianity is located in its capacity to shape local life, rather than to compel local adherence to larger institutional intricacies.

WHAT EPISCOPALIANS BELIEVE

What Episcopalians today believe about the Christian faith and their church's traditions is often the subject of speculation and only occasionally the subject of sound research. A portion of the Zacchaeus Project was dedicated to sending survey questions about Episcopal life and identity to a random sample of about thirty congregations in each of the project's nine selected dioceses.[3] The findings below are clear and revealing. Numbers reflect the percentage of respondents agreeing with each statement.

On matters of worship and tradition:

The Eucharist is central to the life of the congregation.	99%
The Book of Common Prayer is central to the life of the congregation.	95%
Prayer is central to the life of the congregation.	95%
The Bible is central to the life of the congregation.	80%
Small groups and specialized ministries are central to the life of the congregation.	67%
Episcopal traditions clearly define right and wrong for this congregation.	54%
The congregation tries new things without worrying about Episcopal traditions.	28%

On matters of Episcopal identity:

Christian education is central to the life of the congregation.	84%
Episcopalians are more likely to ask questions than to answer them.	78%
The congregation sees itself as part of Anglican Communion.	75%
The congregation actively seeks new members.	72%

What conclusions about Episcopal beliefs can be drawn from this data? First, we conclude that the beliefs of the overwhelming majority of Episcopalians are rooted in worship, the church's traditions, and Scripture. We will discuss worship in detail in the next section of this chapter, but here we will point out the interesting finding that the Eucharist and the Book of Common Prayer draw a more affirmative response than the Bible, though for more than three-fourths of our respondents, the Bible's centrality to their churches is upheld. We do not interpret this statistic as meaning that one-fifth of all respondents disregard the Bible's authority. Rather, we suspect that these statistics reflect the role of the Eucharist or the Bible in the congregation's program life. Thus, to say that the Eucharist is central affirms the primary role of worship in the local church's life. We also suspect that, for one-fifth of those who responded, there may be inadequate opportunity for Bible study, a fact which they would be likely to lament!

We also conclude from these findings that Episcopal tradition matters in local churches. The nature of our quantitative and qualitative data helps to define what most Episcopalians mean by "tradition." For example, almost all of our respondents say the Prayer Book is central to their congregations, and only one-quarter would disregard Episcopal traditions when taking innovative steps in their congregations. We interpret their view of tradition as referring primarily to worship according to the Prayer Book and to the manner in which the Prayer Book upholds and expresses such basic Christian beliefs as the authority of Scripture and the divinity of Jesus Christ. We also include the church's historic pattern of relying upon both apostolic ministry (bishops, priests, and deacons) and lay responsibility as key aspects of its "tradition." It also is striking that three-fourths of the people we surveyed understand that they are part of the global Anglican Communion and not just the Episcopal Church.

The findings from another national survey confirm ours. Hartford Seminary's massive Faith Communities Today (FACT) study surveyed thousands of congregations in all major Christian denominations using written questionnaires usually completed by the congregation's clergy leader. For the Episcopal Church portion of the study, FACT compiled responses from more than seven hundred congregations, not quite one-tenth of all Episcopal churches. From this data, the researchers concluded that Episcopalians have the clearest sense of identity of any of the mainline denominations. In fact, only such staunchly conservative denominations as the Assembly of God or the Church of Christ were found to have comparable or more clearly defined senses of identity. For the FACT researchers, the strength of Episcopal identity relied upon a clearly defined and broadly affirmed set of doctrinal and worship traditions as well as a set of moral values that were "fairly clear."

In this study, most Episcopalians proved to be neither very conservative nor very liberal. Nearly half of those who responded called themselves "moderate," while thirty-two percent were "somewhat conservative" and seventeen percent were "somewhat progressive or liberal." It is interesting that, of the clergy who described their congregations to these researchers, the "most liberal or progressive" proved to have the most vital congregations.[4]

The broader, somewhat two-dimensional information from our survey questionnaire sometimes can—and sometimes cannot—be compared to the more rounded impression of a congregation we gained from our on-site interviews. However, our survey findings cited above do not seem consistent with our interview data in revealing a consensus of Christian belief and church life in the Episcopal Church. To a remarkable degree, Episcopalians express their affirmations of worship, Scripture, and tradition in dynamic terms, by which we refer to the shift toward spiritual dynamism observed by Robert Wuthnow and discussed in an earlier chapter. Today's Episcopalians uphold those very Anglican tenets of worship, Scripture, and tradition, but they do so with a sense of personal and shared spiritual journey, without previous generations' emphases on a static sense of place or unquestioned loyalty to centralized religious institutions. Our research has allowed us to observe this sense of journey and to uncover and to describe its intention: the realization of spiritual community. One church member's sentiments were echoed by others all across the church: "We express our faith in our actions. There are many views of theological and political issues among our members, and that's OK. Underneath all our differences, we are drawn together by a common liturgy to worship the same God. And we understand that he calls us to love one another and serve one another. That's what holds us together. Not tight rules or required beliefs."

Several features of this statement draw our attention. First, there is a clear emphasis on action: hence, we perceive an inherent dynamism in what Episcopalians such as this one now believe. Second, the beliefs of Episcopalians are likely to vary, though belief is important, and there is an underlying affirmation of core Christian beliefs and Episcopal Church traditions. More importantly, there is an emphasis upon seeking common ground through worship while affirming the virtues of tolerance and breadth. This statement—similar sentiments of which surfaced in virtually every one of our conversations across the church—is like a blueprint for the sort of spiritual community Episcopalians seek.

One church member affirmed that, "the Episcopal Church is tolerant, especially on issues of human sexuality and respect." "Being an Episcopalian to me means being non-judgmental," commented another lay person. In a more detailed response, one person who had described some conflicts that had arisen during the formulation of a parish program made this observation: "What was distinctively Episcopalian about how we handled it was that we talked it through. We were inclusive of everyone, and we found a middle way."

These comments suggest the reason for the moderate views most Episcopalians express. The members of Episcopal churches are likely to seek broad forms of consensus that arise through open-ended group processes of discernment and inquiry. Such forms of decision making, rooted in small-group process, pervade the Episcopal Church. Accordingly, parishioners appear less drawn to extreme positions or strident advocacy of particular ideological or theological views. They are far more responsive to shared, open leadership styles than to impersonal, hierarchically defined institutional structures or unilateral forms of decision making.

In fact, there is an acutely felt need throughout the church for leadership that engages tradition and basic Christian beliefs in ways that open up inquiry and discovery. In one church in Texas, this need was clearly articulated: "Our Anglican tradition gives us a strong base to carry us forward as we face new challenges. It offers a rich history of dealing with problems and staying centered on shared worship of the Lord in the middle of all the differences. It's just that, in this situation, we don't see how to make use of that foundation to move ahead with this problem. We're stuck and seem to be not doing much to move forward."

What does "moving forward" mean to Episcopalians? To what end is tradition being put? Through what sort of perspective do Episcopalians read the Bible and explore the Christian faith, as this statement suggests? One historian responds with a compelling interpretation. Episcopalians today, he argues, have not "abandoned faith in God or turned against historic Christianity— far from it." However, they stress "the experiential over the rational," including, we add, the communal over the institutional dimensions of the faith. Thus, while affirming a few key Christian doctrines, Episcopalians view their Christian faith primarily as a "way of life." With worship as their center, contemporary Episcopalians, like Anglicans historically, uphold "a utilitarian attitude toward the faith instead of a speculative one."[5] Or, as one church member put it, "if someone asked, 'what is an Episcopalian?' you'd have to answer, 'come to church and experience it.'"

Another way to make this point is to say that for Episcopalians the goal is to integrate faith and life. That is, Episcopalians generally seek to affirm the core beliefs of Christianity and the traditions of the Episcopal Church in terms of their own lived experience. Not intent on challenging core Christian beliefs on rational grounds or on accepting tradition and belief whole, Episcopalians generally take an optimistic view of the relevance of Christian faith for daily life. Nevertheless, there is not complete accord among Episcopalians on how faith and life should intersect. As we shall describe later in this chapter, conservative Episcopalians tend to fear that culture has become more definitive of belief than Scripture or tradition. Liberals take the opposite approach, typically fearing that contemporary experience is being over-looked in a mindless rush to uphold inherited beliefs and practices. But most Episcopalians of both theological views simply seek a basis for consensus that will unite them in faithful and practical ways.

But putting aside for a moment the debates surrounding the proper relation of life to Scripture and tradition, this emphasis on lived experience can be seen clearly in the importance Episco-palians typically attach to spirituality. For example, when asked what mattered most to them, the members of a church in Missouri gave this answer: "We identified that the Spirit is important, what we have with each other, our dedication, our caring. It's not about a building. We do simple worship, and I have found I can do that—as opposed to more elaborate liturgy—and I like it."

To repeat some useful sentiments from the previous chapter, these comments came from a church in the Southeast: "Being part of this community has become the way I live out my Christian commitment. We are engaged in mutual support and nurturing. It's just healthy personal spiritual growth to be involved in caring for others." Another person added, "I agree. We are learning how to be more trusting in the Holy Spirit and mutually respectful." "We are learning about the strengths in our differences," continued a third person. "We value deeply the spir-itual journey of each individual and recognize that we're all in this together, regardless of how we express it. The principle of community has really come to be central to our identity." When asked about Episcopal belief, the themes of spirituality and com-munity continued to be the primary reference points. As one person explained, "We have Scripture in every service, and value every-one's sense of where God is leading. Those old Anglican ideas of 'tradition, reason, and Scripture' are really vital for us. They allow us to respect and value every person and to join with one another in our journeys." Another respondent added succinctly: "The Episcopal Church is what enabled us to survive and grow. We have become a community because of what the church before us put in place to enable us to come into being."

The centrality of spirituality for Episcopalians accounts for the appeal of such unofficial education programs as Journey to Adulthood, Godly Play, Education for Ministry, and Alpha. In the Midwest, the members of a large, suburban parish were enthusiastic about Alpha's impact. One person described the program in this way: "Part of the vision, once you hear the Alpha process...is what you are called to do. A person with a commitment to spiritual life." Describing Alpha's role in the Christian education of children, one person was explicit: "We see they are [becoming] servants of others, and they have [developed] a personal, active faith." "It was all basic Christianity," added another person. "About having a personal encounter with Jesus Christ and the Holy Spirit and where to go from there."

The participants of this small group repeatedly characterized the Alpha Course as "basic" Christianity, giving us the impression that they considered other (presumably overly denominational) forms of Christianity to be decidedly *less* basic—perhaps even suspect. Having established their wariness of programs and practices that were *too* Episcopal, a curious, paradoxical dynamic overtook their group; three of them proceeded to detail at some length how perfectly Alpha fit into Episcopal tradition and the process of preparing confirmands, which happened to be the sole—and the specifically Anglican—use to which their parish put Alpha! In retrospect, our researchers found their performance doubly paradoxical: first, because of the Anglican origins of the supposedly un-Episcopal course they had chosen; and second, because of Alpha's capacity—and their parish's capacity—to adapt to one another in the most Anglican way imaginable. Far from finding their behavior eccentric, however, our interviewers were struck by their subtlety of understanding of Anglicanism. They, like many other Episcopalians around the country today, filter Episcopal identity through the prism of spirituality; from certain angles, given this prism's bending of perception, the congregation will seem Episcopal hardly at all; from another, that same bending of perception will array the congregation in deep, rich shades of Anglicanism that appear almost old-fashioned.

The emphasis on spirituality and community also explains the role of small groups in shaping how Episcopalians frame Christian belief. One parish on the West Coast was forthcoming about how small groups affected their common life. "The small groups that have worked well for this church include: prayer circle, Stephen Ministry, prayer ministry, planning diocesan programs for youth, and the Taizé service." Another person continued, "Small groups work here because they are small, fun...more personal contact, people cannot be ignored. Small groups foster relationships that make it easier to comfortably fit into the overall congregation." Another person concurred: "Small groups are the foundation for the overall community. They contribute to the connectedness in the wider congregational community."

What is notable from the research we gathered is that small groups set a style for all of the congregation's life. They encourage a different kind of congregational ethos. Yet small groups rarely constitute the center of the congregation's life. Among Episcopalians, belief and common life derive from the experience of worship.

WORSHIP

"Our liturgy is the core," members of a parish in Texas emphasized when we visited them. Not often so succinct but usually sufficiently clear, most Episcopalians would agree. But what do they mean when they say that worship is the "core" of their congregation's life? During an evening in a Minnesota parish, one explanation was expressed with great passion: "The liturgy centers us and defines us as the people of God. Out of that repeated experience flows the motivation to care for others." As will be addressed at length later, Episcopalians instinctively link the character of worship to particular qualities of the Christian life.

This connection between faith and life occurs for Episcopalians in their experience of worship. Simply put, what Episcopalians believe and what they do on the basis of belief is rooted in the experience of worship. When asked what worship means, most reply that worship is response to God. This emphasis surfaces in various ways as Episcopalians describe their common life. For example, the point is often made that the Episcopal Church doesn't "tell people what to believe" but instead "inspires belief." As a result, it is "OK to disagree" on points of interpretation as long as the church's members affirm their unity at the altar. The test of faith's validity is its ability to inspire a common life, and worship is the occasion when that unity must be understood and expressed.

The experience of coming together in worship out of disparate personal circumstances leaves a powerful, lasting impression. Church members speak frequently of their worship as "beautiful," or "spiritually deep," or reassuringly "structured." Conversely, when a church's worship leaves something to be desired, church members speak despairingly or fear that their congregation lacks its necessary center. We have been struck, however, by the extent to which local Episcopal churches speak approvingly of their worship. For instance, in the South, the members of one church stressed that, "our worship reconnects us with God's wonderful love for us. That motivates us to love one another, especially those who are hurting or on the margins." In the Midwest, a lay leader agreed in more elaborate detail: "People come to this church because of the liturgy and the worship. There aren't a lot of demands that you think this way or that. Instead, we worship together and receive the sacraments together. That's the powerful attraction. You are fed and you realize you are growing."

The fact that worship is conducted in a specifically Episcopal way consistently matters. Church members often cite the importance of the Eucharist and the beauty and reverence of Episcopal liturgies. As one Kansas Episcopalian described it, "the Prayer Book and our liturgy hold us together. We have differences about lots of things, but we all meet at the altar." In a number of situations, lay leaders reported to us that the distinctively Episcopal forms of worship structured what Sunday school and adult education classes taught. For instance, the Episcopal emphasis on worship, combined with contemporary interest in spirituality, leads many churches to offer presentations on various forms of prayer and meditation. The Episcopal capacity for breadth and acceptance means that it is not unusual for Episcopal churches to study a variety of other Christian approaches to worship and prayer, as well as the spirituality of other world religions, such as Buddhism and Islam. For Episcopalians, the centrality of worship as response to God provides a perspective that is clearly grounded in a particular Christian tradition, yet sufficiently broad to explore other approaches. It is this combination of breadth and grounding that many Episcopalians value as a basis for spiritual growth.

The basic theme, of course, is that worship serves as the core of the congregation's life, because worship is a collective response to God. Of course, Episcopalians differ over appropriate styles of worship for their congregations—a reality of Episcopal life with a complex recent history, especially in the last third of the twentieth century, when worship was the source of intense conflict. As we have described above, the process of revising the Prayer Book resulted in the approval of sweeping changes. Not only did the Eucharist become central to Sunday worship, but Baptism and the ministries of all baptized persons became definitive of Christian community. This sacramental focus on worship grew out of an unprecedented emphasis on the example of ancient Christian liturgical sources as authoritative standards for refashioning the church's contemporary worship. As we shall explain, this emphasis reflected the triumph of Anglo-Catholicism's historic principles and practices, which began to reshape the church's worship in the nineteenth century.

With Prayer Book revision, Episcopal worship gained new flexibility to adapt to varied local contexts. Somewhat paradoxical patterns of practice developed as a result; although the forms of eucharistic worship that closely follow the Prayer Book tended to prevail, the Prayer Book's flexibility, which adapted easily to diverse local contexts, invited other forms of worship to arise and hold sway over certain constituencies. Among those influential new styles were the Charismatic and Evangelical Renewal movements of the late twentieth century, which have imprinted styles of music and intercessory prayer on many parishes. Liberal emphases on inclusive language and expansive imagery of God also are apparent in many places. In fact, rarely does one style win universal affirmation in a congregation. In the hundreds of Episcopal congregations we have visited, tensions arising from conflicting views of worship—formal versus informal or traditional versus innovative—frequently are found.[6]

But while these tensions are inescapable in most places, and references to them are regularly heard, they are not the principal feature of Episcopal worship. We have concluded that the conflicts over Prayer Book revision have largely been resolved and that worship according to the 1979 innovations is more a source of unity than of tension. As the people in one parish explained, worship "is the place where we all can come together at the Lord's table, whatever our differences."

A WAY OF LIFE

Episcopalians are a religious people whose beliefs are rooted in worship.[7] But how exactly does worship speak to them? Is the experience of worship isolated from other dimensions of personal and congregational life? Or, is there a deep, life-giving connection that takes shape in worship? Asked another way, if being an Episcopalian centers on participation in a distinctive way of life, what is this way of life, and how does worship serve as its core?

Our research reveals that, with few exceptions, Episcopalians see themselves as engaged in building a distinctive way of life that is expressed in worship. Clearly, there is a strong emphasis on spirituality and the spiritual journey when Episcopalians speak in this way. But what is the source of this distinctive way of life, and what sustains it? When encouraged to speak further, many say they feel that God is calling them toward a life they have not fully discovered. Consistently and energetically, the people in Episcopal churches say they often have a feeling that

God is leading them. They are not always certain about this feeling or entirely clear about where it is leading them, even when the feeling is vivid. But they are secure in the knowledge that they are being called by God, and that they are in the midst of understanding what this sense of call portends for them personally and for the churches in which they participate.

This sense of call takes various forms. The primary sense of call urges Episcopalians to follow God faithfully in the person of Jesus Christ. "Somehow, underneath it all, we are called to follow Jesus," someone in Florida stated. This sentiment surfaced often with variations. "We are called to follow Christ and to serve others," was the typical way of expressing it. A California lay leader offered this variation: "Our mission is to produce a Christ-centered community"; and a North Carolina church member offered this more elaborate one: "We are Christ's disciples, finding our way to be obedient to the Great Commission—to go into the world, and make disciples and teach them (and us) to obey his commandments. We are his people, following him and carrying out his plan for the church in the world."

As followers of Christ, Episcopalians instinctively understand that they must demonstrate a certain quality of personal and congregational life. "We are called to be a family, drawn together and led by God. We are to listen to him and follow him," one person said. A church member in the South added this important quality of service to others: "Our sense of God's call is that we love him and love and serve one another. We are the body of believers, called to serve our brothers and sisters, then the whole community, and then out to the world." Another Southerner said, "We are to be faithful to God, to continue following his Spirit, to grow in him, and to serve those in need all around us here."

Frequently, the emphases on being faithful, on growing spiritually, and on serving people in need are juxtaposed. "We are to be nurturing one another in spiritual growth and serving others in need," one lay leader declared. For Episcopalians, faithfully following God's call means more than individual acts of charity or nurture, regardless of how well intentioned or effective. The underlying quality that many try to cultivate is a spirit of invitation, of seeking ways to build connections to other people in ways that promote spiritual growth and strengthen the congregation. "We are to keep on with our efforts to invite people in and find ways to help them grow in faith," said one member. In another church, a similar sentiment surfaced: "We are to invite others in, engage them in service to others, and help one another grow in faith." Or, as another person expressed it, "we should find ways to draw everyone in and make use of their gifts for serving the needs of others and helping them grow." Many voices urge commitment to the local community. "We are called to be Christ's disciples here in this community," one person declared. Someone in Massachusetts put the sense of call in clearly personal terms: "I have always wanted to help people. That is the heart of my spiritual life. It makes me feel good."

The experience of God's call does not conclude a person's— or a congregation's—search for assurance. Episcopalians frequently relish the opportunity to struggle for clarity. Because they value the church's emphasis on breadth and honesty in matters of faith, many understand their call from God as the chance for spiritual growth in the midst of challenges and uncertainties. "God calls us to hang in there, to be present for one another in life's struggles to grow." Various members of a group in California revealed that their sense of call is to be a congregation that "asks tough questions," that "continues to grow," and to "stretch." "We're a church called to continuously live with questions," another of their group stated.

The members of another California parish felt they were called to be "diverse," "resilient," and willing to "engage in discussing the issues." Echoing the earlier Californian who felt called to "hang in there," one of this group characterized spiritual persistence as a "refusal to exit."

Consistently, Episcopalians' personal struggles for clarity about Christian faith find a common outlet. As they seek a deeper faith, they discover the possibility of spiritual growth in a congregation. As they join the congregation and begin to work together to build it, they find practical expression of their faith. As their faith has tangible impact, they grow spiritually in ways they could not have envisioned. Soon, many whose spiritual journeys began personally and inwardly find that the spiritual life has become shared and outward. In the context of an Episcopal congregation, they have discovered a way of life that inspires and sustains them.

Furthermore, Episcopalians who realize consciously that they have been led or called to participate in a congregation usually experience an accompanying sense that they have gained assurance about the Christian faith. For all the emphasis on journey, struggle, and uncertainty, the majority of the Episcopalians we spoke with revealed a deep conviction of their Christian faith. A member of one congregation took care to explain that, "we are an Easter people. The celebration of the resurrection is the high point of the liturgical year and the core of our faith. From that emerges all else we do, especially loving and serving others." Being "called to make Christ known, to be his agent, to offer our best regardless of the circumstances," is how one Missouri congregant expressed it, then added, "To do better, do more. To be open to new ways to contribute."

Not all Episcopalians are clear about how God is calling them. In some places, there is a strong sense that people are seeking clarity; in others, there is a sense of frustration in congregational life due to lack of clarity. In exasperation, one Florida church member said: "Well, I'm no prophet! We're looking for who we are called to be in this situation." At a Massachusetts church, a similar longing for clarity was voiced: "We're in the middle of trying to find out who we are called to be. This is a good question for us. We've found there is a lot of the community we're not involved with. We're finding that you need to educate, communicate." When asked about his congregation's sense of call, one church member in Texas said simply: "I think that's a tough question to answer."

How is a sense of call evoked in congregations? One source is the sermon. Sermon content can be effective in shaping response to God. According to one set of research data, Episcopal clergy emphasize the same few themes in their preaching. They speak of God's love and of personal spiritual growth. Often they frame their messages around accounts of personal experience. There is also consistent emphasis on the mystery of God, combined with struggles for faith and assurance. Less often, there are doctrinal expositions and illustrations of leading a moral life. Only slightly more than a quarter of the clergy surveyed reported that they emphasized social justice.[8]

The sense of call often is sharpened by challenging, practical questions. In the South, a lay leader put it this way: "We are to be faithful, to recognize that it is difficult to be a real Christian. We ask ourselves, 'now what would Jesus want of this assembly of such diverse individuals?' We mature in our faith by sticking with the difficult process of finding ways to respond to one another's needs and those of people in this community." Succinctly, another person added that the congregation's "spiritual life is expressed through its meetings. It is expressed through discussion, reading, and learning to think theologically."

Most often, Episcopalians report that their sense of call originates in the give and take of congregational life, as they wrestle over dilemmas and do the work that sustains their common life. In committees and events and meetings, both personal vocation and common vocation take shape. As one church member in Florida put it, "we are disciples of Christ. That takes many forms and shapes. Everyone's gifts are needed. We need to grow and to serve the many new people coming to us. We want to be hosts, receiving them and helping them to get in touch with the One who calls them. That means following Christ and supporting one another in doing that for others."

A sense of creative give and take was palpable in a downtown parish on the West Coast. The church members who gathered there one evening described their vestry meetings as "amazing" in terms of "community, prayer, and theological insight." They emphasized that, for them, spirituality is expressed through discussion. They have been inclusive about facing issues in their parish, publicizing all meetings as open to anyone who is interested. But they have learned that meetings cannot be productive if they are free-form. Now their leaders see that their time together must be structured, and that there must be strong but sensitive leadership for a truly effective process of discernment. The result is a strong sense of confidence about the parish. "We've worked really hard and don't exactly know what the next step will be," one person ventured, noting that the parish was at a crossroads where a variety of creative possibilities loomed. "But we are willing to listen and move according to the Holy Spirit. We're looking for what is next. We're not setting our own agenda but discerning the needs we face."

Conversely, failures in church life reflect the breakdown of effective ways to address challenges collectively. In the upper Midwest, one church member cited her parish's "failure to get consensus on the small, somewhat insignificant things in church life that make or break churches. Someone donated a picture, and the priest hung it up in the worship area. Some people immediately disagreed with what she had done." A stalemate ensued with little hope of resolution.

The sense of call that emerges from healthy parish dynamics can be surprising. One woman spoke of how a study group in her congregation became involved in consulting with other congregations. "Some of us have stayed together as a resource to other churches. We always are able to ask, 'where do we go from here?' We also can ask, 'what is our mission?' And we're very social! We talk about things you can't talk about elsewhere. This is part of what makes this a very valuable group."

But it was not always so. With little encouragement, the woman revealed that her study group had faced struggles. "There really are no differences among us now. We have had a lot of sorting out to do. I don't know, I guess we were there to sort out feelings. To discover how we could help. Who we are called to be is a hard question. We realized we are called to nurture. To care and show concern. And we found out it's a process."

Consistently, Episcopalians told us that honest conversations clarified their shared and personal sense of call. A member of one

Midwest vestry trying to decide the future of a parish-sponsored neighborhood ministry explained it this way: "Our fault lines were addressed by meeting with the program directors and offering guidance. We see our role as staff support. The neighborhood certainly has problems—it came to us, and we came to it. This situation opened my eyes to see people and circumstances I never realized existed. I listened in the meeting and this put a new spin on it.... For me it was opening my eyes and becoming open." Thus, the process of honest encounter encourages a transformed way of understanding people and situations. The sense of call is clarified because a change in perspective has occurred. But this is usually only the first step. Episcopalians also tell us that, with new understanding and fresh perspective, they realize that they must remake the ways they express their faith practically. To use a concept that has gained appeal in recent years, a sharpened sense of call inspires a revised set of practices to sustain personal and congregational life.

One popular book describes practices as "things Christian people do together over time in response to and in the light of God's active presence for the life of the world." More concretely, practices are "some of the most important activities" that compose the Christian life. Practices "address fundamental human needs and conditions through concrete human acts." Practices have "practical purposes," for example, to heal and to discern. But they are not simply intended to produce specific outcomes. Practices are marks of identity and standards of excellence.[9] For instance, Christian people are called to be reconcilers and healers. It is a mark of Christian conviction that followers of Jesus Christ would be agents of reconciliation. In the same way, other forms of practice arise from the nature of Christian belief and serve as benchmarks for the Christian community. They are the basic forms of expression to which Christians must aspire.

Historically, Christians have identified certain basic practices as integral to the church's life. The foremost of these is worship. For the early church, there was also strong emphasis on Christian witness and on works of mercy toward persons in need. Hospitality was emphasized as was education and basic patterns of faith formation. Together, these practices served to build the Christian community and to endow it with an inherent sense of dynamism. At the very least, the church realized that it faced continuing challenges of ministry and formation. To meet these challenges in ways consistent with their identity as followers of the risen Lord, the early church followed these basic practices.[10]

Contemporary writers on spirituality have found the concept of practices appealing. For people who are seekers—looking not only for clarity but for forms of community and structure that effectively integrate spirituality into their lives—the idea of practices is promising. One set of recent authors has compiled an amended modern list of practices to address current needs. It includes "honoring the body," "household economics," "saying yes and saying no," "shaping communities," and "discernment."[11] While these categories are illuminating, it is not clear how they reflect actual practices of people in local churches. Specifically, if one were to ask what practices are prominent among Episcopalians today, what would one find? And what would these practices reveal about what today's Episcopalians most deeply believe?

We have found that the concept of practices is not abstract for Episcopalians but quite specific, referring to actions that deepen and express their faith. When speaking of joining a committee in her church, one lay leader in Florida gave a detailed example. "Well, I was in a program of spiritual direction at a retreat house near here, so this committee provided me a concrete opportunity to put into practice what I had been studying. The rector asked me to convene and facilitate the committee. That role has drawn upon and deepened my skills in listening and learning to evoke instead of trying to control things." She then cited the benefit of her experience. "For me the committee drew me beyond just intellectualizing about spiritual issues and into practice."

At one North Carolina congregation, the reliance on early Christian examples of practice was articulated with unusual clarity and conviction. "We are trying to model ourselves after the early church as much as possible. That means worshiping and praying together, studying God's Word, sharing our resources, telling others about him, inviting them to join us in following him, and becoming obedient to him in everything we do. It means building one another up in the faith, being a strong and supportive community, and welcoming others to join in. They come and sense the strong presence of God's Spirit among us and want to stay."

Linkages between worship, spirituality, and practice abound in encounters with church members. "We're about right history and right practices," said one lay person, "not right thinking and right behavior." In Massachusetts, one person noted that her parish was "led to who we are and called through prayer." Not surprisingly, for a tradition that is centered in worship, prayer is a major form of religious practice for Episcopalians. There are frequent references to prayer when discussions of personal and congregational spirituality begin. "The basis for me was prayer, how to pray, and how to discern different responses to changes in the situation," one person revealed. "We are called to pray, to be open to one another," another lay leader said. "Are we faithful in prayer, listening, then moving forward in trust that he will lead us and provide for the needs?" another lay leader wondered.

As we have described at several points in this narrative, a cluster of practices are inspired by worship and prayer in Episcopal congregations. The Episcopalians to whom we have spoken cite a spirit of welcoming newcomers to their congregations, of being diligent in the Christian formation of their children and in their own spiritual growth. Because there is a practical emphasis in their spirituality, most Episcopalians cite forms of outreach, especially helping people in need. Invariably, someone in every small-group session pointed out that stewardship means more than fundraising; it means assisting with duties in the parish office, helping with care of the physical plant, or helping to design and conduct the church's worship and music. In whatever form, giving of oneself in response to God through one's congregation represents a basic form of Christian practice. This can be seen in specific applications of one's talents and also in general assistance with all aspects of congregational life.

Based on recent research, the patterns of Christian practice among Episcopalians can be broken down into the following:

- Worship and Praise
- Prayer and Discernment
- Service and Outreach
- Study and Formation
- Pastoral Care
- Advocacy and Justice
- Stewardship
- Evangelism
- Healing

These forms of practice are prominent, throughout the church. Episcopalians now agree only generally on the importance of certain basic practices in the lives of their congregations, but they have found consensus on more specific aspects of Christian practice. For instance, our research shows that the overwhelming majority of Episcopalians understand the Eucharist to be the central form of worship. But there are limits to the consensus on practices. It is not clear how practice conveys belief or how practice forms and sustains mission in a congregation. From one congregation to another there may be energetic new forms of programs, but little consistency in the practices that local leaders adopt to initiate or sustain these programs. Theological views of the practices necessary for a congregation vary widely from one locality to the next, and in each congregation there will be local idiosyncrasies in how one or another practice is conducted, especially worship. Thus, local patterns reveal more breadth than consensus among Episcopalians. But even within congregations, it is not unusual to find disparate views of appropriate practice.

In a Midwestern congregation, one person to whom we spoke said that it was "hard for this particular congregation to understand a sense of call as being about them as a whole." At a Northeastern

church, one lay person described his own sense of call to lay ministry and his work in the parish; he spoke positively about the
tenor of life in his church, but then he hesitated, his face darkened, and he spoke more somberly about those of his fellow
parishioners who were long-time church members: "It disap-
points me when so many do not feel as strongly about it. I will
say, at some point, they are strong in commitment, but as traditional Episcopalians they don't know how to express it. It is sort
of an inner thing. Outside of the Prayer Book, you don't talk
about God comfortably or readily. At the vestry, you talk about
budgets and the economy; you don't talk about how God is
directing and inspiring me, and so I just want to give to God."

Similarly, a lay leader in Texas worried that members of her
church were reluctant to express their faith: "The call of whatever is expressed through words and actions.... If you don't act,
nothing will happen. It takes more than understanding what it is,
what the call is, and having a commitment to it." Such concerns
were echoed often. "We stood back for a long time," was typical
of what we heard. From such hesitations, we learned that the new
ties among Episcopalians and the new kind of church emerging from
them reflect a process that is incomplete. In the pews of Episcopal churches, there is an energetic struggle to define belief and
practice in terms that are both faithful and current. In some
cases, those struggles reflect conflicts over particular practices of
Christian life; in others, struggles reflect the turn of the church
to new priorities of faith and mission. To understand these struggles,
we must ask how Episcopalians handle conflict over belief? What
is the meaning of such battles, and what is novel about current
tensions?

WHEN CONSENSUS FALTERED

Although a consensus of impressive depth and energy unites
people in Episcopal churches on matters of Christian belief and
practices, this consensus has its limits, as we shall explain. Clear
and consistent affirmation of eucharistic worship and the Bible
demonstrates that Episcopalians in large numbers embrace the

historic foundations of Christianity. But consensus of this kind does not represent a return to an institutional view of the faith; neither does it portend a renewal of instinctive denominational loyalty to the Episcopal Church; neither does it signal a revival of the former consensus about how belief inspires practice and how practice encourages mission. Yet there is much about it that is encouraging. Today, the basis for consensus on practice lies in the centrality of the Eucharist in worship, and that is a new emphasis. We have described how the process of liturgical revision, which had its roots in the nineteenth-century debates over ritual, led to revision of the Prayer Book of 1979 and to a decisive turn toward sacramental worship as the primary expression of the church's life. But the church did not change its basic *manner* of belief as a Christian body; rather, it shifted the manner in which worship upheld basic Christian belief, and the manner in which belief functions in the church.

What does this turn mean? Our conversations with Episcopalians inform us that Christian belief functions in the following ways:

- *Affective*: The priority of the Eucharist tells us that Episcopalians seek to worship in ways that engage all of their senses, not only their minds. The sacraments are rich in expressive symbols and dramas;

- *Affirmative*: Episcopalians generally believe that they are called to embrace and minister to the world as they encounter it. They usually are eager to affirm diversity and to discover cultures other than their own;

- *Collective*: The evidence argues that there is more emphasis on the local church and on forming community than at any other time in Episcopal history;

- *Generative*: there is significant emphasis on the role of belief in building local religious community and ministries;

- *Reflective*: the emphasis on spiritual seeking and on building community has produced impressive energy for understanding and living the basics of the Christian faith. Large numbers of Episcopalians now have been shaped by their experience of small groups.

As we have suggested above and will discuss in the last section of this chapter, Episcopalians too often are vague about their belief and their identity. They seek faithfulness, but faithfulness requires deepening knowledge of basic Christian beliefs and Anglican traditional expressions of them. How Episcopalians find deeper knowledge of Christianity in general and Anglicanism in particular, how they express their faith, and how they construe their faith as a basis for congregational life varies from one local context to another. The pitfall of a church whose energies now arise in a new way from the local level is that patterns of common life can become anarchic. All too often, congregations and even dioceses can act as laws unto themselves. Widespread consensus cannot be presumed to create reliable unity, much less order. However compelling, the fact of widespread local vitality provides no sense of how Episcopalians are connected to one another, much less how they are to resolve agonizing conflicts over belief and practice in ways that honor local initiative while ensuring broad unity and faithfulness.

A consensus on belief that secures the church's identity and vocation is an ideal that many Episcopalians deeply desire. As we have noted, many members of Episcopal congregations speak longingly of finding the church's center. That is, they seek assurance that the church possesses a clear sense of its core values and that these core values are rooted in an affirmation of historic Christian belief and practice. Such longing is as practical as it is theoretical, for it is nothing less than a plea for an effective means of mediating between competing, confusing, and occasionally conflicting claims about definitive belief and practice. The ideal of a center represents the glue by which the church is held together and the mechanism by which it can integrate varied experiences and agendas into a coherent identity and vocation.[12] Clearly, the Episcopal Church is seeking a new sense of its center, in theory and in practice, but it is difficult to know how such a center might be found and which of the church's varied groups— feeling that their key affirmations were being threatened in the process of locating this center—would resist. In the past, when the Episcopal consensus on the beliefs and practices underlying its identity and vocation shifted, serious conflict always erupted. To put the contemporary church's patterns of consensus and conflict in perspective, we must look at an earlier instance of conflict and consensus.

It is tempting to view the past as a time of unchallenged consensus, when the Episcopal Church was united in its Christian identity and faithful in its vocation. If there were fault lines in the church, this idealistic view of the past presumes that they were minimal and concerned only secondary aspects of belief and practice. On the essential matters of belief and practice, clarity and unity prevailed.

Such beliefs come easily to Episcopalians, largely because we presume that diversity—whether it is ethnic, cultural, or ideological—is a modern development within the Episcopal Church. In fact, the Episcopal Church has always encompassed a variety of groups and perspectives, each with distinctive and surprisingly unassimilated features. African Americans are one notable example.[13] Native Americans are another. It must be emphasized that African and Native Americans as well as several other ethnic groups in the church developed a sense of distinctiveness in part because of the barriers to full participation put in their way for many years. In each case, their longing for acceptance and equal participation was apparent. But, as a result, each group developed distinctive ways of being loyal Episcopalians. It is a reality that supports our ongoing point that, although the Episcopal Church has achieved clear forms of belief and practice, it has never done so in completely uniform ways. Broad forms of consensus, rather than perfect uniformity, have marked the church's search for a secure American identity and vocation.

Diversity is not incidental to our church's history; one might even go so far as to say that diversity—especially ideological diversity—has been our defining characteristic. From its origins as the colonial outpost of the Church of England, the Episcopal Church absorbed the ideal of "comprehension" (or "comprehensiveness"). Sometimes considered the Anglican tradition's "genius," comprehensiveness refers to the church's ability to embrace "great variety" in belief and practice.[14] Comprehensiveness represents "agreement on fundamentals, while tolerating disagreement on matters in which Christians may differ without feeling the necessity of breaking communion."[15] This key thread in the church's fabric represents Anglican spiritual pragmatism. One of the Anglican tradition's most basic values is the assumption that comprehensiveness is "the normative mode for establishing and maintaining the order of society."

It is characteristically Anglican to believe that the church must mirror society to minister effectively to it. This belief has played a defining, shaping role in Anglicanism from its very inception. From the Reformation of the sixteenth century onward, Anglicanism faced a range of other religious groups in England, including various parties within itself. The church's challenge was to affirm that its belief and practice reflected the essentials of Christian faith while allowing for variations in interpreting and enacting them. How could it be *the* Church of England without reflecting the true diversity of English society? To be England's church in fact, early Anglican leaders such as Richard Hooker realized that it had to "achieve a basic Christian consensus which any reasonable person could accept." Unlike Anglicans today, Hooker "could take doctrinal agreement for granted and defend the national church's corporate reason as a basis for practical uniformity in things indifferent."[16] The challenge was that England's social circumstances changed dramatically, such that, in practical terms, the Church of England could not claim to hold the allegiance of all English people. Significant numbers remained Catholic, and increasing numbers moved toward the Protestant denominations. Some English people were

Jewish, and by the twentieth century, other religious minorities were apparent in England, including Muslims and Hindus. The historic ideal of a comprehensive, truly national church lingered but lost practical application long before the beginning of the twenty-first century. The Church of England's status as the established church bore little relation to social fact.

Episcopalians, of course, could not rely upon the legacy of the established church. As we have seen, an independent United States created unprecedented challenges for survival. But historic Anglican ideals shaped the Episcopal Church's identity and vocation, and the old ideal of comprehensiveness was pivotal. With the church's reorganization after the American Revolution, a broad swath of the church's leaders presumed that the key to an authentic identity and vocation lay in adapting the church's life to American culture. It is significant that these Episcopalians presumed that the church's adaptation to American life could enhance, rather than compromise, its clarity about the Christian faith's essential affirmations. What resulted was a reliance upon the American pattern of democratic process to govern the church and, thus, to legislate on matters of belief and practice.

Episcopalians have not always been sanguine about uncritical reliance on American culture. At its best, the church's leadership has understood that there are inherent tensions between American life and Christian life. When they have been clear about the challenge they face, church leaders also have grasped that they cannot achieve uniformity of belief and practice while valuing comprehensiveness and entrusting their governance to democratic process. At best, the church's leaders have affirmed essential aspects of belief and practice in the form of a broad consensus. The most noteworthy articulation of consensus came in the late nineteenth century when Episcopalians forged agreement on the essentials of the faith after considerable discussion in public and in the church's official channels. The Chicago-Lambeth Quadrilateral was adopted by the House of Bishops of the Episcopal Church in Chicago in 1886 and refined and endorsed by the Lambeth Conference of Anglican bishops in 1888.[17] These four marks define the church's fundamental affirmation of essential belief:

- The Holy Scriptures of the Old and New Testaments, as "containing all things necessary to salvation," and as being the rule and ultimate standard of faith.
- The Apostles' Creed as the Baptismal symbol, and the Nicene Creed as the sufficient statement of Christian faith.
- The two Sacraments ordained by Christ himself—Baptism and the Supper of the Lord—ministered with unfailing use of Christ's words of Institution, and of the elements ordained by him.
- The historic Episcopate, "locally adapted in the methods of its administration to the varying needs of the nations and peoples called of God into the Unity of His Church."[18]

The achievement of the Chicago-Lambeth Quadrilateral and its rapid adoption by the Anglican Communion represent a high water mark for consensus. And yet even these clear marks of the church, as the comment on the episcopate reveals, presume that there are acceptable forms of variation. In the absence of a formal role in the nation, the Episcopal Church has sought other appropriate means of enforcing its standards of belief and defining an acceptable range of interpretation. It has done so in two ways: first, by encouraging consensus on the essentials of the faith; second, by relying upon broadly understood and accepted patterns of governance to address questions of belief and practice and to enforce the resolution of conflicts about them. The democratic procedures embedded in vestries, diocesan conventions, various official committees and commissions and, above all, the General Convention have been the bases of Episcopal order.

But at times, the nature of the Episcopal Church's order has been in dispute. As we have described, agreement on the church's governance was not easily achieved. A fault line appeared between leaders who emphasized the necessity of the church's adaptation to American patterns of organization for the sake of its mission and leaders who prized the distinctiveness of Episcopal identity and were hesitant to accommodate too much of American life.

It was a bold step to grant to democratic assemblies the authority for decisions that could involve essentials of the faith. Generally, Evangelical Episcopalians cheered it as an appropriate way to root the church's identity and vocation in American life. High Church Episcopalians feared that public opinion could become the sole basis for belief and practice. But a consensus held the church together, and that consensus reflected agreement more on matters of church governance than on matters of faith. Certainly, Evangelical and High Church Episcopalians agreed on such basic marks of church identity as the centrality of Scripture, worship, and the apostolic episcopate. But at points where their consensus faltered, Episcopalians looked to the church's forms of institutional procedure and democratic process to sort out their differences.

Before proceeding further, it becomes necessary to discuss the principles around which the High Church and Evangelical parties formed early in the nineteenth century. Like their Low Church counterparts in the Church of England, Evangelicals saw the church's mission and its reliance on the Bible as crucial tenets and often were eager to find common ground with non-Episcopal Evangelicals for the sake of furthering mission. Taking their theological cue from Calvinism, they also retained an emphasis on worship.[19] But they felt that worship should emphasize preaching from Scripture and should be simple so as not to be a distraction. Evangelical Episcopalians encouraged personal piety and conduct and valued the role of lay leaders in the church. By the middle of the nineteenth century, leading Evangelicals, such as Bishop William Meade of Virginia and Bishop Charles McIlvaine of Ohio, believed in the republican political principles of the Whig Party with its emphasis on a mixture of personal rights and personal virtue.

By contrast, High Church Episcopalians typically wanted nothing to do with the republicanism of the Whigs.[20] They located the Episcopal Church's identity in its worship and ministry, rather than in its adaptation to American life. Like the English Oxford Movement, which criticized the church for its proximity to the state, the American High Church party intended to distance the Episcopal Church from accommodation to American culture. More important, High Church Episcopalians cultivated a particular form of piety. If Evangelicals viewed the church as an invisible fellowship of people called to follow Christ, the High Church party valued the church's visible worship and ministry because of their apostolic origins. Like Evangelicals, they cultivated an intense inner piety, but theirs was a piety rooted in the church's sacraments. Bishop John Henry Hobart of New York believed that the church should uphold a distinctive identity as the basis of its vocation. Hobart's ideals and forceful personality drew such notable followers as Jackson Kemper and James Lloyd Breck, whose missionary work expanded the church into the West. The General Theological Seminary in New York embodied Hobart's influence and became an American center for the ideals of Ritualism that transformed the church's worship.

Despite the disparity in the Evangelical and High Church ideals, for the first third of the nineteenth century an uneasy truce prevailed. By 1840, however, the strains between these parties became unmanageable. Each party had acquired strong, regional concentrations and forceful leaders. As they did, the broad consensus on which the church relied was threatened, and its governance offered more of an arena for conflict than the basis for reconciliation and resolution. The immediate cause of the conflict was the American appearance of the *Tracts*, the series of pamphlets that announced the theological positions of the Church of England's Oxford Movement. Although not all High Church loyalists agreed, many of them believed that the *Tracts* made plain the true source of the church's authenticity, namely its apostolic ministry and worship. Evangelicals, on the other hand, feared the *Tracts* would undercut the church's primary reliance upon the Bible and move the church toward Roman Catholic belief and practice. Determined to counter this trend, Evangelicals mobilized for the General Convention of 1844. Several Convention resolutions introduced by Evangelicals intended to compel adherence to particular theological principles, notably the priority of faith, and the representative—rather than literal—efficacy and character of the sacraments.[21]

Despite the Evangelical initiative, it was a Convention resolution introduced by High Church deputies that passed. The resolution struck a note of compromise and, in doing so, acknowledged a reality. It affirmed that the church's "Liturgy, Offices, and Articles" are sufficient "exponents of her sense of the essential doctrines of Holy Scripture; and that the Canons of the Church afford ample means of discipline and correction for all who depart her standards." But the resolution also noted that "the General Convention is not a suitable tribunal for the trial and censure of, and that the Church is not responsible for, the errors of individuals, whether they are members of this Church or not."[22] Thus, the church was committed to a measure of toleration that seems impressive even by today's standards. But if the General Convention did not serve as a forum for determining and enforcing the Episcopal Church's standards of belief, which of the church's offices or structures could do so? If the church's unity relied upon a generalized, consensual determination about the boundaries of belief and practice, that consensus would face severe challenges.

As long as the High Church party derived its identity solely from its theological principles, it was possible to ameliorate differences with Evangelicals. By 1855, some church leaders, seeking to claim a new center for the church, could even cite the beneficial influences of this controversy. Noting the *Tracts'* influence in America, Bishop Horatio Potter was not deterred by the heat of the dispute or by the loss of a few notable leaders on both sides of the Atlantic to Roman Catholicism. In his book *The Catholic Movement in the American Episcopal Church*, George DeMille summarizes the situation by quoting freely from Bishop Potter. Potter considered "the movement which has occurred in the Anglican Church within twenty years" the "most energetic and the most important of any which has been witnessed in that branch of the church, since the period of the Reformation." Controversy compelled the church "to appeal to higher evidence and authority than the accident of a state establishment. She dug down to her foundations. She pointed to Scripture and to the records of the first Christian ages, to prove that her origin was from God, and her power divine." Thanks to the Tracts the "ethos of the ancient church was revived and renewed in the modern." As a result there had been "a wonderful revival of spiritual life and energy."[23]

Although the church had "dug down to her foundations" during the theological firestorm sparked by two contentious parties, ultimately there had been beneficial results; but the spiritual energy that was thrown off in the process soon generated the most profound and extended conflict the church has experienced. Theology was one thing, but when worship got involved, the entire church was engulfed. Worship lies at the core of Episcopal identity, and in the second half of the nineteenth century, the church's worship began to shift. It did so not because of pronouncements from a church party or a change in canon law by the General Convention but rather because of changes occurring at its grassroots—changes that affected its consensus on the basic features of Christian belief and practice. The seeds of conflict were sown as Ritualism brought the principles of the Oxford Movement into the church's life, and one parish after another began to enhance aspects of its worship. Many of these changes would seem inconsequential today: flowers on the altar, vested choirs, acolytes and processions with singing to mark the beginning and end of worship. But by 1850, such influential, centrist clergy as William Muhlenberg had made some of these changes. In a few parishes further steps were taken. At Church of the Advent, Boston, and St. Paul's, Baltimore, pew rents were abolished, regular matins and vespers were conducted, and weekly Eucharists were celebrated. Elsewhere, stone altars with colored frontals replaced simple tables, and candles and a cross adorned them. Clergy wore surplice and colored stole and, in some places, reserved the sacrament for communion of the sick. As one historian observed, these apparently simple innovations were "the indicators of an inner revolution" that would eventually appropriate the center of the church's worship life.[24]

Ritualism became the principal expression of the Anglo-Catholic party in the church. With persuasive advocates such as James De Koven, Ritualism also became something of a grassroots movement. De Koven argued for acceptance of a eucharistic theology as the basis of Episcopal belief. The effect of his influence was the development of theological roots for changes in worship. While Evangelical Episcopalians construed the church's piety as inner and personal and looked askance at elaboration of worship, Ritualists sought acceptance for enhancements of the church's outer manifestations. Such a turn, they believed, would provide the grounding in apostolic life that Episcopalians required. They were convinced that worship must be understood sacramentally as the literal means of experiencing God's grace. In the Eucharist, they stressed Christ's spiritual presence, not his symbolic representation.[25] (Indeed, under the influence of Ritualism, Episcopalians have developed a practical basis for understanding the Incarnation, i.e., the historic Christian affirmation that Jesus was God in human form.) Ritualism also secured the role of worship as the basis of the church's spirituality, especially its sense of the congregation as community.

By the 1860s, the Ritualist outlook and the practices that embodied it had become the source of profound conflict across the Episcopal Church. Typically, the conflict erupted as rectors—imbued with Ritualists ideals by their training in such centers as General Seminary—started making changes in worship, creating suspicion among their parishioners and alarm among their bishops. In some cases, the combination of vestry and bishop was sufficient to suspend liturgical innovation in a parish. At St. Clement's, Philadelphia, for instance, a rector was dismissed for such unfamiliar practices as using colored stoles, singing hymns in procession, bowing to the altar, making private confession, and offering prayers for the dead.[26]

Evangelicalism's opposition to such innovations relied in part upon the sympathies of bishops who were not hesitant to use the authority of their office to discipline or dislodge Ritualist clergy. But innovation in worship steadily moved beyond a few single-minded reformers. Though prominent in certain regions of the country and a few influential, urban parishes, Ritualism also was proving to have broad appeal. By stages, increasing numbers of parishes were adopting aspects of ritual innovation. To prevent a groundswell, Evangelicals turned to the General Convention. Given their tradition of respect for republican principles of government, it was only natural that Evangelicals would seek resolution of their theological and liturgical distress within the church's national legislative arena. But they were to be frustrated with the outcome.

The General Convention of 1868 was the high point of the Evangelical effort to stem the tide of Ritualism. Nearly twenty "memorials" (or resolutions) sponsored by Evangelicals called for "new canons that would restrict specifically Anglo-Catholic ritual practice." One proposed canon would have eliminated any vestments other than "surplice, stole, band or gown," as well as the use of candles, crucifixes, bowing at the name of Jesus other than in reciting the Creed, elevation of the bread and wine during the Eucharistic Prayer, and the use of incense.[27] But the effort came to naught. Tellingly, the Convention encouraged study of the proposed canon and postponed a decision until the next Convention in 1871.

By then, it was too late. The only Evangelically supported resolution that could pass was one by the Bishop of Maryland that left decisions "concerning ceremony and vestments in the hands of each diocesan bishop."[28] By all accounts, it was a moment of Anglo-Catholic triumph. James De Koven stood before the Convention at one point and declared his belief in the real presence of Christ in the bread and wine of the altar. Anglo-Catholic principles seemed to have triumphed, and Evangelicals felt that their convictions and sensibilities had been trampled. One historian notes the anguish of a deputy to the Convention who felt that Evangelicals could "have no relief, no help or comfort to expect from the legislation of the church. We have nothing to look for from the action of our General Convention but oppression...till conscience and loyalty to God and his truth can bear it no longer."[29]

The concluding reference to "conscience and loyalty to God" is significant for two reasons. First, it underscores the failure of the Convention to legislate on matters of belief and practice in ways that would unite, rather than divide, the church. Second, it indicates that the failure of the Convention to endorse one particular platform could motivate some to break with the church. This is precisely what happened. In 1873, Bishop George David Cummins of Kentucky and a few other clergy broke with the Episcopal Church to create the Reformed Episcopal Church.

The creation of the Reformed Episcopal Church promised a setting within which it seemed possible to preserve and perhaps expand the true, biblical principles intended for the Episcopal Church.[30] Its founders believed that the Reformed Episcopal Church could be the catalyst for a union of American Protestants. Such a success would have consigned the Rome-leaning Episcopal Church to history's dustbin. But it was not to be. Although, the schism caused public consternation and prophesies of doom, it had surprisingly little effect upon the Episcopal Church and the American religious scene overall; today, the Reformed Episcopal Church consists of only a few thousand members in a few regional sections of the country, especially the Philadelphia area and parts of South Carolina. However, there is an important lesson to be learned—namely, that belief and practice cannot be legislated. The Reformed Episcopal Church remains as an emblem of the inability of a legislative forum to resolve a bitter conflict at this core level of the church. The center of the church's identity and vocation must take shape in other ways. But that lesson appears to have eluded the two fractious parties of the nineteenth century, and it appears to have eluded those of the twenty-first as well.

In light of the rout of the Evangelicals and the secession of the Reformed Episcopal Church, it would seem only natural that the General Convention of 1874 would have confirmed Ritualism's triumph in 1871. But quite the opposite happened. Although various Ritualist canons were proposed, the one that passed revealed the mood of the moment. It created a process by which a bishop could investigate complaints about the ritual practices of priests in his diocese. It cited such forms of excess as elevation or adoration of the elements in the Communion, and it prohibited the use of any acts not authorized by the Prayer Book. Although the Convention still refused to prohibit particular practices, its decision implied that there could be excessive ritual, and it set forth a means of resolving complaints about ritual at the diocesan level.[31] Thus, the Convention of 1874 indicated a new reality, one that made any wholehearted legislative endorsement of any one party in the church over the other highly unlikely. The 1874 Convention embodied the commitment of a broad swath of Episcopal leaders to articulate a new sense of worship that would secure its central role in the church. While Ritualism was gradually gaining a hold in parts of the church, its influence would only be sanctioned within limits. Thus, the Convention served as a forum for a collective process of mediating among varied local patterns and, over time, seeking a common mind. Convention could not halt the division that became the Reformed Episcopal Church, but it became clear that Episcopalians were in search of a new consensus. Problematically, however, that consensus found its basis in institutional process.

EPISCOPAL FAULT LINES YESTERDAY AND TODAY

After the General Convention of 1874, the clash over ritual in the church subsided. Though Episcopalians of either a strongly Evangelical or strongly Ritualist bent were left unsatisfied, a measure of consensus had been achieved. Indeed, by 1928, the adoption of a new Prayer Book by the General Convention occasioned relatively little debate and no rupture of the church. It seemed that the Episcopal Church had successfully faced a tension over belief and emerged with a coherent identity and vocation.

However, the conflicts over ritual that led to a series of strained Conventions had proven a portent of conflict and division to come. To understand what and how Episcopalians believe now, we must identify the perennial sources of conflict over belief, and the manner of addressing them in the church. Which fault lines represent persistently unsettled issues that threaten further division? Over what have Episcopalians fought, and how have they sought resolution? To what extent have they been successful, and to what extent frustrated, in trying to maintain a coherent identity and vocation?

It is easy to specify what has *not* been the source of conflict among Episcopalians. For example, the conflict resolved by the 1874 Convention was *not* about complete uniformity of practice. At the time, such a goal would have been unthinkable, given that the church appeared to be pulled more or less evenly by the opposite forces of the two well-secured church parties, each so strikingly different in approach to worship and ministry. Even the most confirmed Evangelical or Ritualist of the period realized that the goal was to lobby for a range of acceptable practice or, put another way, the limits of acceptable practice. Each party was attempting to establish the point at which certain approaches to worship would begin to confuse or betray—rather than uphold— Episcopal identity. Even to the most partisan Episcopalians, comprehensiveness was integral to their identity and entailed a striking diversity of beliefs and practices.

Neither was the conflict about belief in any strict sense. The controversy had been less about specific tenets of Christian faith than, as we have already established, authentic forms of church practice. Furthermore, very few Episcopalians—however rabid they may have been about worship practices—were drawn into the intense pitched battles of theology that raged among other Christians of the period. Unlike other mainline Protestant denominations near the end of the nineteenth century, there was no Episcopal conflagration over the Bible. There would be no suggestion of a required list of fundamental beliefs. Indeed, as Fundamentalist movements tore the fabric of other denominations, Episcopalians seemed strangely unaffected, apart from giving ecclesiastical sanctuary to victims of Fundamentalist assaults in other churches.

Although the Episcopal Church apparently escaped the furor of the "Fundamentalist-Modernist" controversy that engulfed much of mainstream Protestantism, the same core issue—the church's relation to American culture—did confront Episcopalians.[32] Like other Protestant denominations, the Episcopal Church had developed a fault line over whether American life offered opportunities or hindrances for the religious life. As we described in chapter two, this was a tension between readily adapting the church to the contours of American life and taking care to guard the church's distinctive identity and vocation from an overly easy association with American life. Although this tension set the stage for the flare-up over ritual, it seemed contained within the broad boundaries established by the Convention of 1874. The basis of broadly acceptable consensus seemingly had been found. It was a consensus that rested upon prevailing assumptions about the basis of ecclesiastical order among Episcopalians. So long as those assumptions held the allegiance of most people in the church, it could channel such tensions into a coherent sense of its identity and vocation.

From 1935 on, this means of consensus began to falter, thus beginning a period of crisis and decline that may well represent the severest challenge ever faced by the mainline church in America. At the time, the crisis was not readily apparent, because mainline religion had achieved a seemingly secure place in American life. But 1935 begins the period for which historians use terms such as "drift and indecision" and "disarray and disaffection" to depict the mainline church's experience.[33] What is striking about this development is that belief was the battleground.

"Modernization" typically refers to the collection of social forces that undercut mainline religious belief. Modernization includes urbanization, technological development, pluralism, and organizational reconfiguration. Evidence of modernization surfaced in extensive shifts in lifestyles, values, and forms of cultural expression. No aspect of American life went unaffected. For mainline religion the most obvious result was the increasing force of secularization. Unbelief—and a set of social circumstances seemingly encouraging it—became the greatest threat to religious life.[34]

Sensing the drift of American life, the mainline churches, including the Episcopal Church, made decisive changes in their styles of belief and practice. First, church leaders, including seminary faculty, placed fresh emphasis on defining the core of Christian belief in terms that seemed to accommodate it to a new cultural day. One product of the effort to restate Christian belief for a new era was the appearance of a series of volumes entitled the *Church's Teaching Series* that appeared in the 1950s. A new series of the *Church's Teaching Series* with new authors appeared in the 1970s, and yet another edition of the series with another set of authors appeared early in the twenty-first century. The popular appeal of these volumes lay in their intention to address the foundations of Christian belief, church history, ethics, and so forth in ways that contemporary lay people could readily understand. The volumes tried to find a centrist position in content and tone; sometimes the perspective was more liberal and affirmative of the general trend of American culture; sometimes the perspective was more conservative and critical of a growing laxity in boundaries. In the opinion of some, the series leans overall in a slightly more liberal direction. Harder to establish is its prevailing stance on the nature of the church's relation to culture—either exactly what that relationship *is* or exactly what that relationship *ought* to be. Over the various editions of the series, a few of its writers have been noted iconoclasts, such as James A. Pike. But most have been Episcopal clergy and teachers whose commitment to the faith has been unwavering but who simply believe that Christianity must be restated with a more critical view of American life.

Such efforts to restate Christian belief and practice and to integrate a more critical view of society have been paralleled by a more aggressively critical approach to American life by the Episcopal Church's official bodies. From 1935 on, diocesan and national conventions in resolutions—and some individual leaders in their pronouncements—became vigorous critics of virtually every aspect of American life, from social mores to wars to the state of civil rights for minority groups. Sometimes these critiques have triggered consternation among church members. But mainline leaders did not relent. They were driven by the urge to respond to the sense of social crisis in ways that—they hoped—would recover the authenticity and the influence of their churches. The social role and repercussions of belief was their central concern.[35]

In chapter five, we noted the rise and influence of "crisis theology" in the Episcopal Church, whose politically oriented practitioners were accused by detractors of trying to be "relevant at any cost." By "relevant," critics of crisis theology meant that its practitioners sacrificed basic Christian beliefs in their rush to accommodate the church to a changing society. In fact, advocates of crisis theology did intend to reframe the basis of Christian faith but with an intensified critique of society, not a more lax attitude toward it.

The theology of crisis and response that gained momentum in America attempted to reconstruct religious belief and practice along socio-political lines. Although the ultimate effect of this approach upon the core of belief in the Episcopal Church is open to debate, the movement did have profound and far-reaching effects on practice—the two foremost examples being the expansion of women's leadership roles (including ordination) and Prayer Book revision. Politically speaking, each of these momentous changes had an equally momentous and opposite reaction, resulting in General Conventions so contentious (and media headlines so blaring) that many Episcopalians despaired. Never had the Episcopal Church seen the like before, and many worried that there might be schism or even worse.

Of course, the church *had* seen the like before and would have done well to have noticed the precedent. Exactly as they had done in 1874, Episcopalians in the late twentieth century sought to make changes in belief and practice through organizational process, especially the legislative processes of the General Convention. That they should do so was only natural, and that efforts at change would prompt increasingly organized opposition was no surprise.

The end result was another phenomenal replay of the past. Exactly as the small group of Episcopalians seceded in the nineteenth century to create the Reformed Episcopal Church, others began to break away in the twentieth. For example, in 1963, James Parker Dees, an Episcopal priest in Statesville, North Carolina, organized the Anglican Orthodox Church. While claiming that the Episcopal Church had "watered down" the Christian faith, Dees's major complaint was the church's stand on civil rights and its turn toward what he viewed as Roman Catholic forms of devotion, such as reserving the sacrament and referring to the bread and wine of the Eucharist as Christ's body and blood. A supporter of right-wing fringe groups, such as the Liberty Lobby, and of a strong national defense as a deterrent to Communism, Dees decried church leadership's position on social issues, including its support of the National Council of Churches, which advocated "disarmament, coexistence with Russia, the abolition of loyalty security laws, recognition of Red China, and forced racial integration."[36]

Dees managed to get consecrated as a bishop by a bishop of the Holy Ukrainian Autocephalic Orthodox Church. He proved himself an adroit organizer and, by 1969, claimed to enroll nearly forty congregations. He eventually linked his movement with small, like-minded movements in several countries, including Rhodesia and the Philippines, but such cooperation was rare; he scorned those groups that later broke from the Episcopal Church over Prayer Book revision and the ordination of women, claiming that their efforts at establishing a "continuing" Episcopal Church were useless, since his movement was the one true continuation of Reformation Anglicanism. Dees also founded Cranmer Seminary at Statesville, North Carolina.

Other groups, most of them tiny, also left the Episcopal Church. For instance, the Old Episcopal Church, formed in 1972 by Jack Capers Adam, a former wrestler of alligators and owner of a small zoo in Mesa, Arizona, never mustered more than a few congregations. Similarly, the Southern Episcopal Church, founded in 1962, claimed that "Christianity is a conservative religion that does not follow every liberal waxing of men's minds and moral laxities" and that "it has always been an acceptable fact that the South was overly [sic] conservative in thinking and moral attitude."[37] Proudly using the 1928 edition of the Book of Common Prayer, the Southern Episcopal Church had four bishops by 1984, but its membership statistics were uncertain.

The pace of dissent accelerated from the 1970s on, as long-anticipated changes in the Episcopal Church were implemented. Other small dissident groups, such as the Anglican Episcopal Church of North America and the American Episcopal Church, appeared and enrolled a few dozen congregations and several thousand members each. Some of their congregations were tiny, new outposts, but some had truly left the Episcopal Church, though rarely did such churches and their adherents like to be described as "breakaway." Like earlier groups, they styled themselves as the "continuing" church; after all, *they* had not left the Episcopal Church; the Episcopal Church had left *them*—and Christianity—when it revised the Prayer Book, ordained women, and took various liberal stands on social issues and theological interpretation.[38] By the early twenty-first century, more than three-dozen such breakaway groups could be identified.

Meanwhile, dissent within the church was highly mobilized. By the late 1970s, the umbrella organization of dissent was the Fellowship of Concerned Churchmen, a collaboration of the Society for the Preservation of the Book of Common Prayer, the American Church Union, and the editors of two magazines, Dorothy Faber of *The Christian Challenge* and Perry Laukhuff of *The Certain Trumpet*. More than most such groups, they were clear about the principles they espoused. These included loyalty to Scripture, the Creeds, and the Prayer Book, and affirmation of the Eucharist, Baptism, and the church's apostolic ministry. Of course, these affirmations would appear to place the organization in the church's mainstream—and that is where they wanted to be, as signaled by their resolve to "taking every step necessary toward the continuation of the Episcopal Church in its historic form."[39]

By the end of the twentieth century a bewildering variety of dissenting groups within the church had appeared, most saying similar things but few able to find common cause with one another. By the beginning of the twenty-first century, a new variation on the theme of being the "continuing" church had appeared. Two new dissident groups, one without the church and one within, had devised a new tactic to underscore their claim to being the true church. In search of legitimacy, the Anglican Mission in America (AMiA) managed to have its initial bishops consecrated by Anglican bishops from Africa and Asia. The rationale for such moves was that the Anglican Mission would minister to those loyal Episcopalians who could not abide the theological drift of the Episcopal Church. By the twenty-first century, most of these groups had dedicated the greater part of their energies toward opposition to the church's official sanctioning of the blessing of same-sex unions and the ordination of homosexual persons, although the issues that had ignited dissent in previous decades were not forgotten. For most dissenters, homosexuality was the latest addition to a long list of apostasies into which the Episcopal Church had fallen. Tapping into the growing discontent, the Anglican Mission in America claimed to have enrolled more than fifty congregations.

Still within the church, Forward in Faith (FinF) continues the work of the Episcopal Synod, which once had served as an umbrella organization for dissident groups. Forward in Faith makes common cause with dissident Episcopalians and with conservative Anglican groups in Britain and Australia. The umbrella organization articulates a set of perceptions and convictions typical of Episcopal dissent in the twenty-first century. It is dedicated to "upholding the Christian faith" and to offering "support of those persecuted for this Faith." Forward in Faith "rejects alteration of this Faith demanded by those who question the authority of Holy Scripture in order to advocate 20th century secular values." Thus, Forward in Faith emphasizes that the primary reality for the church is a crisis over the authority of Scripture. Its organizers perceive that prominent Episcopal leaders believe they "should be able to modify, change, ignore, or eliminate certain passages of the Bible which do not support the prevailing 'modern ideas.'" These "modern ideas" include women's rights and the ordination of women, the "advocacy" of homosexuality, and perceived denials of "the reality of sin" and the "need for radical repentance." Forward in Faith's spokesmen add their concerns over issues of sexual morality, abandonment of the doctrine of the Trinity, compromise of the apostolic ministry by the ordination of women, and endorsement of abortion and euthanasia. The leaders of Forward in Faith qualify their objection to homosexuality by explaining that homosexuality only becomes evil when it is "practiced." They suggest, like other conservatives, that it is possible for homosexual persons to become heterosexual by repentance and conversion. But homosexuality is not the basic issue, although it is a galvanizing one. Beneath the litany of theological woes, Forward in Faith's leaders are convinced that there is a "crisis of belief." The Episcopal Church, they feel, has abandoned historic Christian faith because of its urge to think and act in ways sanctioned by contemporary society. By 2002, over sixty Episcopal congregations had heard the call and enrolled with Forward in Faith. Proclaiming their loyalty, they also declared their commitment to vigorous dissent.[40]

Often reliant on the charisma of a commanding figure, the leadership of such groups usually proves brittle. It becomes difficult for such groups to work together, as each has a slightly different perspective and emphasis, causing most of their encounters to end in theological squabbles, with each claiming the higher ground. Typically, these theological fracases prove unsuccessful, usually because their premises and, indeed, their very reasons for existence tend to be *against*, rather than *for*, something (and, as any seminarian will attest, arguing the negative premise in traditional theological discourse tends to be much more rigorous and challenging than arguing the positive). But the substantive motivation for their protests should not be discounted. Dissent is more than the carping resistance to change; it cannot be dismissed as intransigence or prejudice. Dissenting groups elicit followings because they cite a genuine weak point in the church, namely, its discernment of boundaries. That is, conservatives believe that the Episcopal Church's emphasis on comprehensiveness and its impulse to respond to a sense of social crisis have compromised its identity and vocation.

Conservatives bring an important offering to the church: a clearly grounded and defined sense of order. The conservative urge is to tighten the church's boundaries by declaring certain practices and people out of bounds. Thus, the conservative motivation is to claim the church in all its purity, which they believe existed at some point in the past but has diminished because of modern compromises. Breakaway groups in particular are acting on the conviction that they have a sure sense of the church's true identity and vocation and that they can re-create it as necessary in its intended purity. Ironically, such groups succumb to the very fallacy to which they believe Episcopal leaders are so prone: they disregard the church's authority on matters with which they disagree. In that sense, they are a symptom of the church's problem, not its solution.

THE NATURE OF ORDER

The very existence of such groups reveals the true source of conflicts among Episcopalians over belief: the nature of the church's order. Nothing less than the nature of that order is at stake, but the issue of order is a thorny one because, historically, Episcopal identity and vocation have been rooted in a critical tension between the capacity to embrace a variety of expressions of the Christian faith (in other words, to be "comprehensive") and the requirement to be faithful to Christian tradition (in other words, to be "apostolic"). Indeed, the maintenance of that creative tension classically defines the Episcopal—and wider Anglican—genius. The challenge, of course, has been that rapid social change has compelled adaptations of church life that take some Episcopalians in the direction of being more comprehensive and others in the direction of leaning more heavily on apostolic precedent. Finding a middle ground for these polarized parties has proven very difficult.

But there is a still greater challenge. At a time when increasing numbers of people in the United States are without religious roots and consider themselves spiritual seekers, the challenge is to draw them into a faith community. As we have seen repeatedly in respondents' stories, this transition from spiritual individualism to spiritual community is occurring in a powerful new way in Episcopal churches. It remains for Episcopalians to form a shared commitment to mission on the basis of this new experience of shared Christian life. To do this, Episcopalians increasingly must live with the tension of where to set the boundary between what is acceptable belief and practice and what is unacceptable. Of course, a strong focus on the need for such boundaries of acceptability traditionally has been the provenance of conservative groups within the church. And, given the fluidity of practice and belief in the contemporary world, surely their concern is well placed and legitimate. Even in less fluid periods of our Episcopal past, the church appears to have spent its time and energy wisely whenever it addressed boundaries of belief and practice. As we have shown, the process whereby these boundaries were debated did not necessarily achieve the goal; but the process usually did accomplish something as important—perhaps more important: the creation of a coherent basis for unity and mission. Regardless of whether conservative groups have placed their boundaries at the most appropriate places along the political continuum, they have at least identified the importance of the question and are doing their part to help the church reestablish Episcopal identity in the twenty-first century.

Setting boundaries never is easy. Attempts to do so usually create more questions than answers—questions such as these:

- How are the Episcopal Church's core beliefs defined and enforced?

- How can the church at all levels, from the congregation outward, ensure that its practices reflect the belief it affirms?

- Are there faithful and consistent links between belief, practice, and mission unifying the various levels of the church?

- What set of beliefs and what sense of mission now provide a basis for the church to say it is coherent?

- What steps can be taken to enhance the sense among Episcopalians that they indeed participate in a faithful, responsive, and effective church?

The last question may be the key, and the answer has to do with Christian formation. Historically, the church has relied upon its relation to American culture and upon a distinctive ethos—maintained through forms of worship, ministry, and education in order to help define itself. For example, church-related primary and secondary schools created environments within which young people readily grasped what the church held dear. Even in Sunday schools and youth groups, the church's teaching was clear and could readily be absorbed. But the church's ability to rely on such historic patterns of formation has lessened. The diversity and mobility of American culture and the emphasis of Americans upon a spirituality rooted not in one place but in a continuing journey has eroded the ethos Episcopalians once took for granted. The church's historic identity and vocation have become uncertain. With its ethos in disarray, how can the Episcopal Church now create the conditions in which to faithfully and effectively form people as Christians? What does Christian formation mean today, and how can it be implemented in practical terms? And how can effective patterns of formation in one locality find points of unity with what proves effective elsewhere? By extension, how can Episcopalians then devise the means of forming people as leaders in ways that are faithfully Christian and distinctively Episcopal? The questions are enormous; they reflect the power of the cultural shift that has confronted the church and they concern the future shape of its identity and vocation.[41]

NOTES

[1] Charles Hefling, "On Being Reasonably Theological," in Robert Boak Slocum, ed., A New Conversation: Essays on the Future of Theology and the Episcopal Church (Church Publishing, 1999), pp. 48–59.

[2] Turner, p. 120, 127.

[3] Central Florida, Kansas, Los Angeles, Massachusetts, Minnesota, Nevada, North Carolina, Texas, and West Missouri.

[4] C. Kirk Hadaway, A Report on Episcopal Churches in the United States, Domestic and Foreign Missionary Society, the Episcopal Church, April 2002.

[5] Gardner H. Shattuck, Jr., "Knowing The Tasks," in Robert Boak Slocum, ed., A New Conversation: Essays on the Future of Theology and the Episcopal Church, p. 38.

[6] Hartford Seminary's FACT study of Episcopal churches notes the tension between tradition and innovation that characterizes Episcopal worship today. While formal and structured patterns of worship are widely valued, nearly a third of Episcopal churches responding to this survey describe an emphasis on innovative and lively worship, and claim they have made major changes in their patterns of worship within five years of being surveyed. The study's principal researcher also associates changes in a congregation's worship with its strength and growth. See Hadaway, op. cit.

[7] From its earliest Reformation years, the Church of England, and subsequently its Anglican Communion offspring such as the Episcopal Church, have grounded their life in the concept of lex orandi, lex credendi, or "the law of worship is the law of belief." This is another way of saying that belief arises not through rational formulations but through encounter with God in the experience of worship.

[8] Hadaway, p. 26.

[9] Craig Dykstra and Dorothy C. Bass, "Times of Yearning, Practices of Faith," in Dorothy C. Bass, ed., Practicing Our Faith: A Way of Life for a Searching People (Jossey-Bass, 1997), p. 6f.

[10] Nancey Murphy, "Using Macintyre's Method in Christian Ethics," in Nancey Murphy, Brad J. Kallenberg, and Mark Thiessen Nation eds., *Virtues and Practices in the Christian Tradition: Christian Ethics after Macintyre* (Trinity Press, 1997), pp. 33–42. In the same volume, James Wm. McClendon, Jr., describes the life of the early church and its focus on community formation at length. His chapter is instructive for us because we see a modern focus on community formation among Episcopalians. See his "The Practice of Community Formation," pp. 85–110.

[11] Dorothy C. Bass, et al.

[12] See Liah Greenfeld and Michel Martin, "The Idea of the 'Center:' An Introduction," in Greenfeld and Martin, eds., *Center: Ideas and Institutions* (University of Chicago, 1988), p. ix.

[13] See Lewis, *Yet With A Steady Beat*, op. cit..

[14] Wayne Stuart Frederick Pickering, "Sociology of Anglicanism," in Stephen Sykes and John Booty, ed., *The Study of Anglicanism* (SPCK/ Fortress, 1998), p. 373.

[15] Stephen W. Sykes, "The Fundamentals of Christianity," in *The Study of Anglicanism*, p. 232.

[16] Arthur Stephen McGrade, "Reason," in *The Study of Anglicanism*, p. 109.

[17] Wayne J. Hankey, "Canon Law," in *The Study of Anglicanism*, p. 209f.

[18] Book of Common Prayer, pp. 876–878.

[19] Guelzo, *For The Union of Evangelical Christendom: The Irony of the Reformed Episcopalians* (Penn State, 1994), p. 39.

[20] *Ibid.*, p. 46.

[21] DeMille, *The Catholic Movement in the American Episcopal Church* (Church Historical Society, 1941), p. 59.

[22] *Ibid.*, p. 60.

[23] *Ibid.*, p. 70f.

[24] *Ibid.*, p. 85.

[25] *Ibid.*, p. 94.

[26] *Ibid.*, p. 110.

[27] Guelzo, p. 67.

[28] *Ibid.*, p. 68.

[29] *Ibid.*

[30] *Ibid.*

[31] DeMille, p. 123f.

[32] See the excellent account of the sources of this tension in American religious life in William R. Hutchison, *The Modernist Impulse in American Protestantism* (Duke, 1992).

[33] Sweet, "The Modernization of Protestant Religion in America," in Lotz et al., ed., *Altered Landscapes: Christianity in America, 1935–1985* (Eerdmans, 1989), p. 20.

[34] These trends are summarized by Sweet.

[35] *Ibid.*

[36] See the unpublished manuscript by Donald S. Armentrout, *Episcopal Splinter Groups*, p. 9.

[37] *Ibid.*, p. 12, 7.

[38] See Douglas Bess, *Divided We Stand* (Tractarian Press, 2002).

[39] Armentrout, p. 21.

[40] These positions are detailed in Forward in Faith's brochures, especially "Confronting the Crisis: A Way Forward."

[41] Such questions are asked with unusual clarity by Philip Turner in his chapter, "When Worlds Collide: A Comment on the Precarious State of Theology in the Episcopal Church," in Slocum, ed., *A New Conversation: Essays on the Future of Theology and the Episcopal Church* (Church Publishing, 1999), p. 125.

8

FROM RELIGIOUS INSTITUTION TO SPIRITUAL COMMUNITY
The Challenges Ahead

I f the past is a reliable guide to the future, the Episcopal Church will continue to face profound challenges. We have seen that Episcopalians repeatedly have faced tensions that arise largely because they aspire to two somewhat oppositional goals: the definition of belief and practice; and the accommodation of breadth and diversity. We have found that, at times, these tensions become unmanageable, causing opposing factions to resort to the legislative procedures of the General Convention for resolution. In the process, Episcopalians usually have achieved more clarity about what was *not* to be practiced and affirmed than about what *was*. If the precedent holds, the Episcopal Church will fail to achieve coherence on some—if not most— matters of acute importance in the future; and we will be left to live with ambiguity on pressing issues of belief and practice. For some, such ambiguity will be intolerable, representing an abdication of responsibility for the church's identity and vocation. Loudly they will protest, and loudly some of them may leave the church in search of a safe enclave in which to build the church in a pure form, as their inclinations dictate. But once again—if the past is a reliable guide—their intentions will be frustrated.

It is highly unlikely that there will be a mass exodus from the Episcopal Church as a result of the tensions we face today. Although discontent with national structures and institutional procedures is pervasive, there is a paradoxical corrective at work—namely, the widespread local initiative and vitality that has been our principal focus throughout this book. Given this paradox, what lies ahead for Episcopalians? To find out, we asked people in local Episcopal congregations what challenges they anticipate in the near future.

RESOURCES FOR THE FUTURE

GROWTH

The most significant challenge Episcopalians cited was the necessity of growth in their congregations. By growth, they meant both an increase in the congregation's membership and an enhanced quality of congregational life. The theme of growth surfaced in both general and particular ways. In an East Coast congregation, for example, one member expressed this outlook: "I think we should revisit our mission and vision, get clear about where we're going and why. We talk about growth, but in what dimensions? It's not just numbers; [it's] more important to nurture people in their spiritual growth; disciples building up other disciples."

Frequent references to growth in membership do not appear to indicate widespread interest in an average-church-attendance "numbers game"—that is, filling pews with people as an abstract exercise in evangelism. An interest in growth manifests itself in several ways. Some Episcopalians feel that, if their neighborhood is growing and the parish is maintaining its status quo, then something is wrong. From their perspective, a status quo parish in a growing neighborhood isn't status quo—it's in decline! Others simply want to reach people who need the spiritual and material comforts that a healthy outreach program can bring. From their perspective, growth will happen automatically to a parish that reaches out to its community; therefore, the parish that is not growing is a parish that probably is not fulfilling its mission.

A member of a parish in the Southeast spoke of growth in terms of an influx of young people: "Our young people are increasing in numbers, so we need to expand our programs and resources for them. There are many new families coming in with children, so we are talking about hiring a minister specifically to focus on the children and youth." A member of another parish spoke even more vividly of the challenges of neighborhood growth. She suggested that it no longer was necessary to go forth from the parish looking for the fields of evangelism, because the fields were coming to *them*, almost overwhelming her congregation with opportunity: "Our area is quickly changing from rural to urban. The temporary structure we are in sits on ground that had a barn and pasturage just a few years ago. Now we are surrounded by housing developments and shopping centers. The immigration of people is dramatic."

Others in the focus group echoed their concern about population growth. "Some of those people have found their way here, and our attendance is growing rapidly. We are already bursting at the seams in this space." "We definitely need some sort of new building soon," another person added. "In it, we need educational programs for children, teenagers, adults, older people, the whole range." Another person seemed somewhat more comfortable with growth per se but did worry that the quality of community might be compromised because of it: "We need to find ways to involve our newcomers in activities so they will become a part of the church community."

A member of a parish on the East Coast echoed this concern about membership growth and its effect on spiritual community: "I am confident that we will grow in numbers, which raises the challenge of how to maintain the small, family feeling—the intimacy—in the crowds of people." A similar thought surfaced in the room when the group was asked to identify the challenges their congregation faces. One parishioner answered quickly, "Our biggest challenge is demographics, I think. The population growth is to the south and west of us here. This neighborhood is changing, and it won't be the wealthy area it once was. I wonder how we will deal with that." Her question brought a ready response from another member of the group: "I think our challenge is to stay clear about who we are and why we are here. If our neighborhood identity is changing, that may require different ways of enacting our mission. We already do a great deal of work with one of the inner city parishes, so we have a lot of experience with ministry in a changing neighborhood."

Of course, wherever population is stable or declining, growth takes on an entirely different meaning. In the Northeast, one parishioner mentioned "membership" when asked to cite a major challenge. "Attendance has already picked up," she continued, "but we have a long way to go. There was a time when there was standing room only. We have a very, very long way to go. I would just like to see the pews filled up. I would like to see people in the front pews." Whether the population is growing or declining, the underlying reality for all Episcopal congregations is change, coming at them quickly and in multiple forms. As one lay person expressed it, "Our society is undergoing rapid changes, diminishing intimacy and connectedness and increasing alienation. The church is or can be a major source for rebuilding community and bringing light into darkness."

An urban dweller observed that "this city has many transient people because of the college and the military base, with lots of people moving in for a few years and then moving on. We have a strong core and some slow increase in numbers, but the real challenge is how best to serve those who live here and attend for only a year or two." In a similar vein, another lay leader noted: "There is so much instability and insecurity all around us. I hope we can be a place where people find a sense of belonging, meaning, and affirmation. We are already a source of strength and nurturing to many people. Our worship and the emphasis on the sacraments are key to that. Our mission is to continue being a source of community in a world where that is weak."

Mission and Resources

The challenge of growth is largely the challenge of mission. As the members of an active parish on the West Coast declared, "The Episcopal Church is in a great position to take the Gospel into the culture of the new century. All the parts are there. It is just a matter of mobilizing the church. This is an incredibly exciting time." A hundred miles down the coast, the members of another parish agreed. "We had a discussion about evangelism last Sunday," said one man, "and our group agreed that Episcopalians generally don't spread our faith. We don't pound on doors."

The topic of evangelism energized this group's discussion. One person disliked the image of pounding on doors and was not happy about the word "evangelism." "If this church did that, I wouldn't be a member," she declared. But another person was ready to reply. "Well, about the only time we mention renewing our faith is when we renew our baptismal vows in baptismal liturgy. I know Mormons and Jehovah's Witnesses who actually go out and visit people. They are really going out into the world with their faith."

"How about knocking gently," one person interjected, eliciting chuckles. A person who had been silent said, "I think we demonstrate our faith through our actions." This thought brought quick affirmation: "I agree. Look at the way we act." But for several people in the group, it still was unclear what evangelism meant and how it "relates to us." Defining evangelism in terms of their congregation's life seemed the heart of their challenge. After more tentative thought, one person seemed to speak for the group: "When we say evangelism, we don't mean to have a hair shirt and walk around with a sign. Essentially, it is to share your faith. And we have the best 'product' in the world. The last vestry meeting, we said, 'let's bring a friend to church.' I looked at my neighbors, and they're all Jewish. I ran out of people, but I could have tried harder. I think evangelism is just inviting one person to church. That is evangelism to Episcopalians. Of course, when I was Baptist in the South that was just courtesy!"

Mission and evangelism demand resources, and Episcopalians were rarely slow to describe to us the resources they believe they need. "We really need some useful resources for training lay leaders, including spiritual growth and practical skills in team building," said one person. "We need some good Christian education materials, too," added another person in the focus group. Other tangible needs were apparent. In a number of cases, people spoke of the challenge of raising money. Some cited general needs, such as meeting budgets; others focused on very specific needs. In the Northeast, one church member noted that his parish has "huge maintenance problems. We have a hundred-year-old slate roof. It is leaking like a sieve."

"I understand that," responded a member of another church who was in the same focus group. "We're having all our stained glass repaired now." In another group's discussion, the theme of money was related to opportunities for growth. Asked to name her parish's challenge, one person cited: "Money to do what we need to do and are called to do—maintain and upgrade our facility, extend our Christian education programs, and provide more outreach programs in the community."

Surprisingly, money matters were not emphasized in small groups as often as we had anticipated, but when they were, the underlying issues were mission and leadership. For a parish in a search process, the principal hope was to find a rector

> who is committed to lay leadership and able to teach us how to grow in that area. We are struggling with emerging from our old and familiar culture of centralized authority and becoming mature, adult Christians. It's almost as if we are a family of teenagers who still blame daddy for everything that frustrates us but are not quite ready to take responsibility for ourselves. We're very ambivalent about power and fearful of claiming our own, since that would mean we have to carry greater responsibility.

The theme of lay leadership as the congregation's greatest resource came to light often. "If things are to be done, we must do them," a Southern lay leader said. "Nobody is going to do it for us. We are growing in numbers since people who come here see that and want to be part of it." One person said simply, "We are the best resource."

We heard similar sentiments when we visited a nearby parish. One member said enthusiastically, "Our key resource is our energy and money." After a brief pause, someone described their process for determining what to do with their bountiful resources: "We are trying to rely on God to show us how to move forward."

The practices of spirituality often were cited as resources: "Prayer, listening to Christ, and avoiding traps of quick solutions," offered one person as examples; another mentioned "Developing more small groups for study, prayer, and mutual support."

However, when encouraged to identify tangible resources, many respondents hesitated. "I don't know what resources there might be to help us with these struggles," was one reply that we heard in several variations surprisingly frequently.

Of course, in some cases, our questions about resources elicited the group's discontent with the church's national structures. A lay leader in the South said, "The question frequently comes up about why we send money to other structures of the Episcopal Church when we need them more right here." In the Northeast, one man emphasized that the church's structures must support local initiative. He noted that "the diocese or the national church" often has materials and consultants to offer, but he suggested that it was more important that these church structures

> just respect the individual parishes in what they do and sometimes let them freely do it on their own and give the parish flexibility. What I am sensing, and I am speaking for other people, is, I think they like to do things on their own in the parish and not have too much interference from above in the sense of lording it over. What we are doing as a parish is mixing with four other parishes in the same area and trying to find where we can work together, and that is not coming from the diocese but coming from the parishes themselves as we realize we need to work closely together.

In one Western parish, as lay leaders discussed the national church's use of resources, one wanted to see "real effort and money directed toward lay ministry. Not just mouthing the words. Really thoughtful appreciation and support for lay people and what we are creating and leading the church into." For some people, there was insufficient awareness of good things the national church's structures and offices offer. "Our diocese and the national church do some good things in providing money for missions and world relief in disasters. Most of us don't know much about that, which is too bad. There really should be more effective means of communication, so we would be more informed and engaged in those activities." Many people noted that their congregations used a variety of programs offered nationally by the church or by organizations and agencies affiliated with it.

Some respondents used discussion of the wider church's resources to refer to the combative climate at the national level. "We try to stay out of the sorts of political battles that seem to be tearing apart our church nationally," observed another person. "Those political battles are irrelevant to our mission and purposes. We are into love, not war." Occasionally, a respondent grew angry on the subject of national leadership: "Those guys are approaching a cliff, and it could bring us all down."

In a few cases, the conversation lingered on the subject of national church resources. Usually, however, it was noted briefly and uncomfortably, then dismissed as group members returned to describing their local challenges.

LEADERSHIP AND IDENTITY

Almost all conversations in Episcopal congregations seem eventually to lead to leadership: whenever Episcopalians describe the challenges they face today; whenever they envision the challenges of tomorrow; whenever they discuss growth or mission. Likewise, this book has returned repeatedly to the topic. We have examined leadership as it is defined by creative leaders in congregations relating (or not relating) to the wider church; and we have examined leadership along lay-clergy lines. Within these broad parameters are a nexus of other leadership issues.

One young adult in the Northeast declared that "there is a need for the clergy presence and leadership, and yet, at the same time, the challenge is how to have that leadership and be able to support and pay for it, and also how to blend in lay leadership that can be effective and work together." For a lay person in California the challenge was more specific, having to do with the "shortage of young priests. Three of the larger parishes here are looking for younger assistants. But most of the assistants are over forty. It seems that some dioceses are reluctant to ordain young people." A number of the people with whom we spoke linked the presence of young clergy with expansion of the church's mission to young people. "We need to attract the younger people and keep them there," one Massachusetts lay person stressed.

Most of our respondents linked the need for leadership to a sense of profound change in the church and the world. Without proper leadership, the church sometimes responds to constant change with mere busyness rather than meaningful activity. As a Florida lay leader put it, "we have to find that fine balance between intentional planning and spontaneous emergence of people's interests. We can't get out too far ahead and just announce a whole range of activities and programs, nor can we neglect preparation and just rely on people to come up with programs without leadership from us." With unusual clarity, one young adult perceived that a major transition in the style of church life is underway:

> I definitely think the parish has a future. They may have to be very flexible and recognize that the old ways of just gathering people together, the programs to do stuff together to have a sort of community fellowship, may have gone by the wayside, including the parish fair. It was a way of getting people to do stuff when people had more time. I think the church now, our parish, needs to focus even though people who have been there a long time may disagree.
>
> Instead of getting people together just to get together and have a pot-luck supper or the Women's Guild program, I think, more and more, the church must be distinctive in how it gets people together, so that, when people get together,

> they feel there is something of substance offered, not to just
> have something that will occupy their time with some fun
> and fellowship. But I do think, as time goes on, people will
> come to church if they know that there is something spiri-
> tually unique that the church offers.
>
> More and more, I see it has to be something specifically,
> uniquely Christian and Anglican, Episcopal. It needs to be
> that identity. If we don't have that identity, why bother
> coming to the parish? Why not just worship at home, turn
> the television on, or gather with your friends at the local
> bars?

Identity and discernment of vocation often arose during discussions of leadership. As one lay leader in the Midwest emphasized, "when I grew up, if you wanted to be a leader in the church,
you went to seminary. That didn't seem right for me, but there's
still this little nagging voice saying my career as an accountant
isn't all my life is about. I don't know how one becomes a non-
clergy religious leader. Are the same skills I use at the bank the
ones I should apply here? But here, it's all voluntary, and there
are few rules and no bottom line. How does anyone lead in such
circumstances? How do you get a common goal and then divide
up the work to get there? What do you do when some volunteer
drops the ball? I wish I knew!"

The need to find leadership that will unify the Episcopal
Church was prominently featured in small group discussions
everywhere. One respondent, echoing many others, said that the
goal of leadership was to "create a more cohesive sense of our
unity. Cohesiveness is an important concept. What do we actually
share? How are we the same? The fact that our three worship services
are so different signals that challenge for me."

Also highlighted in small group sessions was the need for
leadership to resolve high-profile conflicts in the church in order
to move forward in mission. In one Southeastern parish, the
exchange was energetic as some members vented their frustration
with the level of contention in some quarters of the church. "Tell
them in New York to settle the controversies and get on with
business," one woman urged. "Their poor press is complicating
life for us here on the front lines."

"No, that's not the place to start," another person in the group insisted. "Our leaders should be about igniting spiritual fires of growth, leading us in prayer and caring, not drawing lines and rules."

"But where will you get real moral leadership if not from the church?" wondered another person. "Look," injected another, "the way to moral leadership isn't through rules and control. It's through prayer and growth in the spirit. The Holy Spirit is the source of real community, not political power."

Laughing, a person who had been silent said, "Well, you can see that we are as divided as we accuse our leaders of being." Her comment was an important one. She and the members of her group were struggling with questions that challenge the Episcopal Church at every level: Is the church primarily an institution that rests upon rules and procedures? Or, is it a spiritual community that exists less by procedures and more by prayer and discernment in the midst of ambiguities caused by rapid change? In this particular locale, members clearly preferred having a spiritual community, even if that meant forfeiting some of the clarity of role and purpose that comes with being a primarily institutional church. The problem with the institutional church—according to these members—is that the church as an institution no longer is capable of speaking with a clear moral voice, much less a spiritual one.

Yet they seem to understand that they cannot be Episcopalians locally without being connected in some way with the wider church. But that connection must be mutual: they must connect with the wider church, but the wider church also must connect with them. Referring to the seemingly endless General Convention resolutions that attempt to moderate controversy, one member said, "Resolutions have to build from the ground up if they are to be lasting." Clearly, the speaker did not believe that the kind of resolutions proposed at General Convention ever would exhibit true mutuality. In general, the group was not hopeful about the church as an institution. "Our whole church is mired in the tension between central authority and mutual ownership, but where—outside this room—are such issues being faced and examined? I believe we are headed in the right direction, even though our path ahead isn't clear. At least we are working on important challenges. I wish I thought anyone in the hierarchy was working on these challenges, too. I suspect they're even more afraid of these things than we are."

Though discussions of leadership among Episcopalians typically produce more questions than answers, there is remarkable consensus on the leadership challenge the church faces. Not only must Episcopalians find the leadership necessary to inspire a new sense of unity, they must also cultivate a new moral influence in society. In the Southwest, one lay leader was specific about this leadership challenge:

> I think the growing economic polarization in our society is something that the national church should be addressing. We have to deal with the consequences here locally and can't do much about root causes. When corporate executives of national companies are getting millions of dollars in bonuses and letting go of workers, surely our national leaders should be speaking out, instead of sucking up to them for donations. Certainly money is important, but the underlying systemic injustices need attention.

The question of the church's ethical voice reflects widespread, local concerns about the coherence of Episcopal identity and vocation nationally. It is tempting to think that local leaders are simply carping about liberal drift in the church. In fact, most local leaders fear that the church's national political entanglements obscure its proper focus. As one lay leader in the South expressed it, "the conflicts and controversies at the national level of our church are undermining us. Everyone reads about the conflicts over things like ordaining women and homosexuals and thinks that's all we do—argue over symbols and slogans. I say come to a conclusion and get it over with. This endless indecision is killing us. That's just poor leadership at the top."

With remarkable clarity, one lay person in Massachusetts rolled everything to do with identity, vocation, and leadership into this simple declaration: "Who God is calling us to be is the issue!"

INTRACTABLE CIRCUMSTANCES

At this point, we wish to review the basic points of the book and then add some final observations that will return us one last time to the constantly recurring themes of conflict and leadership.

We have described how the identity and vocation of the Episcopal Church are undergoing a transformation from religious institution to spiritual community, a shift that began at the church's grassroots and now is widespread. For Episcopal congregations, the result has been the influx of a number of spiritually motivated people. Many of them have little or no familiarity with religious institutions and therefore do not view the local church institutionally. As for the wider church, they often bring with them an American suspicion of institutions generally and religious ones specifically. Ultimately, however, the new participants in Episcopal life are not characterized by suspicion. Increasingly, the people in Episcopal pews arrive as spiritual pilgrims in search of local spiritual community rather than institutional membership. Thus, they approach the Christian life from an entirely different presupposition than institutional loyalty. The spirituality that is prevalent in Episcopal congregations entails a new sense of religious identity and vocation.[1] It represents an aspiration to personal and shared wholeness and purpose that re-visions the church's ends and means while renewing their basis in faith.

An avid effort to recover and reapply ancient Christian belief and practice is apparent in many congregations. Unlike similar efforts in the past which often were used to bolster hierarchical authority within the church, today's attempt at recovery of the past has other applications: to find precedents for spiritual community; to return worship to the center of congregational life (including using worship to enhance the tone of small groups meeting for study and prayer); and to ratify the crucial role of lay leadership.

Patterns of leadership now are collegial rather than hierarchical. Nostalgia no longer stymies creativity or initiative. Our members are deeply invested in forming and nurturing mutually supportive groups for worship, study, outreach, and service. Religious identity now is grounded in local relationships where shared spiritual concerns are addressed in small groups. This sharing is understood to result in personal growth and strong interpersonal bonds, leading to efforts to support and serve those in need, whether inside or outside the congregation.

Rebuilding congregations according to these ideals reflects a pragmatic emphasis on the new spirituality. That is, this contemporary spirituality emphasizes practices that focus on building community and securing a vital sense of local mission. In part, spiritual pragmatism builds upon historic changes in the Episcopal Church that arose from varied sources and have been accepted almost universally. Here we mean the greatly enhanced role of lay leaders that began to take shape in the 1950s. We also note the ordination of women, which gained approval by the end of the 1970s but was decades in the making.

We must emphasize that the new, spiritual ties that have begun to bind Episcopalians are still being secured. The church, like many American organizations of all sorts, is in the midst of a profound transition. We have noted that significant forms of local and national conflict accompany this transition. Despite the popularity of the bleak culture-wars perspective on the church and the current potentially fractious issues relating to homosexuality, we believe that the deeper and more important source of conflict may be found in the disparity between the ideal of the local church as spiritual community and the national church as organization.

THE ORGANIZATIONAL CRISIS IN THEORY

In a sense, this conflict, which might be characterized as a tension between "mission" and "system," should come as no surprise. The experience of the Episcopal Church is like that of any large organization that, over time, begins to lose sight of its original mission, adopting instead a mission of organizational self-preservation. Although the institution may be humming with activity, it usually takes the form of preserving the status quo and protecting all established procedures and offices from change. Consequently, from the outside, the organizational behavior resembles inertia or even hibernation. Such patterns—known as "mission drift" and "goal displacement"—have been observed by sociologists and cultural historians in all organizational contexts.

All organizations face a kind of life cycle. Almost every organization is created by the fervent vision of a few energetic and sometimes charismatic leaders who attract others to share in their commitment to address a problem or concern. Together, they begin planning and then carrying out a needed activity, program, product, or service. As the movement grows and attracts more participants, it develops specialized tasks, creates and differentiates roles, adds staff and offices, and puts systems into place for the orderly conduct of work.

Over time, those in the various roles and offices begin to value the ways in which they carry out their responsibilities more than the outcomes. Their interests turn to sustaining the predictable routines that enable them to get their tasks done efficiently and perpetuate a sense of stability. In organizations with many divisions and subdivisions, this pattern of becoming both increasingly specialized and increasingly regimented at each separate site, office, or department causes the wider institutional connections to begin to deteriorate. Consequently, the original fervor, once derived from a strong sense of common purpose, diminishes.

Of course, the leaders who formed that original fervor and common purpose as well as the later leaders who managed to renew that fervor and purpose eventually move on, causing an increase in institutional regimentation. After all, an emphasis on accountability and orderliness is only natural when a changing of the guard occurs. But the more any organization succumbs to the urge to establish routines, predictability, and clear lines of responsibility, the harder it is for those involved to sustain the organization's original passion and risktaking. The goals that motivated earlier generations of leaders become more and more accommodated to the understandable needs to keep accurate records of resources, link specialized tasks into smooth-functioning systems, and keep the organization operating efficiently.

Tensions between mission and system underlie the activities of all large organizations, whether recognized or not. In the early years of an organization, mission clearly dominates its agenda, but system concerns grow over time until the focus on mission becomes sublimated to organizational procedure. Large institutions often are staffed by people who see changes as a threat to the stability of proven procedures of the past. Changes are tolerated to the extent that they can be fitted into existing procedures; extensive changes are referred to committees that will whittle them down until they fit into the current way of doing things; anyone who objects is branded a utopian dreamer or a troublemaker; anyone who objects loudly is branded a crazy radical.

At some point during this gradual process, growing numbers of people within the organization begin to feel uneasy about what looks to them like institutional lethargy. Small groups of discontent begin to coalesce, some beginning as informally and unofficially as two colleagues going out for a beer after work "just to let off steam." As uneasiness turns to alarm in some quarters, more organized groups begin to form—groups with a plan, not just a beef. The more zealous of these may begin to resemble the original founding leaders, arguing that their effort to change the system is really an attempt to return faithfully to an original mission which has been lost.

Such accusations strike those at the top of the larger institutions as incomprehensible, not to mention ungrateful, since they see themselves as already doing heroic work to keep a huge, awkward system focused on the mission that everyone supposedly is sharing. Furthermore, they would argue that it is extremely difficult (some may say, impossible) to make a huge system work efficiently and at the same time accommodate multiple interpretations of what is needed to carry out the mission. Determined to advance the organization's intention as they see it, those in central, senior positions in the organization become entrenched in their management style.

Divergence between local and central office leaders is a familiar tension in all organizations, regardless of size, irrespective of purpose or product. After all, human nature is such that local leaders everywhere occasionally will feel that one concern or another of theirs has not been heeded sufficiently; and most central leaders tend to believe that they take considerable care to stay in close touch with their institutional outposts. But even when central leaders are truly committed to incorporating local concerns into the common mission, there may be more frustration than resolution. Often the organization responds to local concerns with another program or procedure rather than any real reengagement of the original organizational purpose. The realization that the organization has not changed, despite the assurances of concern by its senior leaders, proves frustrating at every level of the organization. Local leaders become embittered as they sense no practical change. Senior leaders become even more bewildered and defensive, especially when they have taken considerable trouble to address local concerns, albeit doing so only within existing institutional guidelines and procedures. Neither side feels heard or appreciated; neither side knows what to do next. But both sense that the quality of life in their organization has begun to deteriorate. A seemingly irreversible downward spiral ensues.

Organizational leaders who originally tried to accommodate local interests and perhaps even the more militant reformers begin to realize that the situation has deteriorated beyond the point of accommodation. Now real change is demanded. But central leaders often resist making any meaningful changes and devise measures designed only to secure their power base. They deny the legitimacy of calls for change and resolve by one means or another to defuse or even expel troublemakers. Reformers call for coalitions to rise up and take over the organization or else break away to form more a faithful enterprise elsewhere, unfettered by the baggage of the past. Sometimes, they are successful. Then it becomes the reformers' turn to maintain the institutional vision and common purpose, which they do by creating new structures to sustain their new programs. Eventually these reformers will move on or grow lax and, as a result, institutional procedures will begin to tighten as a compensatory measure. Before long, the next cycle of institutional stagnation is underway and continues uninterrupted until new reformers appear on the scene.

A better beginning point for institutional leaders or reformers would be to realize that long-term stability and orderliness are neither necessary nor productive in a large organization. To adapt institutional systems to constantly shifting interests and expectations is a perpetual challenge for every organization that cannot be "fixed" or escaped.

THE ORGANIZATIONAL CRISIS IN THE EPISCOPAL CHURCH

The crisis that confronts the Episcopal Church is similar in theory—if not in specifics—to those that periodically confront all organizations. The elaborate, centralized structures that were created to address the national missionary purpose of the Domestic and Foreign Missionary Society (DFMS), as it is officially known, supported local efforts of mission and ministry efficiently and uniformly for decades, but as times changed and the social context of religious life began to shift, a kind of inertia set in. Church leaders succumbed to a reliance upon institutional procedures, becoming reluctant to modify the structures, forms, and offices that they believed secured the church's identity and vocation. Those in specific roles or offices of the familiar system could not imagine how things possibly could work any other way. Inevitably, their intractability produced would-be reformers. Faced with these critics, they redoubled their intractability.

Most local Episcopal congregations already have come to terms with the new social and spiritual realities that have intruded upon their localities. They pay lip service to their diocesan and denominational affiliation, but their real time and energy is spent addressing local needs and developing the networks necessary to support their own initiatives. Efforts by diocesan or denominational offices to engage them in national church programs and pronouncements or to reenlist them in institutional loyalty and identity are met with indifference at best and hostility at worst.

And yet the church—even at the local level—has become habituated to relying upon institutional procedures whenever tensions arise. The issue of homosexuality, for example, will be addressed in terms of legislative actions, debates, and the prospect of win-lose votes. Lost in the emphasis on procedure will be any sustained attention to the church's mission in light of its identity and vocation. Though some voices will raise the issue, there will be no substantive attention to the question of what is the impact of such debates on those whom the church serves. Procedures and polarizing debates leave no room for attention to organizational purpose, constituencies, or the common good. Nowhere in the process in there any opportunity to reassess the relevance or effectiveness of the church procedures that will bear the weight of addressing such a difficult and potentially fractious topic.

Like so many other American institutions today, the Episcopal Church faces the historic challenge of moving beyond procedural inertia to recover its mission in ways that honor local initiatives and promote a new sense of identity and vocation.[2] While the desire to do so is based largely in local churches, it also is apparent in the initiatives of some institutional staff and bishops. Instead of seeing themselves atop some power pyramid, giving directions to those beneath them, these leaders are working as supportive servants of their people in ministry at the local level. They seek opportunities to bring those people together to exchange ideas and resources and to learn from one another. They suggest links among congregations for developing collaborative ministries and do not insert themselves into those efforts as managers or overseers. They nurture leadership capacities and initiatives among others. They jettison familiar old roles and offices in favor of new, often short-term arrangements that serve emerging needs and concerns of congregations. Once those concerns are addressed, they move on to learn and develop new ways of serving. They articulate the basic mission of the church to demonstrate Christ's love for every person, regardless of condition.

Can such leaders secure a new sense of Episcopal identity and vocation? In the broad context of American life, one writer believes that what is required is a renewed sense of civic virtue and community.[3] In more concrete terms, this means that there must be a binding set of common values linked to a clearly understood sense of purpose. In a pluralistic society, common values and purpose make for a tall order, because notions of community and order must negotiate between often competing priorities. However, at the increasingly pluralistic local level of the Episcopal Church, grassroots Episcopalians have made a start with a sense of mission and community based in a spirituality that is at once brand new and historically Anglican. God is already doing new things; can we not perceive it? (Isaiah 43:19)

THE FUTURE OF EPISCOPAL IDENTITY AND VOCATION

Periodically God has done very new things in the United States. American religious history is often viewed in terms of a series of awakenings, beginning with what has been termed the "Great Awakening" in the 1740s. These periods of religious energy have always entailed spiritual renewal that began locally then spread outward, eventually remaking old institutions and creating new ones. Religious awakenings have promoted entirely new depths of appreciation for what God is doing in the world; new views of religious community consistently result. As one writer describes it, religious renewal always entails "re-enchantment" with the world; that is, seeing the world as bursting with fresh, unexplored possibilities.[4] In that regard, contemporary spirituality clearly is the leading edge of religious renewal. Despite obviously superficial and narcissistic aspects, the wave of spirituality sweeping over American life has produced lasting, Christian results that can be seen in the pews of most Episcopal churches.

The Episcopal Church has tended to remain somewhat removed from the religious awakenings of the past; but it is in the very vortex of today's religious awakening. A growing majority of the people in Episcopal pews define their religiosity by it. Drawn to worship and study, to spiritual community, and to outreach, they are finding the Episcopal Church's emphasis on historic forms of worship, Scripture, tradition, and theological breadth as a spiritually attractive mix. They also value the room for local exploration and initiative that is a hallmark of the Anglican tradition. With a bit of exploration, they soon find that they indeed stand in a rich tradition. The Episcopal Church, in particular, and Anglicanism generally, has long welcomed spiritual sojourners. One of the mid-twentieth century's great English spiritual writers, Evelyn Underhill, followed an extensive path of seeking until finding a home in the Church of England.[5] Finding that mixture of tradition and comprehension that is uniquely Anglican, she became a powerful public voice for Christian faith as the destination of the modern spiritual journey. In the process, she also made an effective witness for Anglicanism.

But what is it that marks the current spiritual surge among people in Episcopal pews as reliably Christian and demonstrably Anglican? Other than consistent verbal references to Episcopal and Anglican traditions of worship and belief, how can we say that the powerful trend we have observed has become grounded in religious identity? What indeed are the marks of a clearly defined religious identity which characterize the patterns of rebuilding the Episcopal Church at the grassroots? For Bishop Stephen Sykes of the Church of England, Christian identity must be understood, first, as rooted in particular experiences set in particular places.[6] Christianity is more than abstractly understood doctrines; Christianity primarily is a set of practices conducted by communities of people in the context of their localities. This reality is both the church's greatest challenge and its greatest opportunity.

Historically, the diversity of the church's local circumstances has meant that conflicting points of view were inevitable. For two millennia, the church has been challenged by the need to reconcile differing views of the nature and the exercise of spiritual power. Thus, Sykes maintains, the question of the "identity of Christianity" is both the most basic and the most persistent of issues that the church faces. Worse, "there has never been one, single, universally agreed methodology for solving the inherent conflicts of Christianity, and we have every reason to suppose that there never will be."[7] We add that this includes solutions offered in the name of institutional order and procedure!

Sykes argues in a clearly Anglican way that the church's identity has rightly been grounded in its worship. Worship, he notes, has certain necessary features: it is in the name of Jesus, it entails prayer and praise, and it is corporate. This means that worship itself usually embodies the differences that seem to sap the church's purpose. Consequently, believers in sharp doctrinal disagreement have been able to come together around altars to give thanks and praise throughout Christian history. It takes a certain kind of religious understanding to see the fixed nature of worship and the church's essentials while living with the ambiguities of diversity and unresolved conflicts. In fact, Sykes argues for understanding Christian life in just that way: agreement on the centrality and necessity of Christian worship, while agreeing to treat matters in dispute as part of the church's ongoing discernment. Worship therefore becomes the core to which the community of faith returns regularly. Worship not only preserves a system of belief and practice but reconfirms commitment and reabsorbs individuals into the church's communal fabric.[8] Thus, the identity of Christian—always both particular and general, both local and beyond—"consists in the interaction between its external forms and an inward element, constantly maintained by participation in communal worship."[9]

We have seen just this approach from the people quoted in our interviews. Their focus is on worship as the basis of building Christian community anew in their localities. In general, their spiritual tenor reflects Sykes's view of Christian identity. But what makes the spirituality of today's Episcopal participants specifically Episcopal and Anglican? On this question, we are informed by the insights of three major Anglican theologians, including Archbishop Rowan Williams. In their views, Anglicanism focuses less upon a doctrinal system than upon the cultivation of a distinctive way of life. The Anglican "way" focuses upon seeking to understand how God now calls people to live holy lives. Thus, Anglican spirituality features "holiness" as God's call and as the standard of the church's response.[10]

Williams and his colleagues acknowledge that there always have been differing points of view among Anglicans about what holiness means and how it should be formed and practiced. But then they make a startling point: Anglicans have continually had to redefine their understanding of holiness, often in the midst of profound disputes. A people who see themselves in dynamic relation to God, Anglicans generally have understood that the nature of belief and the implications for practice must be reconsidered and reformulated. From time to time, however, this dynamic view of faith and faith community must be recovered. Far from being onerous, these repeated renewals bring the vitality of the Spirit into the church anew. Today, just such a renewal pervades the Episcopal Church. A truly Anglican pursuit of holiness engages the ideals and the energies of countless Episcopalians.

Christian life is remade often, sometimes dramatically. Given the dramatic shifts that occur in the Anglican Communion globally and constantly, the reality of change should be apparent to Episcopalians. And at the grassroots—where the transition from religious institution to spiritual community is well underway—apparently it is. The ideal of holiness that Williams and his colleagues describe is actively pursued in one Episcopal congregation after another. Because all enduring forms of belief and practice begin in "local frames of awareness," the transition that absorbs the Episcopal Church has developed firm roots.[11] Because it so clearly follows Anglican patterns and an Anglican agenda, the spirituality that captivates Episcopalians is faithful in its broad outlines. Now the church requires a pattern of leadership that is truly appreciative of this awakening. This new leadership cannot be vested in historic structures or instinctively procedural; it cannot be defined by a sense of crisis or content to offer mechanistic solutions to particular problems; most assuredly, it cannot be the product of a specific ideology. Rather, it must seek to build redemptive connections among disparate communities. The leadership the church requires must be content with ambiguity yet clear about the contours of reconciliation. It must be rooted in "common prayer" yet comprehensive in honoring local experience. It must seek practical forms of discernment on difficult issues, emphasizing not winners and losers, but a common direction on difficult issues. We are encouraged to see such a pattern of leadership taking hold in local Episcopal settings and moving outward and beyond. The church's challenge now is to allow itself to be redefined by such an emerging pattern. To do so, we are confident, would be to participate in a manner of spiritual awakening whose origin and whose destiny is God.

NOTES

[1] The noted sociologist and Episcopalian, Wade Clark Roof, is an astute observer of this trend. See, for example, his article "God is in the Details: Reflections on Religion's Public Presence in the United States in the Mid-1990s," in *Sociology of Religion* (Volume 57, No. 2), 1996, pp. 149–162.

[2] At this point, we are informed by the work of political scientist Michael J. Sandel in *Democracy's Discontent: America in Search of a Public Philosophy* (Belknap/ Harvard, 1996).

[3] *Ibid.*, p. 338f.

[4] Amanda Porterfield, *The Transformation of American Religion* (Oxford, 2001).

[5] Mark McIntosh, "Searching for the Beloved: Today's Spiritual Hunger and Jesus," in Slocum, ed., *A New Conversation*, p. 157.

[6] Stephen Sykes, *The Identity of Christianity* (Fortress, 1984), p. 33.

[7] *Ibid.*, p. 264.

[8] *Ibid.*, p. 281.

[9] *Ibid.*, p. 282f.

[10] Geoffrey Rowell, Kenneth Stevenson, and Rowan Williams, eds., *Love's Redeeming Work: The Anglican Quest for Holiness* (Oxford, 2001), p. xxv.

[11] See Clifford Geertz, *Local Knowledge* (Basic Books, 1983), p. 6.

APPENDIX A

I n anticipation of its fiftieth anniversary in 1999, the Episcopal
Church Foundation commissioned the Zacchaeus Project. At
the end of the twentieth century, the identity and vocation of
the people in the Episcopal Church were no longer certain. It
was clear that the Episcopal Church had undergone far-reaching
changes. It also was apparent that the church faced significant
tensions. But there were anecdotal suggestions that tension
might not adequately characterize the Episcopal Church's life, as
was popularly believed. There seemed to be a great deal of uncertainty about the overall outlook of the church's membership.
The Zacchaeus Project was designed to determine the true nature
of life at the grassroots of the Episcopal Church. In short, who are
Episcopalians today? How do they live their faith? How do they
see their church? What is their role in it?

Typically, national studies of religious life rely upon quantitative data generated by written questionnaires that are adminis-
tered by mail or telephone. In some cases, only a clergy representative of a congregation is contacted. Presumably, the people
contacted offer an objective, broad view of the congregation and
denomination. Usually, it is not possible to check the accuracy of
the response.

A portion of the data generated by the Zacchaeus Project
reflects such an approach. Written questionnaires were mailed to
a representative sample of congregations in the project's nine target dioceses. As we describe in chapter four, the results provided
a clear sense of what Episcopalians believe. For example, in overwhelming numbers Episcopalians see the Eucharist as central to
the lives of their congregations.

The project also relied upon existing data on Episcopal Church attendance, membership, and finances. On the basis of what was unearthed, we concluded that the Episcopal Church's attendance nationally increased by more than 31% between 1974 and 1997. This contrasts with a 36% decline in membership from 1967 to 1997, the sharpest period of decline being from 1967 to 1973. The graphs illustrating these figures can be found in Appendix C.

But the bulk of the Zacchaeus Project's research was qualitative. That is, we attempted to identify patterns of collective activity among Episcopalians, not merely individual actions and attitudes. To uncover what Episcopalians do together and why—especially in their congregations—a team of seven researchers conducted focus groups primarily in nine target dioceses. We asked each group to describe a recent program or event in their congregation that had succeeded. When the group decided upon an illustrative example, we then asked a series of questions about the course of events and factors responsible for its success. For instance, we wanted to know if there had been "obstacles" that challenged the likelihood of success, and how these were overcome. We were most interested in the pattern of collective activity that emerged, and what this activity meant to its participants. We also expressed interest in the "resources" each congregation required for its program life. Then, we asked what made a successful program distinctively Episcopal and what role the church's diocese played in fostering a successful outcome.

Then, we asked each focus group to identify a program in their congregation that had failed. We asked the same questions about their failure that we had asked about their success—questions about obstacles, resources, and whether there was anything distinctively Episcopal about the failure.

Finally, we invited respondents to envision the future of their congregations. What challenges do they anticipate? What resources might they need? And so forth. By this point in the process, most focus groups had become animated. Candid conversations often broke out among them, giving our interviewers a privileged view of the depth and breadth of their congregational lives together.

We also interviewed individuals, asking them the same questions asked of focus groups. This book contains several valuable quotations gathered from these on-on-one interviews, although, given our overall focus on spiritual community, it should come as no surprise that the majority of the quotations we selected came from group interviews.

To make this study truly national and representative, an advisory panel of lay and ordained leaders from across the Episcopal Church worked with a management team from the Episcopal Church Foundation to design the project. An ecumenical group of religious scholars and practitioners also met on one occasion to critique our planning.

Guided by the advisory panel, nine dioceses were chosen as representative of the Episcopal Church. After considerable discussion, the group settled on the following: Central Florida, Kansas, Los Angeles, Massachusetts, Minnesota, Nevada, North Carolina, Texas, and West Missouri. All nine dioceses have a few broad characteristics in common; for example, each has a representative sample of congregations, ranging widely in size, setting, and membership composition. Each diocese has distinctive features. Together, they offer impressive scope. They also serve, to some extent, as demographic, geographic, sociological, and theological "balances" to one another. Los Angeles and Massachusetts are densely populated, urban dioceses, whereas Nevada and Kansas contain large, sparsely populated rural areas. Los Angeles is the most urban diocese in the study and Nevada the most rural. Massachusetts is an older diocese and considered— like Los Angeles—to be "progressive," whereas Central Florida is a relatively new diocese in the rapidly growing sunbelt of the state and generally is considered conservative. Kansas and West Missouri present interesting study opportunities because they are neighboring dioceses with many similarities and many differences; they also interact programmatically to a considerable— perhaps an unusual—degree. Texas and North Carolina compare and contrast in several ways: Texas is particularly well known for a strong commitment to mission, but both dioceses are diverse and growing; together—along with Central Florida—they establish a Southern contingent, but North Carolina also represents East Coast patterns, styles, and tendencies, while Texas also represents those of the Midwest and even the West. Minnesota, overall considered somewhat liberal, makes for interesting study in that there are especially marked differences between urban and rural parishes. Geographically, the focus of the study clearly is the middle of the country with four dioceses represented: Minnesota, Kansas, West Missouri, and Texas.

We also went to several seminaries where we conducted group interviews with students, faculty, and trustees. Finally, we conducted interviews in a smattering of congregations, dioceses, and church-related institutions outside of the nine target dioceses. For the duration of the Zacchaeus Project, from mid-1998 to late 1999, a total of more than two thousand people were interviewed in more than two hundred locations. Analysis of the data from both interviews and the survey were performed by the research team and advisory panel in meetings that occurred periodically throughout the project.

The project's findings may be summarized as follows:

- There is a strong commitment to worship and tradition among Episcopalians.
- There is creative ferment and vitality in Episcopal congregations.
- There are a variety of tensions in the church, but issues of sexuality, doctrinal clarity, and other volatile issues are not distracting Episcopal congregations from mission.
- Episcopalians seek to embrace diversity and change.

Compelled by these findings, the Episcopal Church Foundation began the Emmaus Project in 2000, and it continues at this writing. The purpose of the Emmaus Project is to determine whether new patterns of leadership, especially by bishops, can reduce the sense of disconnect with wider church structures that many Episcopalians report. This research has taken place in the dioceses of Indianapolis, Louisiana, Maryland, San Diego, South Carolina, and Western New York. The Emmaus Project draws upon the findings of the Zacchaeus Project, especially data related to leadership issues, but the Emmaus Project goes even further in examining the new leadership patterns emerging today. The Emmaus Project will produce a report on the state of leadership among Episcopalians and eventually a book-length study of contemporary religious leadership.

Appendix B

Leadership of the Zacchaeus Project

Co-Directors
Thomas P. Holland
William L. Sachs

Advisory Committee
William G. Andersen
Diana Butler Bass
Frederick Burnham
Thomas K. Chu
William S. Craddock, Jr.
Vincent Currie, Jr.
Linda Curtiss
R. William Franklin
David A. Galloway
Carlson Gerdau
Carmen Guerrero
Ben E. Helmer
Sandra A. Holmberg
John B. Lipscomb
F. Clayton Matthews
Wendel W. Meyer
Virginia Paul
Stephanie Cheney

Zacchaeus Research Associates
Diana Butler Bass
Sarah Buxton-Smith
Shannon Leach

Anne Mallonee
Susanne C. Monahan

Ecumenical Advisory Committee

Nancy T. Ammerman
Ian S. Evison
Alvin Jackson
Russell Richey
Wade Clark Roof
James P. Wind
Erica B. Wood

Quantitative Data Consultants

Charles P. Clark
Linda Curtiss
Susanne C. Monahan

APPENDIX C

NATIONAL DATA ON EPISCOPAL CHURCH MEMBERSHIP AND ATTENDANCE

Members
(Since 1947)

Year   The Church Report Company

Average National Attendance
For The Episcopal Church (Since 1974)

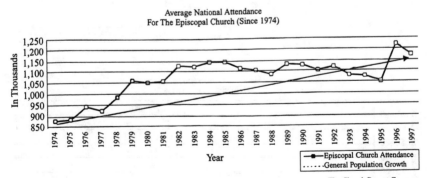

Year
■ Episcopal Church Attendance
..... General Population Growth

The Church Report Company

NATIONAL DATA ON MEMBERSHIP CHANGES IN OTHER DENOMINATIONS

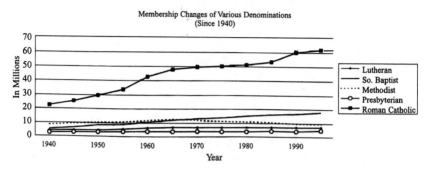

Membership Changes of Various Denominations
(Since 1940)

The Church Report Company

NATIONAL DATA ON EPISCOPAL CHURCH FINANCES

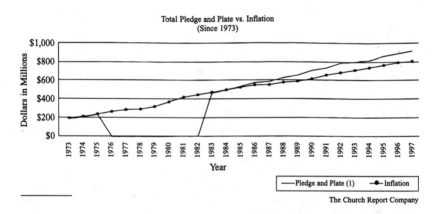

Total Pledge and Plate vs. Inflation
(Since 1973)

The Church Report Company

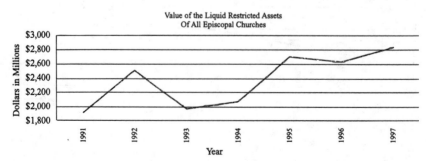

Value of the Liquid Restricted Assets
Of All Episcopal Churches

The Church Report Company

BIBLIOGRAPHY

Addresses and Historical Papers before the Centennial Council of the Protestant Episcopal Church in the Diocese of Virginia at Its Meetings in St. Paul's and St. John's Churches." Paper presented at the Centennial Council of the Protestant Episcopal Church in the Diocese of Virginia, Richmond. New York: T. Whittaker, 1885.

Ammerman, Nancy Tatom, Arthur Emery Farnsley II, Tammy Adams, et al. *Congregation and Community*. New Brunswick: Rutgers University Press, 1997.

Ammerman, Nancy Tatom, et al., eds. *Studying Congregations: A New Handbook*. Nashville: Abingdon Press, 1998.

Armentrout, Donald S. "Episcopal Splinter Groups." Unpublished manuscript.

Bass, Diana Butler. *Strength for the Journey: A Pilgrimage of Faith in Community*. San Francisco: Jossey-Bass, 2002.

Bender, Thomas. *Community and Social Change in America*. New Brunswick: Rutgers University Press, 1978.

Berton, Pierre. *The Comfortable Pew: A Critical Look at Christianity and the Religious Establishment in the New Age*. Toronto: McClelland and Stewart, 1965.

Bess, Douglas. *Divided We Stand: A History of the Continuing Anglican Movement*. Riverside: Tractarian Press, 2002.

Bolman, Lee G., and Terrence E. Deal. *Leading with Soul: An Uncommon Journey of Spirit*. San Francisco: Jossey-Bass Publishers, 1995.

———. *Reframing Organizations: Artistry, Choice, and Leadership*. Jossey-Bass Management Series. San Francisco: Jossey-Bass, 1991.

Briskin, Alan. *The Stirring of Soul in the Workplace*. San Francisco: Jossey-Bass Publishers, 1996.

Burr, Nelson Rollin. *The Story of the Diocese of Connecticut: A New Branch of the Vine*. Hartford: Church Missions Publishing Company, 1962.

Carroll, Jackson W., and Wade Clark Roof. *Bridging Divided Worlds: Generational Cultures in Congregations.* San Francisco: Jossey-Bass, 2002.

————, eds. *Beyond Establishment: Protestant Identity in a Post-Protestant Age.* Louisville: Westminster/John Knox Press, 1993.

Caswall, Henry. *America and the American Church.* Religion in America Series. New York: Arno Press, 1969.

Coalter, Milton J., John M. Mulder, and Louis B. Weeks, eds. *The Organizational Revolution: Presbyterians and American Denominationalism.* Louisville: Westminster/John Knox Press, 1992.

Confronting the Crisis: A Way Forward. Forward in Faith Publications. Fort Worth, TX. No date.

Daly, Lewis C. "A Church at Risk: The Episcopal 'Renewal Movement.'" In *IDS Insights* (Institute for Democracy Studies) (December 2001).

DeMille, George E. *The Catholic Movement in the American Episcopal Church.* Philadelphia: Church Historical Society, 1941.

De Pree, Max. *Leading Without Power: Finding Hope in Serving Community.* San Francisco: Jossey-Bass, 1997.

Douglas, Ian T. *Fling out the Banner!: The National Church Ideal and the Foreign Mission of the Episcopal Church.* New York: Church Hymnal Corporation, 1996.

————. *The Times and Timeliness of Henry Knox Sherrill.* Unpublished. New York: The Episcopal Church Foundation, 1999.

Drucker, Peter F. "The New Society of Organizations." In *Harvard Business Review* (September 1992).

Druskat, Vanessa Urch, and Steven B. Wolff. "Building the Emotional Intelligence of Groups." In *Harvard Business Review* (March 2001).

Dudley, Carl S. and Nancy Tatom Ammerman. *Congregations in Transition: A Guide for Analyzing, Assessing and Adapting in Changing Communities.* San Francisco: Jossey-Bass, 2002.

Dudley, Carl S., and David A. Roozen. *Faith Communities Today (FACT): A Report on Religion in the United States Today.* Hartford: Hartford Institute for Religion Research, 2001.

Dykstra, Craig, and Dorothy C. Bass. "A Theological Understanding of Christian Practices." In *Practicing Theology: Beliefs and Practices in Christian Life,* edited by Miroslav Volf and Dorothy C. Bass. Grand Rapids: Wm. B. Eerdmans, 2001.

―――. "Times of Yearning, Practices of Faith." In *Practicing Our Faith: A Way of Life for a Searching People*, edited by Dorothy C. Bass. San Francisco: Jossey-Bass, 1997.

Eck, Diana L. *A New Religious America: How a "Christian Country" Has Become the World's Most Religiously Diverse Nation*. San Francisco: HarperSanFrancisco, 2001.

Eiesland, Nancy L. *A Particular Place: Urban Restructuring and Religious Ecology in a Southern Exurb*. New Brunswick: Rutgers University Press, 2000.

Finke, Roger, and Rodney Starke. *The Churching of America 1776–1990: Winners and Losers in Our Religious Economy*. New Brunswick: Rutgers University Press, 1992.

Fletcher, Joseph F. *Situation Ethics: The New Morality*. Philadelphia: Westminster Press, 1966.

Friedman, Edwin H. *Generation to Generation: Family Process in Church and Synagogue*. New York: Guilford Press, 1985.

Fukuyama, Francis. *Trust: The Social Virtues and the Creation of Prosperity*. New York: Free Press, 1995.

Geertz, Clifford. *Local Knowledge: Further Essays in Interpretive Anthropology*. New York: Basic Books, 1983.

Goleman, Daniel. *Emotional Intelligence*. New York: Bantam Books, 1995.

―――. "Leadership That Gets Results." In *Harvard Business Review* (March 2000).

―――. "What Makes a Leader?" In *Harvard Business Review* (November 1998).

Greenfeld, Liah, and Michel Martin. "The Idea of the 'Center:' an Introduction." In *Center: Ideas and Institutions*, edited by Liah Greenfeld and Michel Martin. Chicago: University of Chicago Press, 1988.

Guelzo, Allen C. *For the Union of Evangelical Christendom: The Irony of the Reformed Episcopalians*. University Park: Pennsylvania State University Press, 1994.

Hadaway, C. Kirk. *A Report on Episcopal Churches in the United States*. New York: Office of Congregational Development, Domestic and Foreign Missionary Society, The Episcopal Church, 2002.

Hall, Peter Dobkin. "Religion and the Organizational Revolution in the United States." In *Sacred Companies: Organizational Aspects of Religion and Religious Aspects of Organizations*, edited by Nicholas Jay Demerath III and Peter Dobkin Hall, et al. Oxford: Oxford University Press, 1998.

Hankey, Wayne J. "Canon Law." In *The Study of Anglicanism*, edited by Stephen Sykes and John Booty. Philadelphia: SPCK/Fortress Press, 1988.

Hardy, Daniel W. *Finding the Church: The Dynamic Truth of Anglicanism.* London: SCM Press, 2001.

Hatch, Nathan O. *The Democratization of American Christianity.* New Haven: Yale University Press, 1989.

Hefling, Charles. "On Being Reasonably Theological." In *A New Conversation: Essays on the Future of Theology and the Episcopal Church*, edited by Robert Boak Slocum. New York: Church Publishing, 1999.

Heifetz, Ronald A. *Leadership Without Easy Answers.* Cambridge: Belknap Press, 1994.

Heifetz, Ronald A., and Donald L. Laurie. "The Work of Leadership." In *Harvard Business Review* (February 2000).

Hein, David. *Noble Powell and the Episcopal Establishment in the Twentieth Century.* Urbana: University of Illinois Press, 2001.

Herman, Robert D., and Richard D. Heimovics. "Critical Events in the Management of Nonprofit Organizations." In *Nonprofit and Voluntary Sector Quarterly* 18, no. 2 (1989).

Holifield, E. Brooks. *A History of Pastoral Care in America: From Salvation to Self-Realization.* Nashville: Abingdon Press, 1983.

Holland, Thomas P., and David C. Hester, eds. *Building Effective Boards for Religious Organizations: A Handbook for Trustees, Presidents, and Church Leaders.* San Francisco: Jossey-Bass, 1999.

Holland, Thomas P., Donald Leslie, and Carol Holzhalb. "Culture and Change in Nonprofit Boards." In *Nonprofit Management and Leadership* 4, no. 2 (1993).

Hopewell, James F. *Congregation: Stories and Structures.* Philadelphia: Fortress Press, 1987.

Hunter, James Davison. *Culture Wars: The Struggle to Define America.* New York: Basic Books, 1991.

Hutchison, William R. *The Modernist Impulse in American Protestantism*. Durham: Duke University Press, 1992.

Isaac, Rhys. *The Transformation of Virginia, 1740–1790*. Williamsburg: University of North Carolina Press, 1982.

Karon, Jan. *At Home in Mitford (The Mitford Years)*. New York: Viking, 1998.

Killen, Patricia O'Connell. 2002. "Christianity in the Western United States since World War II." Paper presented at the Spring Theological Conference, 19 April, at Pacific Lutheran Theological Seminary, Berkeley, California.

Knauft, E. Burt, Renee A. Berger, and Sandra T. Gray. *Profiles of Excellence: Achieving Success in the Nonprofit Sector*. Jossey-Bass Nonprofit Sector Series. San Francisco: Jossey-Bass Publishers, 1991.

Kotter, John. "What Leaders Really Do." In *Harvard Business Review* (December 2001).

Lewis, Harold T. *Yet with a Steady Beat: The African American Struggle for Recognition in the Episcopal Church*. Valley Forge: Trinity Press International, 1996.

Lindsley, James Elliott. *This Planted Vine: A Narrative History of the Episcopal Diocese of New York*. New York: Harper & Row, 1984.

Markers of Strong and Effective Clergy. Evanston: Lilly Endowment, 2000.

Martin, Harold C. *Outlasting Marble and Brass: The History of the Church Pension Fund*. New York: Church Hymnal Corporation, 1986.

Marty, Martin E. "Introduction: Religion in America, 1935–1985." In *Altered Landscapes: Christianity in America, 1935–1985*, edited by David W. Lotz, Donald W. Shriver, Jr., and John F. Wilson. Grand Rapids: Wm. B. Eerdmans, 1989.

———. *Under God, Indivisible: 1941–1960*. Modern American Religion, vol. 3. Chicago: University of Chicago Press, 1996.

Matthews, Donald G. "The Second Great Awakening as an Organizing Process, 1780–1830." In *American Quarterly* 21, no. 1 (1969).

McClendon, James William, Jr. "The Practice of Community Formation." In *Virtues and Practices in the Christian Tradition: Christian Ethics after Macintyre*, edited by Nancey Murphy, Brad J. Kallenberg, and Mark Thiessen Nation. Harrisburg: Trinity Press International, 1997.

McConnell, Samuel David. *History of the American Episcopal Church from the Planting of the Colonies to the End of the Civil War*. New York: T. Whittaker, 1890.

McGrade, Arthur Stephen. "Reason." In *The Study of Anglicanism*, edited by Stephen Sykes, John Booty, and Jonathan Knight. London: SPCK/Fortress Press, 1998.

McIntosh, Mark. "Searching for the Beloved: Today's Spiritual Hunger and Jesus." In *A New Conversation: Essays on the Future of Theology and the Episcopal Church*, edited by Robert Boak Slocum. New York: Church Publishing, Incorporated, 1999.

Mead, Loren B. *The Once and Future Church: Reinventing the Congregation for a New Mission Frontier*. Washington: Alban Institute, 1991.

―――. "Reinventing the Congregation." *Action Information* (Alban Institute, 1990).

Miller, Donald Earl. *Reinventing American Protestantism: Christianity in the New Millennium*. Berkeley: University of California Press, 1997.

Mullin, Robert Bruce. *Episcopal Vision/America Reality: High Church Theology and Social Thought in Evangelical America*. New Haven: Yale University Press, 1986.

Murphy, Nancey. "Using Macintyre's Method in Christian Ethics." In *Virtues and Practices in the Christian Tradition: Christian Ethics after Macintyre*, edited by Nancey Murphy, Brad J. Kallenberg, and Mark Thiessen Nation. Harrisburg: Trinity Press International, 1997.

Murray, Pauli. *Song in a Weary Throat: An American Pilgrimage*. New York: Harper & Row, 1987.

Niebuhr, H. Richard. *The Kingdom of God in America*. New York: Harper, 1959.

Nygren, David J., CM, and Miriam D. Ukeritis, CSJ. *The Future of Religious Orders in the United States: Transformation and Commitment*. Westport: Praeger, 1993.

Nygren, David J., CM, Miriam D. Ukeritis, CSJ, and Julia L. Hickman. "Outstanding Leadership in Nonprofit Organizations: Leadership Competencies in Roman Catholic Religious Orders." In *Nonprofit Management and Leadership* 4, no. 4 (1994).

O'Connor, Daniel. *Three Centuries of Mission: The United Society of the Propagation of the Gospel, 1701–2000*. London: Continuum International Publishing Group, 2000.

Oswald, Roy M. and Robert E. Friedrich, Jr. *Discerning Your Congregation's Future: A Strategic and Spiritual Approach*. Bethesda: Alban Institute, 1996.

———. *New Beginnings: A Pastorate Start Up Workbook.* Bethesda: Alban Institute, 1989.

Payne, Claude E., and Hamilton Beazley. *Reclaiming the Great Commission: A Practical Model for Transforming Denominations and Congregations.* San Francisco: Jossey-Bass, 2000.

Phillips, Paul T. *A Kingdom on Earth: Anglo-American Social Christianity, 1880–1940.* University Park: Pennsylvania State University Park, 1996.

Phillips, Roy D. *Letting Go: Transforming Congregations for Ministry.* Washington: Alban Institute, 2000.

Pickering, William Stuart Frederick. "Sociology of Anglicanism." In *The Study of Anglicanism,* edited by Stephen Sykes, John Booty, and Jonathan Knight. London: SPCK/Fortress Press, 1998.

Porterfield, Amanda. *The Transformation of American Religion: The Story of a Late Twentieth-Century Awakening.* Oxford: Oxford University Press, 2001.

Prichard, Robert W. *A History of the Episcopal Church.* Harrisburg: Morehouse Publishing, 1999.

Putnam, Robert D. *Bowling Alone: The Collapse and Revival of American Community.* New York: Simon & Schuster, 2000.

———. "The United State of America." In *The American Prospect* vol. 13 issue 3 (2002).

"Researching Episcopal Constituencies." In Roper ASW (2002).

Roof, Wade Clark. "God is in the Details: Reflections on Religion's Public Presence in the United States in the Mid-1990s." In *Sociology of Religion* 57, no. 2 (1996): 149–62.

———. *Spiritual Marketplace: Baby Boomers and the Remaking of American Religion.* Princeton: Princeton University Press, 1999.

Rosenblum, Nancy L. *Membership and Morals: The Personal Uses of Pluralism in America.* Princeton: Princeton University Press, 1998.

Rowell, Geoffrey, Kenneth Stevenson, and Rowan Williams, comps. *Love's Redeeming Work: The Anglican Quest for Holiness.* Oxford: Oxford University Press, 2001.

Sachs, William L. *The Transformation of Anglicanism: From State Church to Global Communion.* Cambridge: Cambridge University Press, 1993.

Sandel, Michael J. *Democracy's Discontent: America in Search of a Public Philosophy.* Cambridge: Belknap Press, 1996.

Schein, Edgar H. *Organizational Culture and Leadership.* San Francisco: Jossey-Bass, 1992.

Shattuck, Gardiner H. *Episcopalians and Race: Civil War to Civil Rights.* Lexington: University Press of Kentucky, 2000.

———. "Knowing the Tasks." In *A New Conversation: Essays on the Future of Theology and the Episcopal Church,* edited by Robert Boak Slocum. New York: Church Publishing, Incorporated, 1999.

Shenk, Wilbert R. *Henry Venn — Missionary Statesman.* Maryknoll: Orbis Books, 1983.

Shepherd, Samuel Claude. *Avenues of Faith: Shaping the Urban Religious Culture of Richmond, Virginia 1900–1929.* Tuscaloosa: University of Alabama Press, 2001.

Stout, Harry S. *The Divine Dramatist: George Whitefield and the Rise of Modern Evangelicalism.* Grand Rapids: Wm. B. Eerdmans, 1991.

Sumner, David E. *The Episcopal Church's History, 1945–1985.* Wilton: Morehouse Publishing, 1987.

Sweet, Leonard I. "The Modernization of Protestant Religion in America." In *Altered Landscapes: Christianity in America, 1935–1985,* edited by David W. Lotz, Donald W. Shriver, Jr., and John F. Wilson. Grand Rapids: Wm. B. Eerdmans, 1989.

Sykes, Stephen W. *The Identity of Christianity: Theologians and the Essence of Christianity from Schleiermacher to Barth.* Philadelphia: Fortress Press, 1984.

———. "The Fundamentals of Christianity." In *The Study of Anglicanism,* edited by Stephen Sykes, John Booty, and Jonathan Knight. London: SPCK/Fortress Press, 1998.

Thomas, George M. *Revivalism and Cultural Change: Christianity, Nation Building and the Market in the Nineteenth-Century United States.* Chicago: University of Chicago Press, 1989.

Trumbauer, Jean Morris. *Sharing the Ministry: A Practical Guide for Transforming Volunteers into Ministry.* Minneapolis: Augsburg, 1995.

Turner, Philip. "When Worlds Collide: A Comment on the Precarious State of Theology in the Episcopal Church." In *A New Conversation: Essays on the Future of Theology and the Episcopal Church,* edited by Robert Boak Slocum. New York: Church Publishing, Incorporated, 1999.

Van Buren, Paul Matthews. *The Secular Meaning of the Gospel, Based on an Analysis of its Language.* New York: Macmillan Company, 1963.

White, William. "The Case of the Episcopal Churches in the United States Considered." In *A History of the Episcopal Church*, Robert Prichard. Harrisburg: Morehouse Publishing, 1999.

Wind, James P., and James W. Lewis, eds. *American Congregations: New Perspectives in the Study of Congregations*, 2 volumes. Chicago: University of Chicago Press, 1994.

Wind, James P., and Gilbert R. Rendle, with The Leadership Initiative Team. *The Leadership Situation Facing American Congregations: An Alban Institute Special Report.* Bethesda: Alban Institute, 2001.

Winter, Gibson. *The Suburban Captivity of the Churches: An Analysis of Protestant Responsibility in the Expanding Metropolis.* Garden City: Doubleday, 1961.

Wolfe, Alan. *One Nation, After All: What Middle-Class Americans Really Think About God, Country, Family, Racism, Welfare, Immigration, Homosexuality, Work, the Right, the Left, and Each Other.* New York: Viking, 1998.

Woolverton, John Frederick. *Colonial Anglicanism in North America.* Detroit: Wayne State University Press, 1984.

Wuthnow, Robert. *Acts of Compassion: Caring for Others and Helping Ourselves.* Princeton: Princeton University Press, 1991.

———. *After Heaven: Spirituality in America Since the 1950s.* Berkeley: University of California Press, 1998.

———. *Loose Connections: Joining Together in America's Fragmented Communities.* Cambridge: Harvard University Press, 1998.

———. *Sharing the Journey: Support Groups and America's New Quest for Community.* New York: Free Press, 1994.